1940: THE LAST ACT

1940
THE LAST ACT

*The Story of the British Forces in France
After Dunkirk*

by
BASIL KARSLAKE

Leo Cooper
LONDON

First published in Great Britain 1979 by
LEO COOPER LTD.,
*196 Shaftesbury Avenue, London WC2H 8JL
Copyright © 1979 by Basil Karslake*

ISBN 0 85052 240 4

*Set in 11/13 pt Times New Roman by Inforum Ltd
Printed and bound in Great Britain at
The Pitman Press, Bath*

To
The memory of
Lieutenant-General Sir Henry Karslake
and
Brigadier-General A. B. Beauman

CONTENTS

Author's Note xi
Introduction 19

I	3 September, 1939 – 9 May, 1940	37
II	10 May – 16 May	51
III	17 May – 22 May	63
IV	23 May – 31 May	93
V	31 May – 6 June	121
VI	7 June – 13 June	152
VII	14 June – 20 June	191
VIII	The Final Phase	209
IX	Summary	228

References 242

Appendices

A	Order of Battle on the L of C	247
B	Administrative Position in B.A.F.F. at 1800 hrs, 2 June, 1940	252
C	Sir Henry Karslake's Report	253
D	The Breton Redoubt and the Cotentin Redoubt	264
E	The Armistice Misunderstanding of 17 June, 1940	268

Bibliography 271
Index 273

ILLUSTRATIONS

1	Lieutenant-General Sir Henry Karslake	*facing page* 64
2	Major-General P. de Fonblanque	65
3	Brigadier A.B. Beauman	65
4	Major-General V. Fortune	65
5	Lieutenant-Colonel R. Gethen	65
6	Brigadier F.E. Morgan	65
7	Lieutenant-Colonel A.L. Cameron	96
8	Lieutenant-Colonel J.H. Roberts	96
9	Major A.G. Syme	96
10	Major G.M. Elliot	96
11	CQMS J.S. Brown	96
12	12" Howitzer in France, 1940	97
13	Troops of the 51st Division on the River Bresle, 8 June, 1940	160
14	Conference at Neuborg, 9 June, 1940	160
15	The Surrender of the 51st Division	161
16	Arkforce leaving Le Havre	161
17	The CIG's final instruction to General Karslake	192
18	General Laurencie's Rebuke	193

Illustrations Nos 8, 13, 14, 15 and 16 are reproduced by kind permission of the Imperial War Museum.

AUTHOR'S NOTE

IT may well be questioned whether yet another book about the Second World War is necessary, or even desirable. It has been written because, hitherto, only fragmentary accounts have been given of the parts played by the British Forces operating along the Lines of Communication during the period 10 May to 20 June, 1940.

When my father returned to England from France on 13 June he was, at first, very reticent about his experiences. However, as it was necessary for him to submit a Report to the War Office, he gradually unburdened himself. I was on leave at the time and he employed me in typing out his report. Naturally, for its composition, it was necessary for him to expand on certain matters so that the sense could be conveyed in précis form. This required extensive notes to be made. These notes, designed to act as *aides-mémoires*, contained much detail that had, of necessity, to be omitted from the final draft, containing, inter alia, references to individuals who had signally failed in their duty and to events that did little credit to those who had participated in them.

Some years after the War I returned to England from India. I then began to learn more of the curious 'fog' which enveloped the period concerned. As various books were published containing references to the War in Europe during 1940, including the *Official History*, it became evident that much important detail had been omitted. Whether this was deliberate was difficult to discover. What, however, was quite definite was that many of those who were worthy of recognition had been ignored, and vice-versa. As the result of a large number of interviews and a massive correspondence, some astonishing facts emerged. In this context my grateful thanks are due to the BBC, who kindly permitted me to use their facilities to appeal for information.

It was not until 1970 that the Public Record Office made the relevant Official files available for study. From this point on it was possible to check on details. However, it soon emerged that whole files and certain important documents were missing. It appeared that this had occurred either as a result of enemy action or because someone was anxious that they should not be seen. If the latter, then certainly in one case, this was thwarted. A copy existed *outside* the Official records. From such copies 'out of captivity' it has been possible to explain certain episodes that otherwise would remain mysteries. Also they expose myths that, up to now, have been accepted as facts.

It is possible that some people may not care to learn that their 'idols' had, during this part of their careers, 'feet of clay'. However, if the whole truth about what occurred during those days is to be told, it is essential that the published accounts by some of those involved should be corrected. Without these corrections it would be impossible for the reader and, perhaps most important of all, the serious historian, to obtain a true picture of the last days of that part of the BEF remaining in France after the evacuation from Dunkirk.

It is hoped that the following account will, at long last, fill a gap in the history of the Second World War, thereby completing the story of the BEF in France.

I would like to give my thanks to the late Mr A.J. Norris of the Public Record Office, who helped me to avoid the snares and pitfalls of locating and examining files; Mr Ronald Lewin who gave much of his valuable time in reading various drafts and advising on their modification and construction; Mr Brian Bond, whose specialized knowledge of both military history and the command of English enabled me to correct many passages. He also edited the work as a whole. Finally, my thanks are due to all those Officers and ORs, their wives, widows and relatives, who generously contributed so much in the way of information and introductions.

'Our God and soldier we alike adore
When on the brink of ruin, not before.
After deliverance, both alike requited:
Our God forgotten and our soldiers slighted.'
                              Francis Quarles (1592-1644)

'History does not rate very highly men in key positions who allow their judgement to be influenced by their personal likes and dislikes.'
                              Rommel, Desmond Young,

INTRODUCTION

This nation had yet to learn the important truth
That the most splended bravery of our Soldiers cannot always
Atone for the neglect or incompetence of those in high places
                          Hayens, after the loss of Menorca in 1756

It is not the purpose of this book to discuss whether Great Britain should, on political grounds, have declared war on Germany in 1939. However, it can be considered whether or not the country was in a position to engage in war with a major continental power at that time. For years it had been the custom to rely upon France to provide the necessary field force should a conflict break out with Germany, Britain, certainly at first, contributing a largely token force, the main effort being directed to the provision of a fleet and, later, air power. Indeed, it was not until April, 1939, that the British Government decided that an expeditionary force should be organized. Up to that time the Army's role was confined to Imperial commitments and home defence. It will be appreciated that the equipment of a force destined for a continental war was very different from that hitherto considered necessary. The provision of armour and the heavier calibre artillery for service in such places as India was on a very small scale. For war with a European power such equipment was vital in very large quantities.

As late as 1938 the manufacture of heavy equipment was of the lowest priority, the provision of medium and heavy guns being quite inadequate to equip even the existing small establishment. At the time of Munich the Committee of Imperial Defence stated categorically that Great Britain was quite incapable of waging any type of war — let alone a continental war. Mr Chamberlain therefore had no alternative but obtain the best terms he could, if only to gain the necessary time. The CID calculated that it would take at least eighteen months, probably two years, before the Army was in a position to go to war if a major rearmament programme was begun at once and at full pressure.

But it was not only from a dearth of equipment that the Army suffered. When war was declared, on 3 September, 1939, the British Army possessed only one officer who had commanded a formation on active service. This was General Sir Edmund Ironside who had commanded the British Expeditionary Force in the Archangel Campaign in 1919. All the other senior officers, owing to accelerated promotion, found themselves in command of formations for which they had had little practical training or, indeed, experience.

In February, 1940, a book was published entitled *Leaders Of The Army*. Its object was to give the public confidence in those senior officers who were responsible for the conduct of the war on land. The officers selected for special mention were Ironside (CIGS), Gort (C-in-C), Kirke (Director-General, Home Forces) and, at the author's insistence, Wavell (C-in-C, Middle East). While little difficulty arose in providing convincing details about three of the above, the chapters dealing with Lord Gort had largely to be confined to accounts of his outstanding gallantry as a junior officer and padded out with details of operations by the Germans in the First World War. It does not take the reader long to discover that Gort possessed no qualifications whatsoever for the important post he was suddenly called upon to occupy.

Many reasons have been put forward as to why the Secretary of State for War, Mr Hore-Belisha, selected, and the King approved, Gort for the appointment of Commander-in-Chief. The most logical one is that Belisha and Gort had been at loggerheads for some considerable time. Belisha had considered every possible method of removing him from the War Office, but had been warned against them, particularly as he had made the appointment in the first place. The chance, when it arose, was too good to miss — and it was one that the King would accept. Belisha jumped at it. Little did he realize that he had exchanged 'King Log' for 'King Stork'. It is to be wondered if he ever considered the effect that his action might have on the future of the Army.

As no major manoeuvres had been held in England since the early 1930s, few officers had had the opportunity to command actual 'bodies' on the ground. Only paper exercises had been carried out and these had been most unconvinving. General Wavell had the advantage of having been GSO I of the 3rd Division on Salisbury Plain in the 1920s and of having taken part in major manoeuvres, even though he had not had a similar opportunity when he was GOC-in-C Southern Command just prior to the war. Unquestionably, apart from Ironside, he was the best fitted to undertake a major command, as he was to prove later in North Africa. Though General Dill, as GOC-in-C Aldershot Command, had commanded a Brigade during the 1920s, the final period of major manoeuvres, his record had been mainly one of staff work in England from the time he had served on Lord Haig's staff during the First World War. None of the other senior officers who led the various formations into France in 1939 had had command experience with actual troops in the field. In due course, as is well known, many of these officers proved themselves highly competent. At the time, however, the situation was most unsatisfactory and, indeed, dangerous.

The danger was, of course, enhanced by the lack of suitable equipment. For years no definite conclusions had been reached as to the type of weapons needed, owing to the Government's failure to decide on the role the army was to play. So no firm orders were given to manufacturers. A great deal of time and money was expended on experimentation but, owing to lack of decision, no effort was made to ensure that the Army was properly equipped.

One result of the purge of senior officers carried out by Belisha in 1937 was the abolition of the post of Master General of the Ordnance. As a result the Army found itself without a major spokesman on equipment. Instead, when it was decided to fit out the Army on a continental scale, all that was considered necessary was to extract the scale of arms from the war establishment of a formation, say a division, and to place orders for such weapons with sundry contractors, parts for the same weapon, for example, being manufactured by a number of different firms. When the guns had to be assembled it was often found that the parts did not 'marry up'. Ultimately, formations received those arms which were 'laid down' but were not necessarily of the type and on the scale required for the particular enterprise on which the formation was to be employed. In fact, as was subsequently proved, much of the equipment was totally unsuitable. What was worse, no provision had been made to build up a reserve. This was aggravated by the fact that the factories were still working on a peacetime schedule and influenced by Trade Union attitudes. Even after the outbreak of war employees were still governed by Union rules.

Until Mr Chamberlain resigned in May, 1940, the Labour Party pursued an obstructive line because they were not prepared to collaborate with a Conservative Government headed by Mr Chamberlain. It can be imagined how this attitude was reflected in the Trade Unions.

There seems little reason to doubt that the Germans were fully acquainted with Britain's lack of preparation. Indeed, it must have staggered the German Government that the country had the temerity to issue an ultimatum over Poland.

To the uninitiated the appearance of the BEF in France during September and October of 1939 was impressive. However, some senior officers, who could see beyond the turnout of the troops and the bright new paint on the vehicles, described the forces as a 'Whited Sepulchre'. Where were the 3" mortars, the 2" HE mortar bombs, to say nothing of pistols, binoculars and other items? After the arrival of III Corps, the shipment of arms, as opposed to necessaries, virtually ceased. Other than the arrival of the three superheavy batteries at the instigation of Mr Churchill, there is no sign that any further guns were landed in France (except the two batteries of A/T guns belonging to the Support Group) until after 7 June, 1940, on the arrival of the 52nd Division. It was only in the vast empty spaces in the Ordnance gun parks that the absence of any reserve of artillery began to be noticed. It was brought home, however, when units sent in their guns to Ordnance for reconditioning and discovered that there were none to replace them. Representations were made to the War Office but without effect. In this connection, reference should be made to a booklet, *The Battle of Flanders*, issued by the War Office in 1941. The relevant passage reads:

'But [says Lord Gort] the situation as regards equipment, though there was latterly some improvement in certain directions, caused me serious misgivings, even before men and material began to be diverted by the needs of operations elsewhere. [This refers to the

Norwegian campaign.] I had, on several occasions, called the attention of the War Office to the shortage of almost every nature of ammunition, of which the stocks in France were not nearly large enough to permit the rates of expenditure laid down for sustained operations in War.

'Grave words. As matters turned out, the ultimate operations lasted for too brief a period for these shortages to be felt. Our disasters arose from other causes. But it is none the less uncomfortable to speculate here as to how our resources would have stood the strain had the Battle of Flanders been prolonged for twenty-five weeks instead of twenty-five days.'

The War Office booklet continues:

'The shortages were not primarily the fault of the War Office, nor for that matter, the Ministry of Supply. They were the fruit of our national predilection for a policy of *laissez faire* and wishful thinking'.[1] (It might have been added that it was also the fault of the Secretary of State for War and the CIGS who had both held office for the few years prior to the outbreak of war.)

While the above quotations may seem surprising, it must be remembered that the reinforcement schedule required the British to provide fifteen divisions by the end of 1940 at the latest. As it was essential for these divisions to take the field both trained and equipped, the guns, as they became available, were to be allotted to them.

For the first months of the war no actual hostilities took place, so the provision of reserve artillery was not pressed at that time and if the equipment schedules had been capable of being implemented, the situation might not have been so bad.

The opening of the Norwegian campaign caused much valuable equipment to be diverted. So when three of the divisions being formed were ordered to France they were neither trained nor equipped — nor did they possess any artillery. This, after seven months of war! It was not until two months later that another division was sent over; this was only partially trained but at least it had its full complement of artillery. A further division, the 1st Canadian, was also ready for despatch. It is said that this latter formation had been equipped at the expense of a British division — but where was this British division? The truth is that there was no British division ready to proceed overseas. The units that had returned from the abortive Norwegian campaign had lost most of their equipment and much of their cohesion; they could contribute little of benefit to the new units. This is confirmed by the fact that, when the 3rd Division was being prepared, after its return through Dunkirk, to reinforce the new BEF it was found possible to equip it with one Field battery only!

It has been said that artillery was sent to France in advance of the new formations. This is incorrect as the example of the Support Group will show. When the Group moved to France its Commander was informed that the Bofors guns belonging to his two AA batteries, which had had to be left in England as part of the Air Defence of Great Britain, would be replaced on arrival. In fact there were no spare Bofors guns in France.

The situation as regards armour was even worse than the artillery. Little was done, prior to the outbreak of war, to provide a real armoured formation. Certainly those officers who were interested in such matters were largely ignored. Indeed, it seems that a definite policy was followed to pass over any officer who had a specialized knowledge of this arm. This is proved by the selection of Commanders of the Mobile, and subsequently, Armoured divisions. Unsuitable vehicles were produced and those that there were had few spares and no replacements. Training had been minimal. When the 1st (and only) Armoured Division made ready to proceed to France, its establishment was suddenly changed at the last moment. Up to then the 2nd Armoured Brigade had been classified as 'Light' and equipped and trained as such, the 3rd Armoured Brigade being the 'Heavy' Brigade. Now both Brigades were made homogeneous; neither had the necessary experience of this new establishment before being called upon to engage in hostilities.

Owing to the lack of both training and equipment the Division was quite incapable of being employed in battle until a considerable amount of 'settling down' had taken place. Its piecemeal employment under an inexperienced commander was bound to end in tragedy; particularly as the Division, in addition to its other disadvantages, had been 'milked' of some of its most important elements on the very day it left for France.

One of the most vexed questions was the role of the Royal Air Force. For many years prior to the war a number of senior Army officers had been agitating for the Army to have its own Air Service, as did the Royal Navy. Notwithstanding the fact that it had been agreed, when the Royal Air Force was first formed, that the Army should have a major say in its composition, employment and equipment, those at the head of the RAF were able to use their not inconsiderable influence to obtain their own requirements. In the early days the RAF had co-operated thoroughly with the Army in support of ground operations, but by the end of the 1920s (except in India) this spirit of co-operation had evaporated. When, therefore, the BEF went to France, the Air Component that had been allotted to it by the RAF to fulfil the various essential tasks required by the Army Command was found largely wanting. Undoubtedly the personnel of this Component did their utmost to fulfil their intended role, but they had no training or experience in close co-operation with ground forces. Indeed, most of the aircraft were totally unsuitable for this role, so the results left much to be desired.

The other, and completely independent, part of the RAF in France, the Advanced Air Striking Force, also had no training and experience in operating with ground forces. It had always been the opinion of the leaders of the RAF that their role was essentially strategic in character — long-range bombing in no way connected with tiresome battles that might occur on land. They made it quite clear that they considered that the Army's role, as far as they were concerned, was to provide them with supplies, labour and ground protection only. This attitude was brought out by the fact that, when it was decided to abandon an airfield owing to German advances, the RAF personnel would fly out and leave the Army to clear up the mess with no instructions or directions. AA batteries found themselves suddenly alone on empty airfields in imminent danger of being captured. Several units were lost in this way.

It is amazing, in the light of the reports submitted to the Secretary of State for War after the German manoeuvres of 1937, that this attitude was tolerated. As is now known, Hore-Belisha never bothered to read the reports. Soon afterwards came his 'non-selective purge' when at least two of those officers who had submitted reports were compelled to leave the army.

After Dunkirk, the assistance rendered to the troops fighting south of the Somme by the RAF was negligible. The available airmen did all they could but they were far too few and too widely spread to influence the situation. Also the system required the deployment of the RAF from England, rather than by those on the spot, which ensured that it was rare that planes were available at the times and places they were most urgently needed.

From the beginning of the German offensive on 10 May, 1940, it quickly became apparent that the efforts of the Government, and the Secretary of State in particular, to provide a Field Army with its essential requirements were far from satisfactory. No reserve of artillery existed in France. Certain types of ammunition barely existed, notably that required by the Armoured Division that Lord Gort was urging to be sent to France. As is now known, when the 2nd Armoured Brigade landed they found the greatest difficulty in finding any ammunition for their Besa guns. In addition, there was a severe shortage of trained personnel in reserve. The reason for this is not far to seek. The shortage of equipment in England effectively prevented training being undertaken both by the troops required to act as reinforcements for those formations already in France and those who were being prepared to form the new divisions intended to be sent over in the near future.

The abolition of the post of Master General of the Ordnance had a very serious effect on the Army. The loss of a gun meant that, for an indefinite time, the unit was without its full compliment. When the L of C was finally severed, the total guns found to be available for the defence of the south consisted of twelve Field guns returned by the 51st Division for reconditioning by Ordnance, one 6" Howitzer, that had no recoil mechanism, 40 A/T guns and eight A/T guns borrowed from the French. When one considers that there were eleven divisions in France, including eight in action, it brings out the utter unpreparedness of the country for war on land. The French have been sneered at for declaring that they had no reserves — but Great Britain had none either.

If the Army lacked much in the way of logistics, nevertheless, in two aspects it possessed considerable superiority over both its allies and its foes. Owing to the troops being constantly employed in constructing defensive works or in training, their health was second to none. Secondly, the Army's supply system in France was unquestionably most efficient. It was only during the last few days in France that the system showed signs of collapse, and this was owing to internal rather than external pressures.

There is little doubt that the insistence by Lord Gort that three untrained divisions be sent to France as 'labour' in April, 1940, was a 'straw in the wind'. Indeed, it showed quite clearly what might be expected to develop in the future. His failure to curb what amounted to over-enthusiasm on the part of the supply services in demanding the construction of larger and larger depots and equivalent services meant that the 'tail' was beginning to 'wag the dog'. Even after the isolation of the BEF the GOC L of C was instructed to continue developing railway sidings and increasing the capacity of the depots. As late as 12 June, vast supplies continued to flow into his area through the southern ports, requiring the use of troops who could have been gainfully employed in fighting the enemy, to unload and stack them — supplies that were ultimately to be lost to the enemy.[1] The remains of the 35th Brigade, on orders from London, continued to work on new sidings until 7 June. Even had there been a reasonable prospect of a reconstituted BEF returning to France in strength, all this additional work was quite unnecessary. Time after time this was represented to the War Office but to no avail.

When, on 15 May, orders were received from GHQ by the HQ of the L of C to arrange for the forwarding of the two 'labour' divisions, the 12th and 46th, who were under their administrative command, they did little to prepare them for the forthcoming ordeal. Though they were fully aware of the divisions' shortages, no effort was made to try and provide them with essentials. Though small arms were available, none were issued to bring the divisions' compliment up to war strength. No ammunition was provided; no maps, though the main map depot was in Paris. Indeed, other than the provision of the minimum of rations, the divisions moved forward with only the poor equipment with which they had originally been issued. The actual move, however, was in conformity with the efficiency previously displayed by the Movements section of the L of C. No blame can be attached to them that the results did not come up to expectations. They were not to know that the Germans were going to anticipate them by taking Amiens. The move via Abbeville was, at first, quite correct, but the misfortune of a faulty telephone line and the 'jumpiness' of one man completely upset the operation. The failure of the divisions to arrive at their destinations complete was advantageous to the defenders in the south. Had the 37th Brigade been able to pass through to the north, it would not have been available to carry out essential work later on. Unquestionably, had the 37th managed to join up with those in the north, it would have been eliminated to no purpose. Other units, also, were gainfully employed which otherwise would have been lost.

Much scorn has been poured on the Beauman Division[2], yet, as is now known, the French Commander-in-Chief, North-eastern Armies, General Georges, considered that its services were vital. He was fully aware of what it was composed and was not misled by its nomenclature into thinking that it was a full-strength fighting division. It cannot be emphasized too strongly how well this makeshift formation performed. In spite of its lack of equipment, it caused considerable discomfort to the enemy.* Had it been disbanded on 1 June, as ordered by the War Office, 'A' Brigade would not have been available to reinforce the 51st Division. It is interesting to note, when considering this 'irregular' force, that General Brooke received orders from the War Office on 14 June to organize similar formations![3]

It is said that it is easy to be wise after the event. In view of this the reader may well wonder what is the value in considering, once again, what might have happened if things had been different. The answer in this case is simple. Had there been errors of judgement, and undoubtedly there were many, and on them only was criticism made, then the examination would be of very little value. In the event, this is not so. Many of the actions taken were deliberately taken, not from military considerations but purely personal ones. This is emphasized when one comes to consider the individual who was responsible for such a situation having arisen. The error that produced the events described occurred as far back as 1938 when Gort became CIGS. Having accepted the Belisha purge, it is quite evident that either General Wavell or General Dill should have filled the post. Of the two, Wavell was by far the more experienced. Dill had had very little field experience and was not in the best of

---

* Lord Alanbrooke, in his foreword to *Then a Soldier*, confirms the undoubted value of the Beauman Division.

health. If Wavell had been appointed, Ironside would have become C-in-C in France. Possibly Gort might have been given a corps, though, through his lack of experience as a commander of troops, a division would have been more appropriate. In due course he might have become a valuable commander of a higher formation in the same way as Alexander or Montgomery. It did not take Belisha long to discover that his earlier purge had created a problem as to how to obtain good commanders for his projected Army expansion. But now it was too late. It was to be another two years before really qualified men made their appearance. The sending of Wavell to the Middle East undoubtedly saved the situation in that area. Nevertheless, his absence from England during the opening stages of the War was sorely felt by the British Army in France. Furthermore, the appointment of Gort, first as CIGS and afterwards as C-in-C, caused a great deal of ill-feeling and jealousy among those who considered that these posts were rightfully theirs, both through seniority and experience. The appointment of Ironside to succeed Gort at the War Office also caused strong feeling. When Dill ultimately achieved his ambition by being appointed CIGS he made quite sure that instructions issued by his predecessor were cancelled, irrespective of whether those instructions were right or wrong. As is well known, after his return to England after Dunkirk, Lord Gort was condemned to virtual obscurity. Bearing the above in mind, it can be readily imagined what effects personal feelings had on the conduct of affairs in France after 26 May, 1940, when Ironside relinquished his post as CIGS.

One example of this was the situation that arose over the Commander of the Lines of Communication.

On 21 May General Ironside had no reason to believe that the BEF would be permanently severed from its L of C. He realized, however, that the L of C themselves, together with the massive and valuable stocks distributed along their length, were imperilled by the progress of the German advance, particularly through the capture of Amiens. He was also aware that there were virtually no troops available in the south capable of putting up much in the way of defence, should the enemy decide to push in that direction. Until, therefore, Lord Gort was in a position, once again, to exercise control and afford adequate protection to his vital lines of supply, it was essential to be prepared for any eventuality. To do this, it was imperative to organize the L of C as a separate operational command under an experienced officer. While it was admitted that the forces immediately available were minimal, it was hoped that in due course they would be reinforced. In the meantime, all superfluous and vital stores and equipment should be evacuated as quickly as possible. The CIGS selected for this almost impossible task Lieutenant-General Sir Henry Karslake. Karslake's job, at first, was not primarily to engage in hostilities; indeed it was recognized that the forces available to him were negligible. As a result, it was not then thought necessary to issue him with similar terms of reference as those issued to Lord Gort. In any case, such troops as there were, other than the 1st Armoured Division, were under his direct command and not under the French, save that the General himself was under the command of General Georges.

It was not until General Karslake returned to France after his meeting with Ironside on 25 May that the CIGS decided that the situation had so changed that the L of C should be reorganized as a Corps. He had approved of the measures Karslake had taken as regards the raising of additional infantry and the forming of a force on divisional lines. Immediate action was taken to arrange for experienced officers to be sent from England to take command of the newly formed brigades. He also decided that the time had come for Karslake to be issued with new terms of reference. Accordingly orders were issued for the necessary documents to be drawn up for signature by the Secretary of State. Unfortunately, these documents were not ready until 27 May. By that time, Ironside had left the War Office to assume his apointment as Commander-in-Chief, Home Forces. Dill, the new CIGS, cancelled Karslake's appointment and the arrangements Ironside had made for the requisite Headquarters staff to be sent out. Fortunately, the posting of the officers to the new composite division had already been acted upon, and they had left for France. It would seem that for some reason the news of the cancelling of Karslake's appointment was never made known, as in the War Office booklet *The Battle of Flanders* appears the following paragraph:

'By 21 May, enemy penetration into the rearward areas had increased to such an extent that communications across the Somme were finally severed. On 23 May, therefore, the War Office appointed General Sir Henry Karslake to command the defences of the Lines of Communication: in other words, the whole of the above-mentioned force ...'

'The above-mentioned force' consisted of 'the 51st Division, now returning from the Saar, and the Armoured Division which had at last arrived in France. There were in addition some nine battalions of the 12th and 46th Divisions, and the troops of the Pioneer Corps.'

Had this force indeed been under General Karslake's command, a command structure would have been essential and the 'terms of reference' vital. As it was, of course, this was far from the case. There was no unified command.

To understand how such a curious situation could arise, it is necessary to examine in some detail what had happened during the period between the arrival of the BEF in France and 10 May, 1940. In the spring of 1940 General Dill, then commanding I Corps, returned on sick leave to England. During most of the period between the arrival of I Corps in France and General Dill's departure, there had been a whispering campaign directed at both Hore-Belisha and General Ironside. A major row had developed over some remarks made by Belisha about the BEF's apparently weak efforts in the construction of field-works along their sector of the Belgo-French frontier. This had resulted in the replacement of the Secretary of State by Mr Oliver Stanley. From every available personal account of the period, the feelings among the senior officers in France were that Ironside should go as well. There is little doubt that approaches were made to the Monarch in this direction. However, Mr Winston Churchill was adamant that Ironside should remain as CIGS. But eventually sufficient pressure was brought to bear during March, 1940, to appoint Dill to the post of VCIGS. In April, therefore, Dill handed over his command to General Barker and assumed his new appointment. He was now but one step from his ultimate objective, which he had always thought should be rightfully his. Furthermore, he was now in an extremely sound tactical position, having the ears of many influential persons both in and out of the Government. All these persons were in a position to further his career — not least Mr Anthony Eden who succeeded Mr

Oliver Stanley as Secretary of State for War in Mr Churchill's administration on 10 May, 1940.

There is little doubt that the senior officers in France were greatly influenced in their opinion of Ironside by the opening of the Norwegian campaign. They considered that Ironside was deliberately depriving the Army in France of essentials both in manpower and material. It would seem that they did not appreciate that Ironside was making every effort to provide what was required and also having to subscribe to orders that he was receiving from his masters in the Government. Ironside was fully alive to the inadequacy of the Army to undertake a major confrontation in France and, at the same time, to provide for such other enterprises in which the Government might see fit to engage. In fact, he was placed in an impossible position. It is difficult to see how, if he had been replaced, his successor could have done better.

MAPS

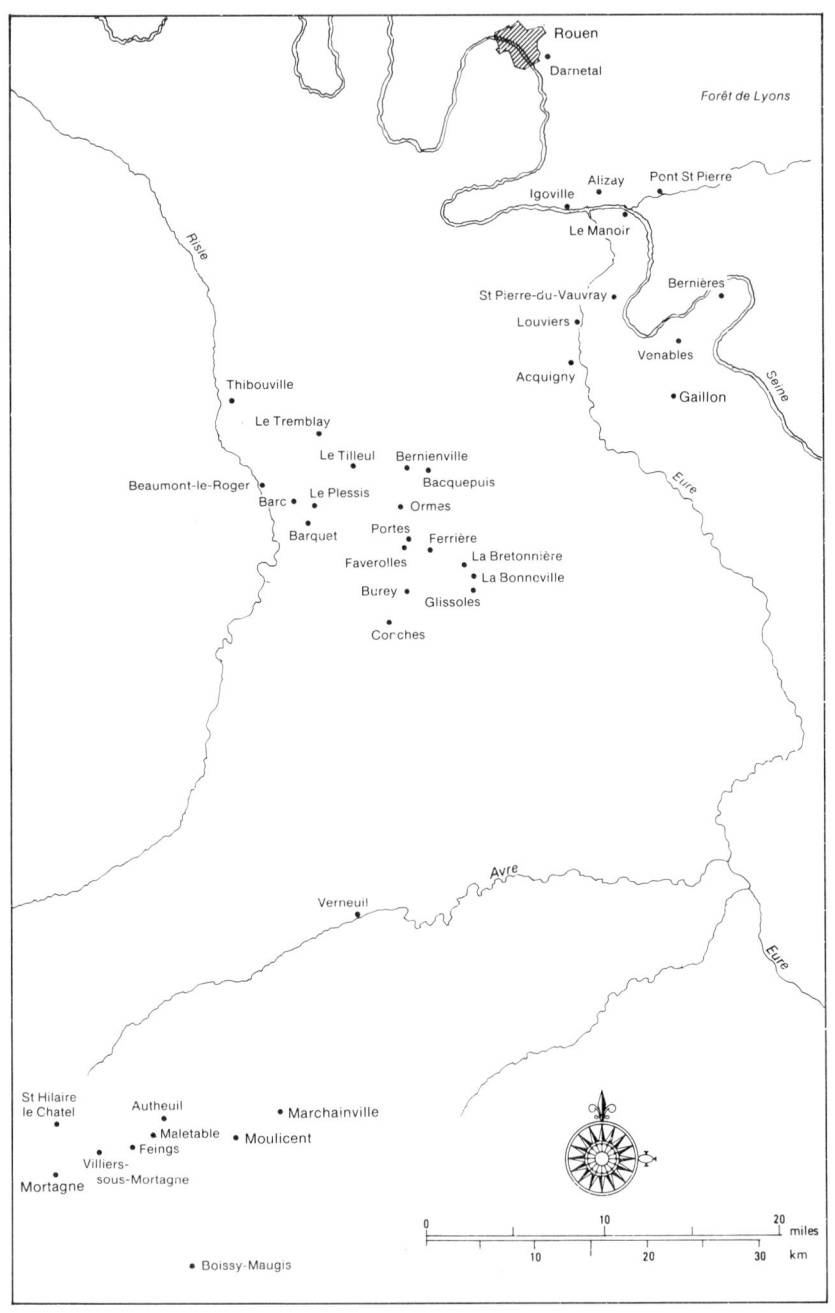

I

3 September, 1939 — 9 May, 1940

As a result of the growing danger from Germany, it was agreed that Staff talks should begin in March, 1939. The French laid down the principle that, from the outbreak of war, all the French frontiers should be safeguarded until such time as the joint Armies were in a position to undertake an offensive; how long this would take was not decided. Further, it was agreed that Great Britain would provide initially four complete divisions followed by further formations so as to reach a total of at least fifteen divisions by the end of 1940. It will already be appreciated that the strain imposed on the British Army to fulfil these obligations would be considerable, not only as regards the provision of trained men but also in the supply of adequate weapons and other necessaries.

While all these matters were being discussed the War Office instructed the Quartermaster-General's Department to examine and, thereafter, plan both the movement and supply of four divisions and the eventual build-up to the full commitment. This was an enormous task and required visits to France by numerous officers to examine the lay-out of ports and to select sites for dumps and camps; in addition, of course, it was essential for there to be a high degree of liaison between the opposite numbers on the Staffs of both countries.

Lest it be assumed that action of the above kind took place only on the actual outbreak of war, it should be pointed out that at the War Office a 'War Book' was maintained. The War Book consisted, in considerable detail, of plans to be put into operation during various periods of readiness culminating in the outbreak of the war itself. It will be appreciated, therefore, that the greater part of the basic planning had been done already. However, the organization for any specific event naturally required certain modifications to be made appropriate to the situation. As far as a campaign in France was concerned, the organization presented many problems over and above the normal ones as, in addition to that of language, there was the difference between the road and rail systems to be considered. Even the standard of accommodation for the troops was different. It was fortunate, therefore, that there were still five months to pass before the Staffs were to be called upon to put their plans into operation.

The duties of the Quartermaster-General's Department were wide and varied. In addition to transportation of all kinds, it was responsible for the supply of all food, clothing and ammunition. Also, Mr Hore-Belisha having abolished the Master General of the Ordnance, the Quartermaster-General had to take all Ordnance supplies under his wing, except for the actual ordering and provision of supplies by the manufacturers.

In peacetime the number of personnel required to carry out these multitudinous duties was small compared to the number needed in war. It will be appreciated, therefore, that there were very few, either officers or men, who were fully conversant with all the ramifications of each of the branches of the Department. It was necessary, on mobilization, to recruit personnel through the medium of instructions issued over the signature of the Army Council, to both Formation and Unit Commanders. These instructions required that the names of all those deemed suitable for incorporating into the Movement Control, Billetting and General Administration duties in 'Q' Branch should be submitted. Such appointments were regarded by Commanding Officers as necessary evils. This attitude frequently produced either very young and inexperienced officers or those who their Commanding Officer regarded as 'difficult' or inefficient. It can be readily appreciated what difficulties were experienced by the senior members of the various 'Q' sections when they found themselves saddled with this vast number of inexperienced officers and men. These they then had to convert into an efficient team for the purpose of conducting a series of most complicated procedures. Notwithstanding the foregoing, it should be understood that, in addition to misfits, there were a very large number of men who were of the highest standard but whose 'faces did not fit' and had been rejected by their units. These turned out to be invaluable when employed in other spheres.[1]

The actual area covered by the Lines of Communication was

considerable. It ran approximately from Arras in the north to Marseilles in the south. The main line can be compared to a river fed by a series of tributaries from the West. These feeder lines connected the main line to the ports. Along its length were numbers of dumps and camps in which stores and personnel were accommodated pending their being forwarded to the fighting formations along the Franco-Belgian Frontier. In due course, as will be seen, this main line was to become the longest Line of Communication in the history of the British Army — over five hundred miles in length and, as a result, increasingly vulnerable to interruption by enemy activity.

From the establishment of L of C Headquarters at Le Mans in September, 1939, until November of that year the L of C Area was divided, for administrative purposes, into sub-areas, each commanded by a Brigadier. These sub-areas contained branches of all the Services, e.g. RE, Ordnance, RASC. As long as any of the fighting formations or units was within his sub-area, the Brigadier was responsible for its feeding and supply and, eventually, for its onward transmission. These Brigadiers were mainly retired officers who had had considerable experience of administrative command and, though probably over the average age for their rank, were ideal for the positions that they were called upon to occupy. They had, however, to train their staffs for their various duties. In some cases this proved a herculean task, as can well be imagined, but there are very few recorded instances when these commanders failed to achieve their object.

The administration of the whole of the Lines of Communication was conducted from a château near Le Mans under the command of a Major-General. This officer had been selected with the greatest care but Major-General Philip de Fonblanque was, unfortunately, not the ideal officer for the position he was given. There was one gap in his experience which was to have serious consequences in the months to come. This was the fact that, except as a very junior officer in the First World War, he had had no combatant experience or war training, nor had he ever held any form of combatant command.[2] However, as an administrator of the normal functions carried out by the various branches of the L of C his work was beyond praise.

Before relating the various activities in France it is necessary to turn to England for a moment. Besides the announcement that Great Britain was at war with Germany, 3 September, 1939, was noteworthy for the most peculiar event in the history of the British Army that has ever occurred on the very day when the Army was called upon to enter a major conflict.

Up to the afternoon of 3 September, General Ironside, as Inspector-General of the Forces, had been led to believe that he would be appointed Commander-in-Chief of the projected Field Force to be sent to France. He had made every preparation for the moment when the appointment became official, even to the extent of sending his Staff to Camberley. He then received a message from the Secretary of State for War asking him to come to the latter's office. He assumed that it was to receive his appointment. There he was told that he was to become CIGS in place of Lord Gort and that Lord Gort was to become Commander-in-Chief. When he was informed of this development, and Lord Gort entered the room, Ironside states, 'I could hardly believe that I was hearing right'.[3]

There is no doubt whatsoever that the appointment of Gort as C-in-C came as a great disappointment to Ironside, particularly as he had been led to believe for so long that he was to hold the post. Also he felt that he was quite unsuitable for the position of CIGS, having had no experience of the War Office, but he considered that he was eminently qualified to conduct operations in the field. While the appointments came as a shock to the officers concerned, others were equally astonished. General Sir John Dill, the third senior general in the Army, was GOC-in-C Aldershot Command. When he heard the news he could scarcely credit it. This was his second great disappointment in recent years. Being a strong supporter of Hore-Belisha's 'youth at the helm' policy in 1937, he had assumed that he would receive the appointment of CIGS on the removal of Sir Cyril Deverell. The appointment of a junior Major-General to this important post came as a staggering blow. Now, once again, he was prevented from assuming what he considered to be his rightful position; in fact, he had been pushed further down the ladder.

Lieutenant-General A.F. Brooke, General Officer Commanding-in-Chief Southern Command, naturally became Commander of II Corps in the BEF. This was the customary procedure in the event of war. His reaction to Gort's appointment can be understood and appreciated. He now found himself under the command of an officer far junior in age to himself and, what was worse, an officer who had had no experience in commanding a formation of *any kind*. Gort's promotion to full General when he became CIGS meant nothing. In fact, other than holding the 'local' rank of Lieutenant-General when he was Military Secretary for a short time, Gort was still only a junior Major-General. He was, in fact, two years senior to Brooke in that rank.

It was in this somewhat strained atmosphere that Great Britain's Army went to war against the most formidable military power in Europe. It did not augur well for the future.

On 4 September, 1939, advanced parties sailed for France to prepare the way for the reception of the British Expeditionary Force. The first troopships arrived at Cherbourg and St Nazaire on the 10th. With the exception of a few minor errors in calculation, many of which could not have been foreseen, the whole programme for the landing of the two Corps was carried out satisfactorily. Between 3 and 12 October both Corps had moved north from their assembly areas to their appointed positions between Maulde on the east along the Franco-Belgian frontier and Halluin in the west, with a defensive flank along the River Lys from Halluin to Armentières. The lay-out of the L of C in conjunction with the 'Fighting Line' was in strict conformity with basic military principles, namely it was at right-angles. This ensured the uninterrupted supply of troops and stores to the front. The principal ports were those south of Dieppe, because such ports as Boulogne and Dover were within striking range of the Luftwaffe. It should be noted, however, that as the 'Phoney' war progressed these latter ports were fully employed, if mainly for the movement of leave personnel owing to the regular Channel ferries being still available; also these ports provided the shortest crossings.

Both during and after the arrival of the troops, massive quantities of supplies of all kinds poured through the ports into the L of C area. These were quickly disposed of into the various dumps which were being constructed. The whole system was based on that of the First World War when, after the first few months, there was not the least likelihood of a renewal of mobile operations. In fact the whole command was carried on in a First World War atmosphere. There was no sense of urgency as the enemy had shown no inclination to undertake any offensive measures.

The entire scheme of the war had been based on the static guarding of the French frontier and allowing the enemy to break himself on massive defences such as the Maginot Line and the subsidiary lines that were being constructed along the front facing Belgium. Probably one of the best examples of the First World War attitude was when Mr Winston Churchill authorized the dispatch to France of three super-heavy batteries, each equipped with 9.2" and 12" howitzers. These guns were to be mounted in concrete emplacements. The chances of their being moved was considered remote. Light railways were constructed to feed these monster weapons from special ammunition dumps; all was set for a three-year war of slogging. In fact, these weapons were destined never to fire a round and ultimately fell into the hands of the Germans. Had they been fired, they would have been the largest pieces of ordnance to be used in the campaign.*

As the months passed and the dumps grew bigger so did they become more vulnerable to pilferage. The possibility of their being destroyed by parachutists or Fifth Columnists seems to have been barely considered, but it was decided to provide guards, if only in some cases of a 'stick' type. Hitherto such guard duty as had been carried out had been undertaken by Corps personnel working in the dumps. This had now become too big a task for the men available, particularly as they were expected to carry out their normal duties as well. Arrangements were made, therefore, to replace them by Second Line Territorial battalions from the United Kingdom. These battalions were composed of officers and men who, nevertheless, possessed a great deal of enthusiasm. It was felt that, after a very short time, they would prove their worth.

In view of the foregoing it is important to note the advice given to the Commander-in-Chief, Lord Gort, by the CIGS, General Iron-

---

* They were incorporated into the German Army being described as: 'Haubitzer 30.5cm 631 (E) and 24.4cm 546 (E)', E standing for English. Actually, the largest gun in France at that time was a 52cm railway mounted howitzer of 1916. This was, also, incorporated into the German Army as 'Haubitzer eisenbahn 52cm 871 (F)', for French. (Ian. V. Hogg).

side, on 10 September, just before the former left for France:

'I had a farewell talk with Gort and Dill [then commanding I Corps] . . . I told them of all my strategic ideas, and I then made an appeal to them to see that their men and transport did not expose themselves to air attack. *Anywhere behind the fighting line is the battle line. Nowhere is anybody safe. All must dig in and disperse themselves. This is particularly necessary amongst the Army Service Corps and the Army Ordnance Corps.*'[4]

While it is admitted that many of the dumps were widely dispersed, notably the great ammunition dumps near Buchy and St Saens, a minimum of protection was either provided, or indeed, designed for those in the rear areas. This failure to heed Ironside's warning was to have dire consequences in due course.

The first three Territorial units designated to provide guards and patrols were as follows:

1/5th The Sherwood Foresters was commanded by Major E.D. Shaw. This unit had been embodied on the outbreak of war but had been 'milked' under the Belisha scheme for doubling the Territorial Army. It landed in France on 7 November and took up its position in the neighbourhood of Nozay.

The 4th Border Regiment was commanded by Lt-Colonel T.W.A. Tomlinson. This unit was one of the first of the Territorial units to be mobilized; it came into being on 1 Setpember. It, too, arrived in France on 7 November and was stationed at Morlaix.

The final unit was the 4th Battalion of the Buffs. This battalion was mobilized on 3 September and was commanded by Lt-Colonel F.A.J.E. Marshall. It did not land in France until 17 November. The unit was widely dispersed, its HQ being at Nantes, with one company at St Nazaire and yet another at Le Havre. Its final company was at the disposal of HQ L of C at Le Mans. The chances of it receiving any training was therefore minimal. Yet when the time came, all these units were to uphold the honour of their regiments and the British Army in an exemplary manner.

These three battalions brought with them either their bands or corps of fifes and drums. By so doing, they were able to maintain the morale of the local population by giving concerts or displays in the way of 'beating retreat' in the nearby towns. It may be remembered that, at home, orders had been given that no bands should play, in order, it was said, to show that the country was grim and earnest in its determination. Fortunately, soon after Mr Churchill became Prime Minister these orders were rescinded.

Before leaving these three battalions, it is as well to correct an error that appears in their Regimental Histories together with certain other books that have been published concerning this period in France. In these it has been stated that these battalions formed the 25th Brigade in France. This was not so; they had, in fact, formed the 25th Brigade *in England.* Before they left for France they were un-brigaded. On arrival they became L of C Troops. The 25th Brigade was reformed and became part of the 50th (Northumbrian) Division under Major-General G. le Q. Martel.

By the end of November, 1939, the number of troops and dumps on the L of C had grown to such an extent that the War Office decided to decentralize the command. General de Fonblanque should remain in overall command but the area should be divided into two Districts, Southern and Northern. Unfortunately, through the slow moving of the War Office, it was not until March, 1940, that the new organization actually became a reality. As it is with the Northern District that we are most concerned, the general lay-out is given below:

District Commander	Brigadier A.B. Beauman
Boulogne Sub-area	Brigadier Griffin
Boulogne, Calais and Dunkirk	
Rouen Sub-area	Brigadier Barry
Rouen, Le Havre and Fécamp	
Le Mans Sub-area	Brigadier Wilmer
Dieppe	Colonel Wilson RAMC
Undefended Medical Port	
Arras Sub-area	Colonel Usher
Amiens Sub-area	Brigadier Barry
Cherbourg Sub-area	Brigadier Thorpe
Cherbourg and Caen	
Rouvray	Colonel C. Vicary
1 and 2 Infantry Base Depot and General Base Depot	
Auxiliary Military Pioneer Corps Group	Colonel Diggle

In addition there were the large ammunition depots at Buchy and St Saens, the Motor Transport depot at Rouen, the RASC Dump at Le Havre and Ordnance and RASC dumps in and around Abancourt.

Though the command was so considerable and the various sub-area commanders were in the main brigadiers, the commander of the District was not given the rank of Major-General. It was particularly fortunate that all these Sub-area commanders had the greatest respect for one another and for their District Commander.

On 23 February, 1940, yet another guard battalion arrived in France. This was the 14th Battalion of the Royal Fusiliers, commanded by Lt-Colonel J.S. Heselton. It had been mobilized on 7 November, 1939. While based on Le Havre its units were positioned at the Poix and Crécy airfields and the great ammunition dump at St Saens. Again this battalion was widely dispersed, thereby preventing any serious training from being carried out.

During this period the War Office was doing its best to raise new divisions to fulfil the obligations that had been entered into with the French. The actual assembling of the men presented little difficulty. The provision of equipment was a different matter. The armament works were, in no sense, working to capacity and production was falling further and further behind. This resulted in a reduction in the amount of training that could be given to the newly-raised units. The chances, therefore, of formation training being undertaken was remote in the extreme. The French were pressing for further formations to be sent over. When it was pointed out that it was quite impossible to send unequipped units overseas, the French offered to disband some of theirs so as to provide the necessary arms. The disbanded troops could then be utilized in their factories for arms production. The War Office declined the offer as they felt that the arms so provided would be totally unsuitable for use in the British Army. However, the CIGS was able, by the most strenuous efforts, to send forward sufficient divisions between December, 1939, and April, 1940, to complete a third Corps, and this in spite of Mr Churchill's diversions in Norway. This gave a total of (more or less) ten divisions ready for operational duties at the time of the opening of the German offensive.

As the stores mounted up and more and more aircraft became

available GHQ found that the accommodation for both was becoming increasingly inadequate. Though the French had placed a number of airfields at the disposal of the RAF they were found to be unsuitable until concrete runways had been laid. The BEF found itself in no position to cope with all these demands for labour; this notwithstanding the formation of massive groups known as the Auxiliary Military Pioneer Corps. As a result Lord Gort pressed General Ironside to release some of the new divisions that were being raised in England. In France the situation was further aggravated by the necessity for providing additional guards and, in the case of airfields, AA defences, these latter being under the direction of the RAF. The CIGS was extremely reluctant to allow any of his embryo formations to proceed overseas. He felt that to do so would put back their state of training to such an extent that it would be months before they could be considered fit to take their place in the Line. However, great political pressure was brought to bear upon him. He finally and reluctantly agreed to send the 12th, 23rd and 46th Divisions to France, for 'labour' purposes. As these three divisions were both unequipped and largely untrained, General Ironside obtained an assurance from Lord Gort that they should receive as much training as possible and were not to be used in an operational role until they had received their full state of equipment. In March, 1940, arrangements were made for the three divisions to proceed to France. In addition a further garrison battalion, the 12th Royal Warwicks (Lt-Colonel G.S. Miller), consisting mainly of elderly ex-servicemen, was sent to France to operate as guards on Vulnerable Points. The companies were distributed over a wide area, at Rennes, Cherbourg, Le Mans and Caen.[5]

The divisions destined for work on the L of C were largely unequipped. Each battalion had not more than three anti-tank rifles (with six rounds apiece) and five Bren guns. Few of the men had ever fired a weapon and the officers had come stright from civilian life. None of the divisions possessed any form of artillery or signals. They did however, have a number of engineer and medical units.

It will only be necessary to follow the fortunes of those units which became involved in the operations that occurred south of the Somme. The remainder were able to join up with the main part of the BEF and their activities are, therefore, beyond the scope of this book. In all cases their original histories are similar. The 23rd Division can be disposed of immediately. On arrival in France it was despatched north of the Somme. Its story can be obtained from works dealing with the BEF.

The 12th Division (Major-General R.L. Petre) landed in France on 21 April, 1940. Its Headquarters was set up at Gamaches. The 35th Brigade, consisting of the 2/5th, 2/6th and 2/7th The Queen's Royal Regiment, was stationed at Aumale. The 2/5th (Lt-Colonel A.F.F. Young) worked on railway construction at Forges-les-Eaux. The 2/6th (Lt-Colonel E.F. Bolton) and 2/7th (Lt-Colonel F.E.B. Girling) were railway-building at Abancourt, the great regulating centre for all northbound traffic.

The 36th Brigade was another formation engaged on railway construction, again at Abancourt. The 2/6th East Surreys (Lt-Colonel H.S. Burgess) did not remain at Abancourt long, one company being employed to guard the great chemical warfare dump at Fécamp. The 6th Royal Sussex (Lt-Colonel E.K.B. Wannup) and the 7th Royal Sussex (Lt-Colonel R. Gethen) remained at Abancourt until their fateful move, which will be recounted in due course.

The 37th Brigade, being one of those formations which joined the BEF, need only be referred to in passing. It was engaged in hut and accommodation construction near Rouen.

In the Southern District there arrived, on 29 April, the 46th Division commanded by Major-General H.O. Curtis. The 137th Brigade, consisting of the 2/5th West Yorkshire Regiment, the 2/6th Duke of Wellington's Regiment (Lt-Colonel E.H. Llewellyn) and the 2/7th Duke of Wellington's Regiment (Lt-Colonel G. Taylor), was stationed in the Blain-St Nazaire area. This brigade was engaged in the handling of stores and, subsequently, preparing anti-aircraft defences (see Chapter VII). The 138th Brigade contained the 6th Lincolnshire Regiment, the 2/4th Yorkshire Light Infantry (Lt-Colonel J. Hodgkinson MC,TD) together with the 6th York and Lancaster Regiment. They were located in the Rennes area and employed in the handling of stores and ammunition together with the construction of railway sidings in the Forest of Tenouarn. The 139th Brigade was also in this area.

The total strength of these divisions amounted to 18,347 officers and men. As compared to normal divisions, they were far below strength. Nevertheless this discrepancy can be accounted for by the absence of their normal divisional troops. Actually, the battalions were well up to strength. With their arrival the numbers of troops on the L of C rose above 150,000. During the final stage the numbers became even higher.

It should be appreciated when considering the story of the L of C that the area covered and the strength of commands in actual bodies was very much greater than in the operational part of the BEF. For example, the total number of men under the direct administrative command of the Commander of Northern District just before the German offensive exceeded 40,000, plus medical services and attached troops. Of these a vast number consisted of 'useless mouths' when the time came to reckon the number of troops available for active operations. Even then, of those who could be classified as 'fighting men', few had had any form of training, even to the extent of firing a rifle. What was worse was that the more 'civilian' labour that was undertaken the more the troops reverted to being civilians.

It can easily be understood why the morale of these erstwhile keen and enthusiastic Territorials and Volunteers suffered severely, and why their appearance, discipline and performance deteriorated. No senior officer from GHQ ever visited the rear areas or took the slightest interest in the personnel who were stationed on the L of C. As long as the organization continued to function apparently efficiently it was felt unnecessary to inspect the various formations of which it was composed. During the whole period when the BEF was stationed along the Franco-Belgian frontier no thought was given by GHQ to the safe-guarding of the L of C. This is excusable to the extent that the General Staff was fully engaged, at first designing the defences on the frontier, and subsequently planning a projected advance into Belgium. Not even an emergency 'skeleton' plan was produced in the event of a sudden appearance of parachute troops descending behind the lines as they were to do in Holland.[6] As far as the guarding of depots was concerned this was mainly of a token nature. In fact, in some cases the troops who were supposed to safeguard these vulnerable points were only 'stick' guards. But even if they had been armed it is doubtful if any determined attacker would have been influenced by their presence. No strong points were constructed or road blocks prepared until long after the German offensive had begun. It was never envisaged that, one day, these same troops might be required to undertake a more active role. One can understand why the troops referred to the staff of the L of C, irreverently, as the 'Grocers'. In fact, General de Fonblanque and his Chief of Staff were known as 'Mr Fortnum and Mr Mason'.

North of the Somme the BEF was preparing to put Plan 'D' (the advance to the River Dyle) into execution if the Germans began an offensive against Holland and Belgium. Much rehearsal was undertaken so that the troops could be moved in the shortest possible time — into an unknown land over unreconnoitred routes. Needless to say the rank and file were surprised that, after all these months of hard work on defensive construction, they should now face the prospect of abandoning it all.

Meanwhile, in England during the first week in May the Chief of the Imperial General Staff was not happy. While agreement had been reached with the French as to their disposal of the troops and to the implementing of Plan 'D', Ironside could not help feeling that he, and not General Gamelin, had been right in his appreciation of what form and where the likely German offensive would take place. This pivoting on the Maginot Line near Sedan, besides drawing the Allied Armies away from their prepared positions into unknown territory, brought the fighting line parallel to its L of C. This contravened one of the most important basic principles of war. If he was right, and Gamelin wrong, could the French hold a massive attack through the Ardennes? If they could not, what then? The prospect was too ghastly to contemplate. Gort, of course, had the right of appeal to the British Government if he thought that any orders he might receive would endanger the forces under his command. It was unlikely, however, that he would use it if he received orders to move forward. Gort was spoiling for a fight. General Ironside called to mind Newbolt's *Admirals All*.

> Essex was fretting in Cadiz Bay with the galleons fair in sight,
> Howard had last to give him his way and the word was passed to fight,

> Never was schoolboy gayer than he since holidays first began,
> As he tossed his bonnet to wind and sea as under their guns he ran.

Gort, Ironside felt, was just like an over-grown schoolboy; Belisha must have been mad to select him as Commander-in-Chief. Another thought struck him. Suppose the Germans did manage to break through; had Gort taken his words to heart and arranged to keep a reserve in hand to safeguard the L of C? Of course, there were the three 'labour' divisions — but they could be of very little value. Then there was the 51st Division, stationed in the Saar, serving very little useful purpose. The General hoped that Gort would exercise his undeniable right and request Georges to return it to his command. The French could hardly refuse, as it was part of the agreement that British formations should not be widely separated. Ironside was doubtful that Gort would have given this idea much thought; his mind would be taken up with trivia and not concentrating on the over-all strategic plan. How then could he be expected to be concerned with one of his divisions so far removed from his direct gaze?[7]

It was 9 May. When Ironside went to bed that night he never dreamt what would be the first news he would receive in the morning.

II

10 May — 16 May

'*Friday, 10 May, 1940*
Very hot day. Germany invades Holland, Belgium and Luxembourg simultaneously, without any ultimatum or warning. Air raids on French towns and on cities in Holland, Luxembourg and Belgium. Also in Basle, Switzerland. Went to BEF concert at Rennes at night with party of men. Good concert, afterwards Dick, CQMS K--- and another Sergeant had a stroll in the city and supper. Supper very poor. Back to camp in truck, the fellows singing all the old war songs in addition to the latest ones. News that the Boche was expected during the night. But nothing transpired.'[1]
So Sergeant Brown wrote in his diary of the opening gambit of a campaign that was not to end until all British troops had left France.

The French High Command issued a warning order at about 0545 and this was confirmed half an hour later. Plan 'D' was to be executed. British GHQ therefore issued orders for the Plan to be put into operation. The first troops, the 12th Royal Lancers, were to move across the Belgian frontier at 1300. The reason for the time lag was because the troops had been standing to for the past three days and had been stood down on the night of the 9th.

Though, on the outbreak of hostilities, the Germans employed the Luftwaffe to attack aerodromes, rail junctions and other key points, thereafter they made little attempt to interfere with the advance of the Allies towards their projected positions along the River Dyle; this in spite of the fact that the Allies found it necessary to travel during both night and day if the positions were to be attained in the time scheduled. Their extraordinary good fortune in enjoying this uninterrupted movement did not strike the Allied High Command; it was much too engrossed in carrying out the Plan to notice any phenomenon, however curious it might be. It was just thankful that the whole move was made with the minimum of causalties. General Ironside, however, was much disturbed when the above facts were brought to his notice. 'Something is wrong here', he thought. 'No enemy in his right mind would allow a hostile force to assemble without interruption, thereby presenting a strong continuous front fully supported by reserves immediately in the rear'. In spite of the mass of work that required his attention, Ironside continued to puzzle his brains over this apparently illogical action on the part of the German High Command. 'The Germans are not an illogical people,' he thought. 'There must be a reason.' He ran over the Appreciation he had made when he had discussed the proposed advance into Belgium with Gamelin. Gamelin had pooh-poohed the idea of the enemy moving armour through the Ardennes. Then his mind returned to Lord Gort's Report that the *whole* of the BEF (including the III Corps) had moved successfully forward. The more he considered the matter, the more worried he became. 'Suppose that he had been right and Gamelin wrong; that the Germans did make an advance through the Ardennes. Were there any reserves to counter such a thrust? Gort, certainly, had none.'[2]

Lieutenant-General Sir Henry Karslake, after his retirement at the age of 59 in 1938, had decided to set up his permanent establishment in the little village of East Wellow near Romsey, in Hampshire. On the outbreak of war it was only natural that he should take great interest in the progress of hostilities. In addition to the normal news media he was fortunate in being in touch with a number of his erstwhile colleagues who were serving with the BEF in France. He adapted his study into a sort of 'War Room' by pinning up on one wall a series of maps covering the whole front. These maps were those that he had used between 1914 and 1918. While they were not in any great detail, nevertheless he was able to show a reasonably clear disposition of the Allied forces engaged. Up to 10 May, of course, there had been little movement; the line of flags was continuous from the end of the Maginot Line proper along the Belgian frontier to the sea. It appeared, from the information he had received, that the defences along the Belgian frontier were of some strength. Eight months had elapsed since the troops had taken up their positions. During that period the troops had spent the greater part of their time constructing field works in the form of pill boxes and anti-tank ditches, to say nothing of erecting masses of barbed wire. An enemy attack on these lines would prove a most costly affair.

In view of the fact that so much emphasis had been laid on the next war being one of movement, it seemed strange that right at the beginning 1914-18 methods were being adopted. All the writings of Liddell Hart were, apparently, being ignored. The tank as such barely registered. But, as a Gunner, he was even more disturbed by the fact that so little provision had been made for this arm. As Representative Colonel Commandant he had toured every Artillery unit in the United Kingdom. While the personnel appeared to be good and, indeed, the new 25pdr Field piece seemed excellent, he had been unable to find any reserve of guns. It appeared, therefore, that if, as is inevitable in war, a number of guns were lost, there would be none to replace them. When, in due course, he was called upon to command a force in France, he was to find his worst fears realized. As he was to remark to General Ironside on his return to England at the end of May, 1940, 'God knows what all those bright young men at the War Office were up to after they had been given the chance by Hore-Belisha. There is absolutely nothing done to back up the troops in the line.'

Early in the morning of 10 May the General, as was his custom, entered his study and switched on the wireless. It was confirmed that the German armies had crossed the frontiers into Holland and Belgium and that the Allied forces were advancing to engage the enemy side by side with our new Allies. At this time little detail was given of the movement of the troops. It was not until the following morning that anything in the way of dispositions were given. The General corrected his flags and then stepped back to survey the result. One who was present says, 'As he studied the map the colour drained from his face. He went deathly white. Without saying a word, he began to remove the flags. Then he carefully unpinned the maps, which he folded up and returned to a draw in his desk. Only when the whole job was done did he speak. "The war is over," he said. "Gort and Gamelin have committed the one strategical error that even the most junior officer is impressed on avoiding; they have brought their fighting line parallel to their Lines of Communication. If the Germans attack here," he pointed at Sedan on the general map of France that lay on his desk, "and manage to thrust their way westwards, they will cut off the fighting troops from their supplies. From what I saw of their Army in 1937, that is just what they will try and do. Then God help us all!" After a pause, he went on, "I can understand Gort making such an error; he is just spoiling for a fight, to wave his sword and win another VC, but I am surprised at Gamelin.'"

On the 13th the fears of General Ironside and General Karslake were realized. The Germans crossed the River Meuse. The French 9th Army, consisting largely of inferior troops, had not been able to advance to its battle positions. Even if it had done so, it is doubtful if the outcome would have been different.

The French 2nd Army, which was very little better than the 9th, and located on its right, was likewise unable to achieve its positions. The German thrust, coming as it did through the 'impassable' country of the Ardennes, continued to advance with the minimum of opposition.

While these shattering events were taking place many miles to the north, the L of C troops were continuing to undertake their constructional and 'grocering' activities. Nevertheless, the 'labour' divisional commanders were trying to make their formations more military, as is shown by Sergeant Brown's diary:

'Sunday, 12 May, 1940
Orders received at breakfast time that everyone must immediately draw his steel helmet and gas mask. 8.30am orders received for issue of gas capes. Later heard that enemy planes were within 5 miles of Rennes.

Monday, 13 May, 1940
Orders received that steel helmets, respirators and gas capes to be carried when out of camp. Bren guns mounted to engage enemy aircraft. Battalion standing-by for immediate move.'

The statement 'Battalion standing-by' is of considerable interest. It would seem that the Divisional Commander of the 46th Division, Major-General H.O. Curtis, had decided that his formation could be better employed in fighting the Germans than in working on the L of C. He therefore telephoned Lord Gort. At the same time he ordered the preparation for movement of all units under his command. On speaking to the Commander-in-Chief, he said that his Division was fully operational and suggested that he should bring it forward to engage the enemy. This statement regarding the readiness of the Division was, to say the least, over-optimistic.[3] Fortunately, Lord Gort declined the offer. However, it must be wondered if this conversation did not subsequently influence him in his decision to order the 'labour' divisions forward. If so, then General Curtis has a lot to answer for!

During 14 May the Southern German advance continued with a minimum of resistance. Indeed, the movement had been so rapid that von Rundstedt, who commanded the Group, which consisted largely of Panzer formations, considered that his southern flank was becoming too vulnerable. He gave orders, therefore, that a halt should be called on the River Oise so as to enable the motorized infantry and supply columns to catch up with his armour. As a result a breathing space took place on the 15th.

It is now time to examine the position of the BEF. All the fighting units and formations, with the exception of the 51st Division which was still in the Saar, were along the River Dyle in the vicinity of Brussels. In addition to the troops directly engaged on the Dyle there were two divisions in reserve but well forward from the French frontier. *There were no other British troops on whom the Commander-in-Chief could rely.* In addition to the problem of finding a further reserve it should be noted that, if the BEF was cut off from its L of C, the latter would be quite defenceless. Admittedly there was a prospect of the 1st Armoured Division arriving in France, the projected date being the 16th, but even then it would not be sufficient by itself to withstand a determined German attack.

Though the German thrust westwards had slowed down on the 15th Lord Gort soon began to realize that his southern flank was likely to be exposed. It had become quite obvious that the French would be unable to bring up either the reinforcements from the south or the field force supporting the Maginot forts, to prevent the Germans advancing and thereby interposing themselves between the BEF and its L of C. One wonders if at that moment Lord Gort realized that the movement of all his three Corps forward had been a mistake. Had he retained one Corps near his original line it might have helped to solve the problem by holding the advancing Germans until the French reinforcements arrived. It is appreciated that it is now known that such reinforcements as the French possessed were quite inadequate to the task. At that time, however, it was assumed that the French had a '*Masse de Manoeuvre*' available for such an event.

As it was now too late for the movement of III Corps to the rear, in desperation Lord Gort thought of the three 'labour' divisions working on the L of C. Knowing that they were both untrained and largely unequipped, and bearing in mind the undertaking that he had given to the CIGS for their non-employment on active operations, he issued orders for their advance to cover his southern flank. He must have been aware that he was sending these unfortunate men to their death. The contribution to his defence, he must have known, would be minimal. Above all, he must have realized that, by withdrawing them from the L of C, he was leaving that organization even more defenceless.

When the news of the German invasion of Holland and Belgium and the advance of the BEF reached Headquarters of the L of C at Le Mans the Staff were ready. It did not take long for the plans that had been carefully prepared beforehand to be put into operation. The lines that had railheads at Arras and further west were duly advanced. The carriage of stores by road increased. Indeed, it was not long before supply trains were moving northwards from the various depots. The whole operation was carried out with maximum efficiency. Actually the event did little to affect the normal running of the L of C. It was just an anticipated extension of the lines. In fact, as far as the Staff was concerned, the war was being carried an even greater distance from them. Provided the railways and roads were not affected, there was no reason why their routine should be disturbed.[4]

Each day, ships bringing further stores and personnel were arriving at the ports. The size and number of the dumps and reception centres were increasing. A long war had been planned for and new depots and further railway tracks were being constructed. Owing to the reinforcement programme, considerable numbers of additional troops could be expected before the end of the summer.

No adverse criticism can be levelled at the basic organization of the L of C. The fact that they were completely insulated from reality was no fault of their own. As long as supplies and other requirements were coming forward in sufficient quantities, GHQ did not concern itself with the finer details of the organization. Lord Gort had the fullest confidence in the officer responsible. Also, as the HQ of the L of C was far removed from the actual seat of war, it was not considered necessary to keep it informed of the progress of the campaign except in the most general terms, indeed only to the extent that it affected the maintenance of supplies to the fighting front. Actually, it was this very distance from the Front that caused the Chief of Staff, General Pownall, to say that he considered that an L of C of over 500 miles was somewhat excessive.[5]

On 14 May the 2/6th East Surreys who, it will be remembered, were garrisoning Le Havre and providing guards for a number of VPs in the district, were informed that, with the exception of D Company, which was guarding the highly secret poison gas dump of Fécamp, they were to be relieved by the 5th Buffs. They were then to proceed to the Saar where they were to be absorbed by the 51st Division and used for guard duties in the rear of that formation. On receipt of the warning order the Quartermaster set about trying to bring the battalion's equipment up to war establishment. In this he was only moderately successful. He found a great reluctance on the part of Divisional HQ to provide the additional requirements. In fairness, it should be said that Divisional HQ, in its turn, received no help from HQ L of C. However, the Quartermaster was able, by the greatest exertions and a deal of 'scrounging', to raise the holding of automatic weapons to twenty Bren guns and eight anti-tank rifles, but with only 500 rounds for the former and a dozen each for the latter, far below the recognized establishment for an infantry battalion. In other respects also the battalion was in a most unsatisfactory state in the way of equipment. It had neither 3" mortars nor carriers, no grenades, revolvers or compasses, no binoculars or maps, and very little signalling equipment. It will be seen, therefore, that the battalion was in no fit condition to proceed to an area in which action could be expected. It should also be remembered that the battalion had had very little other than basic training.

Though the move was cancelled two days later, the effort had not been wasted. Besides the extra equipment the battalion had had the opportunity to practice packing up and making ready for a move. This was to prove invaluable in the days to come.

As mentioned above, the 5th Buffs had also had orders to move. Nevertheless, as the situation appeared to be deteriorating, the battalion was ordered to construct a road-block on the Pont St Pierre road to the east of Alizay, also to send out patrols as far as Pont de l'Arche. It was thought possible by the District Commander, Brigadier Beauman, that there was a danger of parachutists dropping in the area. Brigadier Beauman also ordered the 14th Royal Fusiliers to move to Le Havre as he considered that the various depots, including the great ammunition dumps between Buchy and St Saens, required additional protection.

To enhance these protective measures, Brigadier Beauman was able to obtain a French battalion, the 32nd Depot Battalion, from General Dufour, the French Commander of Rouen District. It is interesting to note that this battalion remained under Brigadier Beauman's command until 25 May when it was decided to form the Beauman Division with a full complement of British troops.[6]

Having said that the amount of up-to-date information received on the L of C was small in the extreme, it may well be wondered what influenced Brigadier Beauman to undertake such action. As part of his District he had visited his sub-area of Arras on 13 May. He hoped that, as this was the seat of GHQ, he would be able to obtain some reliable information. In this he was disappointed. Everyone appeared to be well satisfied with the advance of the BEF and, indeed, with the way the campaign was developing. It seemed that they were quite unconcerned by the fact that the Germans had crossed the River Aisne. However, he received very disquieting information from French sources. This he considered to be sufficiently alarming for him, on his return to his HQ at Rouen, to issue the precautionary orders mentioned above. He also informed HQ L of C of his feelings in the matter. It would seem that his warnings made little impression at Le Mans, no orders being issued for any precautions to be undertaken for the provision of additional safeguards at the various ports and depots.

Whether it was owing to the over-optimistic statements made by General Curtis or not will probably never be known. Sufficient is it to say that on 14 May the Headquarters of the 46th Division received orders from GHQ to forward first the 139th Brigade and then the 138th Brigade. The 139th Brigade duly concentrated on the 15th and entrained for Seclin; the 138th Brigade, less the 2/4th KOYLI, following later the same day. No effort whatsoever was made to provide these Brigades with the necessaries of war. It was assumed by the troops that they were merely moving from one labouring site to another. This feeling can be appreciated as only about 75% had fired a rifle and very few had ever manned a Bren gun; their experience with a Boyes rifle was infinitesimal. Training above platoon level had never been undertaken owing to the wide distribution of units and the great demand made on their labouring services. The moving of these two Brigades, while leaving one Brigade and Divisional HQ behind, is an example of the shocking system which permeated the whole of the BEF, namely the use of formations 'piecemeal'. It was a most pernicious system and had dire consequences for all those whom it affected. Formations lost their entity and, on many occasions, divisional commanders found themselves commanding units belonging to others and losing their own without any prior knowledge. The system had another serious by-product; the Movement Control organization, who were working at the highest pressure, received trains of troops at their regulating stations for onward transmission to the appropriate destinations. On many occasions these trains would contain troops of first one division and then another, then back again to the original division. It can be understood why trains were routed to the wrong assembly areas and formations found unexpected units with them and their own units missing. The situation was not improved by the failure on the part of the telephone system at vital moments.

On the 16th Brigadier Beauman received an urgent summons from Arras sub-area Headquarters. On his arrival he found a conference in progress. A Staff officer from GHQ stated that the Germans had effected a complete breakthrough north of Sedan and that it had been decided to form a defensive flank with the only troops that were available, namely the three 'labour' divisions. The balance of the 46th and the 12th Divisions were, therefore, to be forwarded as quickly as possible.

On his way back to his HQ Brigadier Beauman decided to call in at the French HQ at Amiens in order to discover, if possible, the true seriousness of the position. Though the French commander expressed his fullest confidence in the French being able to hold the advancing Germans, Brigadier Beauman noticed that great efforts were being made to destroy large numbers of files in the courtyard. He left Amiens with great unease. The roads were becoming seriously congested with refugee traffic. This in itself was a pointer. On his way north the roads had been reasonably clear. He considered that the chances of moving troops north at any speed was most unlikely. The railways, also, were beginning to feel the strain. The routes to the north over both the Abbeville and Amiens bridges were becoming choked with either refugee trains or trains packed with Belgian troops moving south to their assembly areas. So great was this southward movement becoming that it reduced the trains carrying supplies northwards to a trickle. Fortunately, the Royal Engineers had been able to give the highest priority to trains carrying ammunition and food-stuffs on the instructions of the Quartermaster-General; as a result it had been possible to build up reasonable stocks of both commodities at the railheads before the forwarding of troops and the influx of southbound traffic made the task almost impossible. The French seemed incapable of organizing any form of one-way traffic that might have eased the situation, though facilities for such a system existed. Though the Royal Engineers had constructed a magnificent regulating station at Abancourt most of their efforts were thwarted beyond that point. So bad, in fact, did the situation become that trains could, without warning, be switched to other lines, purely on local decision, causing them to arrive at the wrong destinations; even, in some cases, coming face to face with oncoming trains. To this day it is not known whether this state of chaos resulted from panic, sheer stupidity, or was due to the influence of Fifth Columnists.

From his vast stocks of reserve transport vehicles, Brigadier Beauman began to equip a number of battalions within his District as highly mobile units. He felt, rightly, that speed of movement was essential if hostile columns appeared. As a result a complete Brigade of the 12th Division, together with the 2/6th East Surreys, received an avalanche of brand-new 3-tonners, thereby converting them to motorized infantry. What they lacked in arms they made up for in mobility. Brigadier Beauman's first 'flying column' consisted of the 4th Buffs and the 2/6th East Surreys, the latter having been transferred from Le Havre on the arrival of the 14th Royal Fusiliers. As a sort of Brigade Group, it was placed under the command of Lt-Colonel Heselton of the Royal Fusiliers. The 5th Buffs, meanwhile, had advanced north with the rest of their Brigade.

Even as late as the 15th the equanimity of HQ L of C was unruffled. It had been decided that, when the BEF had established its new line on the River Dyle, the Headquarters should move further north so as to be more or less midway between the fighting line and the rear of the L of C territory. Preparations went ahead as planned. Orders were issued on the 15th that the whole Headquarters would move to Mantes on the 16th. In spite of the reports submitted by Brigadier Beauman the whole caravanserai duly moved forward on the 16th. On its arrival it was met by a further report from Beauman in which he gave details he had received at the conference at Arras that morning. Then, and only then, did General de Fonblanque decide to reverse his decision to set up his HQ at Mantes. Orders were issued for the whole staff to return to Le Mans at once. The General himself, with a small staff, did not return there until the 20th.[7]

During this period the Luftwaffe had made a series of attacks on the northern ports but without causing much damage; the exception was Calais, where no anti-aircraft guns had been provided. This latter attack effectively stopped the cross-Channel ferries. However, as this system had been used mainly in connection with leave personnel, its elimination caused little interruption to the movement from England of stores and reinforcements.

As it had now become obvious to Brigadier Beauman, if to no one else, that the situation was deteriorating rapidly he decided to take further steps to protect the valuable stores and other sites for which he was responsible. He summoned Colonel Vicary, the chief reinforcement officer for the BEF, to a conference at Rouen. He suggested that the men in the reinforcement camps should be armed and formed into battalions. In addition, all those personnel reputed to be machine-gunners should be organized into platoons and attached to the various battalions, equipment to be drawn from the Ordnance Depots. Neither officer was to know the difficulties they were to experience in this operation. However, Colonel Vicary did his best and it was not long before a number of curious units made their appearance. This combined 'formation' was to be known as Vickforce, Beauman's own formation being Beauforce.

III

17 May — 22 May

They learn from you the lesson plain,
That life may go, so Honour stay.
The deeds you wrought are not in vain.

Lang

WITH the exception of the units of the 36th Brigade, all the other battalions of the 12th Division had to travel by train. Everyone was in the highest spirits. For months they had been working on various construction jobs. As one Sergeant described it, 'it was just like being on permanent fatigues'. Except for having to march to work and wearing denims, there was little which separated them from ordinary civilian labour. They never carried anything more lethal than a spade or pick-axe. There is little doubt that many of the officers and men had become slack in their appearance and habits. They had lost their original enthusiasm; discipline was slack.

However, when orders came to move, an amazing change came over everyone. Backs straightened and heads were held erect. Instead of those depressing denims, battledress was assumed once more. Badges and boots were polished. Rifles, and their few other weapons, were taken from the racks, cleaned and oiled. Webbing was blancoed and brasses (quite contrary to regulations) polished. Quartermasters checked their stores and ammunition, such as there were. The RQMS of the KOYLI remarked, as he issued the seven rounds for each of the three anti-tank rifles, 'It looks as if we are going to annual camp, not to war!'

Between the warning orders and the actual move very little time elapsed — just sufficient to pack up what was immediately available but none to try and obtain anything else.

It was, however, with a gay heart that the men strode out behind their Regimental bands. As one old reservist muttered, 'Just like bloody 1914 — and look what happened then!'

It should be borne in mind that very few officers and NCO's had had any active service experience. The fact that they were to do so well was, therefore, all the more creditable.

THE BLOOD-LETTING AT AMIENS

Though the 37th Brigade had received orders to entrain at Abancourt station in the early morning of the 18th, it was found that this was impossible owing to the 35th Brigade having had similar orders. This latter, less the 2/5th Queens, being closer to the station, had entrained first.

At 1025 the 6th Royal Sussex marched to Abancourt and entrained. Their destination, however, had been altered from Abbeville to Lens. This change caused some surprise to the commanding officer as all arrangements had been made for the battalion transport and rear party to meet the battalion at Abbeville. It was now too late to send new orders back to the camp. A further delay in starting was occasioned by the derailment of a wagon at the points immediately in front of the train. As a result the train carrying the 7th Royal Sussex, which had entrained further down the line, was diverted on to the 'up' line, thereby passing its sister battalion and altering the 'line of march'. Little did the 6th Sussex realize how fortunate the action of a careless shunter was to be to them — they just chafed at the delay![1]

Eventually, at 1256 the train carrying the 6th Royal Sussex, the rear details of the two battalions of the Queens, together with the 264th Company RE and the 182nd Field Ambulance, pulled out of the station. By now it was a considerable distance behind that bearing its sister battalion.

At about 1500, the train carrying the 7th Royal Sussex stopped at St Roche station, a mile from Amiens. This was unfortunate as it coincided with a severe air-raid on Amiens. This raid overlapped St Roche and a bomb fell on the tender of the train and the coach directly behind containing the officers.

This bombing effectively prevented any further movement northwards. Many officers were either killed or wounded. Colonel Gethen himself was wounded. However, he ordered the battalion to detrain and to withdraw some 700 yards to the north of the rail-

1 Lieutenant-General Sir Henry Karslake.

2 (*above*) Major-General P. de Fonblanque as a 2nd Lieutenant.

3 (*above right*) Brigadier A. B. Beauman.

4 (*right*) Major-General V. Fortune.

5 (*below*) Lieutenant-Colonel R. Gethen.

6 (*below right*) Brigadier F. E. Morgan.

way. He felt that it would be safer to have his men deployed until the line was cleared. The position selected was on rising ground, slightly wooded, with a few farm buildings; a few hedges broke up the open ground. Here the battalion took up defensive positions though not anticipating any direct confrontation.

Just after 1500 the train bearing the 6th Royal Sussex approached St Roche station. As an air-raid was in progress, the train stopped. It was the same raid that had affected the 7th and had prevented their train from proceeding. When the raid had ceased, the train was switched to the 'up' line and passed through the station. The troops saw the damaged train but did not connect it with their sister battalion. The train then proceeded into the marshalling yards at Amiens as there were persistent rumours that the enemy were advancing on the city. However, as these rumours appeared to be untrue, the train started off again. It was soon discovered that the track ahead had been severely damaged and no further progress was possible for some time. The local authorities, therefore, decided that the train should return through Amiens and be switched on to a siding at Ailly-sur-Noye, some miles to the south of the city, pending further orders.

Since it had been presumed that all units would have taken but a short time to arrive at their destinations, little in the way of rations had been brought other than 'the unexpired portion'. But it was now evident that the halt might be prolonged, so Colonel Gethen sent a party, on foot, into Amiens to try and obtain supplies. In this they were unsuccessful but, by good fortune, Colonel Gethen was able to contact the supply centre at Saleux. At about 0300 the following morning a number of lorries arrived, bringing sufficient for his needs. He also tried to contact his Headquarters to obtain orders but to no avail; however, he learned that the Germans could be expected to enter the city at any moment.

Though the 6th had been able to detrain a small truck and had sent it into Amiens for supplies, by the time it arrived the roads proved impassable owing to the refugees. It was impossible to contact anyone in authority and no food was to be had. The Commanding Officer, Lt-Colonel Wannup, therefore decided that, until the situation clarified, he would withdraw his men from the siding, which was in an exposed position and liable to enemy bombing, and disperse them in a neighbouring wood.

On the return of his truck Colonel Wannup decided to send his second-in-command (Major Walkington) to try and locate either Brigade or Divisional Headquarters or, indeed, any other unit or formation which might be able to provide food and information.

In the meantime the raids were increasing as the enemy advanced into the city, their object being to gain the river crossings and form a brigdehead on the southern bank of the Somme.

Colonel Gethen, not having been able to contact any Headquarters and obtain orders, decided that he must remain in his present position. It was not until 0330 on the 20th that the enemy appeared. A column of motorized infantry, accompanied by tanks, approached his position from the east. The battalion's positions had been noted by a spotter plane. The Germans decided that it was essential to eliminate this possible threat to their advance.

It should be remembered that the 7th Royal Sussex, in common with all the other battalions of the 12th Division, had very few arms other than rifles; also, that their experience of handling even these was very limited. The Battalion's supply of ammunition was minimal. No effort had been made by their divisional staff to ensure that they were properly equipped before they were sent into battle. Nevertheless, the men of the 7th Battalion Royal Sussex engaged the enemy as if they were a well-found battalion.

The enemy were quite unaware of the weakness of the force opposed to them. From behind every bit of cover these gallant but doomed men fought their one-sided battle. A lucky shot from one of their few anti-tank rifles put a tank out of action. This caused the enemy to become wary. The German infantry deployed and both heavy mortars and a battery of field artillery were brought into action to add to the deluge of shells being poured out by the encircling tanks.

The thirty-two rounds from the anti-tank rifles were soon expended. The small-arms ammunition for the ten Bren guns and the rifles did not last long; there was no reserve. Even when the fire slackened the enemy were reluctant to advance for the kill. They called up dive-bombers to help them. However, the outcome was never in doubt. As the afternoon wore on the casualties increased. Finally, at about 2000 hrs, with every round fired, the survivors reluctantly surrendered. Of the 701 officers and men of all units that had left Buchy station on the 18th, only 70 survived to be taken into captivity. Not even during the murderous engagements on the Somme or at Passchendaele had any unit suffered such casualties. But their sacrifice had not been in vain. It had so discouraged the enemy from penetrating southwards that it saved their sister battalion from a like fate; also a Moroccan Regiment that was not far off.

Colonel Gethen was taken prisoner by Oberleutnant Gerhard Richter who, in due course, conducted him to his Commanding Officer, Major-General Erwin Rommel, commanding the 7th Panzer Division, a section of which had been detailed to eliminate the threat posed by the 7th Royal Sussex. In 1949 Colonel Gethen received a letter from Richter in which the writer expressed his admiration for the fighting qualities of the battalion.

Colonel Wannup, meanwhile, was quite unaware of what was happening to his north. He had two alternatives. First, he could try and obtain a locomotive for the train, the original engine having been removed when the train was shunted on to the siding. He could then move southwards. Secondly, he could march westwards in the hope of meeting up with other British troops. The second alternative appalled him! He was fully aware that his men were quite unused to marching and he had no motor transport. In addition, his men had had no food for the past twenty-four hours other than what they carried in their haversacks. As all the railway staff at Ailley had long since fled, Colonel Wannup sent his Intelligence officer down the line to St Just-en-Chaussée in the hope of finding an engine and a skeleton staff to work the signals and switches. At 2100 the Intelligence officer returned with the welcome news that a locomotive would be coming up within the hour. On its arrival it was agreed to move the train to a less exposed site. Though now on the main line it was effectively screened from enemy spotter planes by a thick wood. At 2200 the men gathered all their possessions together and boarded the train. Luckily it was a full moon and most of the equipment was loaded without mishap.

It would be as well, at this point, to complete the saga of the odyssey of the 6th Royal Sussex. At 1700 on 21 May it arrived at the rest camp at Achères, on the outskirts of Paris. There it stopped for the night. The CO went into Paris to try and obtain some orders from the British Military Attaché, Lord Malise Graham. As a result, the following day at 1330 the battalion left Achères for Blain near Nantes. En route the train stopped at Le Mans where a report was given of the events to HQ L of C*. Also information was obtained as to the battalion's future employment. It was to form part of the L of C reserve, to be used as labour for stacking ammunition and petrol which was still entering the country through Nantes and St Nazaire. The battalion took no further part in the campaign.[2]

THE ABBEVILLE AFFAIR

It is now time to return to the 35th Brigade. It will be remembered that two battalions had left Abancourt before the battalions of the Royal Sussex, en route for Abbeville. The third battalion, the 2/5th Queens, being stationed at Rambures and therefore much closer to their destination, had had orders to prepare to move at an hour's notice. It did not actually move until the 18th and then by road.

The trains reached Abbeville by noon. A conference was held at which the Divisional operation order was issued by the GSO III. It was to the effect that the 35th Brigade was to be disposed east and the 37th Brigade west of the Somme. The troops were to be ready to move at a moment's notice and to arrange for the construction of road-blocks and all round defensive positions. Even as these orders were being issued the local RTO arrived. He said that new orders had been received from GHQ, at Arras, that the Brigade was to proceed to Lens. This appeared quite incredible to all present. The two battalion commanders decided to contact GHQ with a view to getting the order confirmed. A telephone call was put through and, though the line was bad, the reply they received certainly appeared to confirm the fact that their destination was indeed to be Lens.

The situation was now very difficult. The Brigade Commander, who was travelling by road, could not be contacted before the trains left for the north. Also it would be some time before the 2/5th Queens could have their arrangements changed. Even worse was the fact that, as the destination had previously been so close, no arrangements had been made to take on rations; none were avail-

* It was stated, inter alia, that the bridge at Ailly was intact.

able at Abbeville at that time as they had not arrived from base. Faced with this apparent decision by GHQ, the GSO III of the 12th Division had no alternative but to permit the two trains to proceed; also to try and contact the 2/5th so as to redirect them. It should be borne in mind that neither Divisional HQ nor any of the lower formations were equipped with wireless. Division, therefore, was totally unaware as to the fate of the 37th Brigade, even though its Commander, Major-General Petre, was at GHQ at the time.

The trains duly arrived at Lens at 1900 that same evening. They were quite unexpected and nothing had been laid on for their reception. On contact being made with GHQ, it was found that their move to Lens was, indeed, an error. It appears that the order should have been 'proceed Doullens' not 'proceed *to* Lens', the object being to support the right flank of the 36th Brigade.

The Brigade was therefore ordered to return to Abbeville at once as it was now too late to adopt the original course.

Owing to the probability of air attack it was decided to postpone the move until the following morning; the tired and hungry troops bedded down in the local parks. No food was to be found in Lens. At 0600 the following morning the two battalions entrained, moving south to Arras. Here the two COs were lucky enough to meet their Divisional Commander. On the situation being explained to him he was able to arrange for their trains to travel on a single line, via St Pol, the main line having been damaged by enemy action. Unfortunately, in spite of all his efforts, he was unable to provide for their most urgent necessity, food.

The trains finally reached Abbeville at 2000, the men having had no food for two days. The battalions quickly settled in to their new quarters as follows:

2/6th at Drucat and the 2/7th at Vauchelles. One is happy to relate that the battalions' Quartermasters took immediate action to obtain rations and to provide the starving men with a hot meal.

After a hot and tiring march, through shortage of transport, the 2/5th Queens arrived at their billets, with their HQ at Château D'Epagne. They were fortunate that they had not been involved in the nightmare train journey of their sister units. Also, fortunately, Divisional HQ had received a telephone call from GHQ informing them of the error which had occurred. As a result no order had been issued for a move to be made on the fruitless journey northward.

The Brigade was now once more reassembled. A glance at the map will show its distribution. It now proceeded to do its utmost to implement its original orders. Road-blocks were set up, though much impeded by the constant influx of refugees and disorganized Belgian and French soldiery. In any case the road-blocks were likely to be of scant use as the ground on either side of the roads was quite passable for tanks and other tracked vehicles.

Notwithstanding the events recounted above, GHQ had sent neither orders nor information to the HQs of the 12th Division. It was not aware, for example, that its Divisional Commander had been permanently removed; no alternative Commander had been appointed. Indeed, it was not until 1030 on the 20th that it was decided that Brigadier Wyatt, the Senior Brigade Commander, should succeed General Petre.

Before this event occurred, however, Division had issued a curious order to the 35th Brigade. The order reads as follows:

'Billeting areas to be allotted east of the Somme within four miles of Abbeville. The positions are not to be tactical, but areas to be allotted with regard to the fact that the Brigade may have to defend Abbeville.'

It will be appreciated that this order, being of a contradictory nature, confused rather than helped the Brigade Commander. COs were at a loss to understand how it was intended that they should employ their troops. It was therefore decided to erect road-blocks and put their sectors, as far as possible, in a state of defence. There is no doubt that no one considered, indeed could not believe, that it was likely that they would be called upon to engage the enemy. As far as they were aware the Germans were at least a hundred miles to the east!

However, during the morning of the 20th, enemy aerial activity increased. Abbeville and the bridges over the Somme were severely attacked. Nevertheless, it could not be credited that an enemy ground attack was likely. Indeed, it was not until 1630, when a party was sent by the CO of the 2/6th with a message for the 2/7th, that the grim truth was brought home to all ranks. This party ran into a German patrol. One member was killed but another, Sergeant Toster, managed to return to the battalion to warn his CO that the enemy had penetrated between the 2/6th and the 2/7th.

From this time on the battalions were subjected to all forms of attack, including tanks. Their establishment of weapons and ammunition was no better than that of their sister units. It soon became obvious that the position was rapidly becoming precarious. Orders, therefore, were issued for the battalions to retire behind the Somme. By this time, however, it was easier said than done, all bridges in the vicinity having been destroyed in the aerial attack. As a result both the 2/5th and the 2/7th suffered severe casualties before their remnants gained the southern bank of the river. The 2/6th had better luck. Travelling, by the one compass they possessed, across country, it was found that the bridge at Port-le-Grand, some distance westward, was still intact. As a result Colonel Bolton was able to withdraw the battalion almost complete. Only the platoon acting as rearguard suffered casualties. Indeed, the whole of that unit was either killed, wounded or captured. By their action, however, they had managed to delay the enemy sufficiently to enable their comrades to achieve the comparative safety of the southern bank. The CO then marched to Fressenneville, where the HQ of the 12th Division was then located, in the hopes of obtaining orders and rations.

Very few men of the other battalions survived the crossing of the Somme. Notwithstanding acts of the greatest gallantry by all ranks, many were overwhelmed and either captured or killed.

From this time onwards not only was the 35th Brigade, as such, non-existent but also the remainder of the 12th Division, including its HQ, the enemy having penetrated to Fressenneville. The balance of the Brigade made its independent way to the River Bresle. It was not, however, until the 23rd that all the survivors had reached the base depot at Rouen.

The final count of survivors of this gallant, if futile, affair was as follows:

- 2/5th 17 officers and 161 ORs
- 2/6th Complete save for one platoon; one company being employed elsewhere on special duty.
- 2/7th 12 officers and 344 ORs

Thus, out of a total strength of nearly 2,400 all ranks, only 1,234 survived.

So far we have only examined the activities of the 12th Division. It is now time to see what was happening to the 46th Division, the second of the three 'labour' divisions.

The 138th Brigade, less the 2/4th KOYLI, and the 139th Brigade had safely passed over the Somme, and therefore no longer concern us. The remainder of the Division was awaiting orders to move. When it was heard that the Division was to be employed in an active role, the Divisonal Commander was 'full of fight'. He declared that his Division was ready and able to take on anyone. As will be seen, this was a case of extreme wishful thinking.

Notwithstanding that it was known by all ranks as early as 15 May that the battalions were about to move to an area in which action could be expected, no effort was made by Divisional HQ or HQ L of C to ensure that they were equipped for the enterprise. COs tried to obtain additional arms and ammunition to bring them nearer to establishment. In all cases their requests were ignored or they were informed that they were not available. It seemed that those in the rear echelons refused to face reality. The old Quartermaster's attitude of 'We haven't got any. What do you want?' was paramount. Doubtless those responsible claimed that they were unaware of the full implications of the projected move. The real truth was that none of those responsible had any real appreciation of the necessities of war. They continued to be bound by regulations which had been drafted for peacetime administration; they were determined not to be diverted from them. The fact that the establishment, on arrival of the labour divisions in France, showed that there were four anti-tank rifles and eight Bren-guns per battalion proved to those administrators that that was all those battalions were entitled to. This applied equally to ammunition. No more over and above this standard could therefore be issued. As a result of this decision the battalions advanced to battle with sufficient arms and ammunition only to combat a local rising amongst some uncivilized tribe. Indeed, they only had sufficient ammunition for two hours fighting; less, of course, for the anti-tank rifles for which only seven or eight rounds each were available!

Before recounting the adventures of the remainder of the 46th Division it is necessary to look at the activities of that part of the L of C which was located nearest the Somme. It will be remembered that this northern district, which ran from Amiens to the Seine, and comprised all the area between the Somme and the Seine westwards to the sea, was under the command of Brigadier A.B. Beauman. It was his responsibility, among many others, to safeguard this area against both aerial and ground attack. It may well be asked how he, with the forces available to him (officially), could possibly carry out such a task. Fortunately this officer, unlike most, if not all, of the officers of the BEF, (not excluding the most senior) had commanded a brigade in action as a permanent and not an emergency Brigadier. This was on the Italian Front during 1918.

In spite of what must have appeared unsuperable difficulties Brigadier Beauman proceeded to organize a defence force. His first efforts in this direction have already been reviewed.

While engaged in these, he was required, as we know, to forward the various elements of the labour divisions as and when they arrived in his district. He, like many others, was appalled at their state. Indeed, when the 36th Brigade arrived, he scoured his area in the hope of providing it with some artillery. In this he was fortunate. He discovered four 18/25 pdrs which had formed part of a batch returned to Ordnance for re-conditioning by the 51st Highland Division. He then obtained some gunners from the reinforcement depots. The limbers were duly filled with ammunition and this troop was sent forward with the Royal West Kents. The movement of these labour divisions was a forlorn hope. Nevertheless, it is gratifying to learn that someone made some effort to improve their very slender chances when engaged on what was bound to be a fruitless task.

Soon after Beauman had assembled his 'flying column', to his consternation an order was received from GHQ for him to forward (to Boulogne), at once, any organized force under his command. Fortunately, this force was well equipped with transport and supplies. It set off at 0330 on 20 May, orders for the move having come through just before midnight. The little column travelled on the road to Abbeville via Forges-les-Eaux.

Just as they were preparing to make a dash through the town, the force commander was met by a representative of the 12th Division. This officer told him that as all the bridges had been wrecked and that it seemed that the enemy could be entering the town at any minute it had been decided that the column should be diverted to Le Translay to cover the road between there and Gamaches. Colonel Heselton was not happy about this change of plan and decided to go to the HQ of the 12th Division. In the meantime, with commendable promptitude, the whole column of some two hundred vehicles turned about in a road choked with traffic, and reached Le Translay about 2100 hrs. Unfortunately the column commander had not yet returned from Division so the force was without orders or instructions. However, an officer from 12th Division then arrived. He said that the plans had again been altered, that the column should proceed westwards to the coast, the East Surreys to Le Tréport and the Buffs to Eu. Once again the column started off, this time in the opposite direction. After a nightmare journey during the hours of darkness, the column reached its new destinations. Its stay was to be of the shortest. Brigadier Beauman, who had been apprised of the situation by Colonel Heselton (who had borrowed a dispatch rider from Divisional HQ), decided to form a sort of protective line based on the River Béthune. Both battalions were directed to Arques-la-Bataille and thence to the neighbourhood of St Germain, some twelve miles inland from Dieppe. There they were joined by the 1/5th Sherwood Foresters. These three units were directed by Colonel Heselton, who had by then rejoined his command, to prepare defence positions along the line of the Béthune from the sea for some fifteen miles along its southern bank.

Brigadier Beauman appreciated that so small a force was quite inadequate to safeguard the massive store-depots in his area. He decided, therefore, to do everything possible to raise additional troops. He first instructed Colonel Diggle, who was in overall command of all the Pioneer battalions in the area, to assemble these and to equip them as a fighting force. These units contained a large number of over-age reservists. They had been sent out in the early days of the war for labour duties on the L of C. While not as active as their younger colleagues they had the advantage of having had experience of soldiering. Colonel Diggle managed to raise some two and a half thousand of these men for whom he was able to supply rifles. These troops were then disposed along the line of the River Andelle, a distance of some fifteen miles.

There were in the Rouen area the three main reinforcement depots. These contained a considerable number of troops, some awaiting posting, others returning from leave to their parent units with the BEF to the north of the Somme. As it was now patently impossible for any of these men to proceed forward, it was decided to use as many of them as possible, or at least as many as could be armed. As a result, five 'battalions' were formed which were named after their commanding officers, Perowne, Wait, Ray, Davie and Meredith. In addition four machine-gun platoons were raised from men experienced with those weapons. Curiously enough, two of them were manned completely by men of two regiments, the Cheshires and the Gloucesters. The whole force was placed under the command of Colonel Charles Vicary, the Reinforcement Officer of the BEF. It was placed so as to fill the gap between the headwaters of the Rivers Béthune and Andelle.

Brigadier Beauman took one further step to cover the approach to the Seine. The fronts mentioned above were used to form the arcs of sectors connecting them to the Seine. These sectors were placed under Royal Engineer officers, the Béthune sector being under Colonel Doyle, the centre sector under Colonel Alms and the Andelle Sector under Colonel White. It was the responsibility of these officers to ensure that every bridge and culvert was prepared for demolition and road-blocks formed at all tactical points. Fortunately, owing to the very large number of RE personnel available, it was possible to provide an officer and a detachment at nearly every point.

It can be fairly said that all steps which could be taken in the time, namely the 16th to the 22nd, were taken to safeguard the approaches to the L of C and its depots with the resources which were then available. It must be admitted, however, that it was unlikely that the force could put up much resistance to a determined attack. The most that could be expected of it was that it would delay the enemy sufficiently to allow time for the French to transfer the necessary reinforcements which, it was assumed, they were assembling to the south and east. These, it was hoped, would become available within the next few days. Already the new French Seventh Army, under General Frère, was forming along the line of the Somme as far as Amiens. With the transference of the Colonial Divisions from North Africa, the line would be extended westwards.

Through the centre sector of the Beauman 'Defence Line' ran the main road and railway linking Rouen and the great regulating station of Abancourt. A few miles short of Abancourt the road crosses the railway by means of a brick-built viaduct, the railway passing through a cutting at this point. The viaduct had been well-prepared for demolition, all charges being in position and primed.

On the 19th the battle of Amiens was in full swing. In addition German bombers were attacking roads and railways running south and westwards. Enemy patrols had also penetrated south-westwards. Owing to lack of facilities, including aircraft, information was scanty as to the amount of penetration. All that anyone knew for certain was that the enemy had crossed the Somme.

Whether the officer responsible for the destruction of the viaduct panicked or whether he genuinely thought that the advance guard of the German forces was approaching his position will never be known. Sufficient to say that he gave the orders for the charges to be fired. With a tremendous roar they exploded. The charges had been well placed and the huge bridge collapsed into a vast pile of rubble athwart the railway lines, effectively blocking them in both directions. So massive was the block that it was obvious that it would require some days of considerable effort to clear it.[3]

The trains carrying the remainder of the 46th Division had cleared Rouen station by 2000 hrs and had started on their way to Abbeville via Abancourt. Suddenly orders were given to halt. A telephone call had been received by Rouen sub-area HQ informing the Commander of the complete blockage of the line northwards. This situation produced a most serious problem. The only alternative line passed through Rouxmesnil junction, just outside Dieppe. Dieppe was a registered Red Cross Port. Under International Law it had been granted immunity from hostile action. A decision had to be taken whether or not to risk the immunity of Dieppe in order to forward the troops to the north. Owing to the apparent urgency of the situation it was decided to use the Dieppe route. As a result the trains were reversed and diverted on to the Dieppe line.

During the morning of the 20th a German spotter plane noticed the convoy of trains approaching Dieppe. As they were travelling north it was obvious that they could not contain casualties — they must be troop trains. As if to confirm this conclusion, the trains which previously had been moving south through Abancourt were being re-routed through the Dieppe junction. It was known that these trains contained Belgian and French troops retiring from the Front. Orders were therefore issued by the German High Command for the bombing of Dieppe. At the beginning the bombers concentrated on the railway line, but, as time passed, it was seen that an increasing number of troops were entering the town. The bombers then attacked the port in strength.

The trains carrying the troops forward were subjected to a number of aerial attacks but luckily escaped damage. The troops had no knowledge of the German advance to Abbeville. As far as they were aware the fighting was taking place far to the east. As the trains approached Abbeville dense columns of smoke could be seen rising from the burning town. Trains passed them going south loaded with Allied troops, who made significant 'throat-cutting' gestures — to the mystification of the British.

The leading train, carrying the HQ of the 137th Brigade and the 2/5th West Yorkshire Regiment, passed through the blazing inferno of the town and was able to get clear before the Germans arrived. However, that carrying the KOYLI, arriving at 1630, was forced to halt outside Abbeville station. With the Germans entering the town it was quite impossible for it to proceed. A block of three trains now extended westwards down the track.

The Commanding Officer of the KOYLI decided that the only hope of his being able to advance was on foot. He managed to get his command across the Somme by a footbridge which was still intact. Until he was able to discover precisely the situation he placed his men in defensive positions not far from the river. Having made a reconnaissance, he found that the enemy was encircling the town. He had no alternative but to withdraw. Meanwhile the 2/6th and the 2/7th Duke of Wellington's Regiment had come to the same conclusion, though they had not actually crossed the river. It was now found that, owing to the action of Fifth Columnists (who had become most active in the area) and to enemy bombing, it was only possible to reverse the trains after considerable delay. Also the locomotives were running out of water, necessitating the drawing of their fires. Gathering together everything they could carry, the three battalions started to march back along the railway track. It was not long, however, before the lack of marching experience began to tell. Many men had to be carried on improvised stretchers or helped along by their comrades. Food there was none; even worse, there was a complete lack of drinking water.

This terrible march is graphically described in a contemporary diary. After describing his unit's activities north of the Somme the diarist continues:

> We reached the road, which was congested with vehicles, civilians and troops and crossed the bridge over the Somme. We then inclined right and moved northward between the river and the railway. We halted here to get the Company together, and while we rested we were informed that German tanks had entered the town. By this time it was dark but the light was good, owing to the brilliant moon. We moved off again in single file at the right-hand-side of the railway track. The going was very rough owing to the big stones which had been laid as ballast. Also dozens and dozens of big petrol drums lined the track for several hundred yards, which made progress difficult. Captain — pressed us to take a very quick pace. By this time I was exhausted by my heavy equipment, pack and thirst and sore feet were troubling me. I pressed on panting and only the thought of home kept me going.
>
> After travelling some distance I had to abandon my pack, just taking some socks, handkerchiefs and a tin of cigarettes, groundsheet and my hairbrush and case and Balaklava helmet. I was in a very bad state on account of thirst and had difficulty in speaking. At the rear and to the left of us we could see the glare of burning Abbeville, and enemy bombers were nearly constantly passing overhead. Bombing was also going on. We stopped at a cross-roads where I lay on my back on the wet grass.

Fortunately, with the help of an RE detachment which had accompanied the trains, it was possible to construct some ramps. This enabled two motor vehicles to be unloaded. Food being of the utmost urgency, and having learned that the hospital at St Valéry-sur-Somme was unoccupied, one vehicle was despatched thence in the hope that some food would be found. It returned, some time later, loaded with many invalid delicacies, including chicken breasts in aspic!

The battalions gradually drew nearer to Dieppe. The men were nearly worn out by the long march. Many had discarded much of their equipment and units were mixed up, not to recover cohesion until they reached the town. It was now that an incident occurred which proved that 'it is an ill-wind that does no one good'. A party arriving at a station on the railway line looking for water were informed by a French railway engineer that a hospital train had been derailed just down the line. He asked for help as, though a breakdown train was on its way, immediate assistance for the wounded was essential. The party, returning to their units, reported the incident to their COs. At once orders were given to proceed to the scene of the accident. The following extract from a diary graphically describes the incident:

> Whilst travelling along the line we came upon a wrecked ambulance train. The train appeared to have been bombed and machine-gunned. There were dead people, men, women and children, scattered by the side of the train. The engine-driver had his head off. A small ambulance car had toppled off the train and lay in the road on its roof. Steam was hissing from the engine.

By the end of the day the train had been returned to the track and the track itself restored. The engineer, learning that the battalions were making for Dieppe, suggested that if they could squeeze into some cattle-trucks which were standing on a siding, he would couple these to the train and take as many of the troops as possible to their destination. The men squeezed themselves into the confined space. They were prepared to suffer any discomfort to avoid prolonging that hellish march! So, on the 22nd all three battalions were safely in Dieppe.

The removal of immunity from Dieppe had serious repercussions as the following extract shows:

> We then took a roundabout road to Dieppe which we reached at 4.00pm (on 21 May). We walked to the harbour, and Captain — left us to find transport to take us to camp on the outskirts of Dieppe. We remained against the bridge. At 4.30 a number of aircraft came over from the direction of the sea. There was no AA fire (the port, of course, was undefended) and I thought that the planes were either

French or ours. They were very high flying in formation. My first intimation that they were enemy aircraft was two violent explosions on the Hospital Ship, *Maid of Kent*, which was moored about 100 yards from us. A big piece of stone, thrown up by a bomb splinter, struck me on my right knee and I was knocked down. We took cover the other side of the bridge. In front of me lay a French officer and another one fell nearly on me. A number of bombs were dropped. The only return fire was from LMGs made by French soldiers but the planes were far too high for the fire to be effective. After dropping their load of bombs the planes cleared off. We got up and moved back to the bridge. The *Maid of Kent* was on fire and a huge column of black smoke was issuing from it. A hospital train lying on the quayside had its rear coaches on fire. A piece of bomb casing had gone through the window of a café near to which we had sheltered and a girl had been struck by splinters all over her face and neck. A small boy, about eight years of age, had been struck on the ankle. Wounded and sick men were on the *Maid of Kent*, and they were carried off. A few minutes later a second batch of enemy planes came over and bombed. This time we took shelter under the bank of the river. After the raid was over, we came from our shelter, but were driven back by another flock of enemy bombers. The raids lasted until 5.30pm — the *Maid of Kent* was sinking fast and still on fire. The wounded were being transferred onto the hospital train, and we were held up until the train moved off. We left Dieppe at about 6.00pm and, on passing the Military Hospital, we saw where a bomb had struck the lodge. We later heard that the Hospital had been bombed and machine-gunned, that some of our fellows were in it at the time.

Brigadier Beauman, having learned of the arrival of the three battalions in Dieppe, decided to send two of them to the reinforcement depots south of the Seine near Rouen. The KOYLI and the 2/6th Duke of Wellingtons, therefore, set out once more on what was to be a journey very little less arduous than that which they had already experienced. It was largely by begging lifts from passing refugee cars that the exhausted men were able to reach their destination. Again the lack of water provided a major problem. Few estaminets were prepared to give them any.

Brigadier Beauman retained the 2/7th Duke of Wellingtons at Dieppe to act as garrison. Though the port was bombed periodically, their life as garrison troops was by no means unpleasant. The Battalion settled into its new role nicely. It had brought its band, which now played regularly in the square. This did a great deal to maintain the morale of both the troops and the local inhabitants. The troops themseves spent their time constructing defences and building up stocks of ammunition and other necessaries in case of attack.

While these events were taking place in the area of the Somme, HQ L of C was not, until the 21st, unduly disturbed. This was due to the fact that very little information was filtering through from the north. Indeed, any that did come through of an alarming nature was largely discounted. Neither GHQ at Arras nor the War Office had supplied any information which they felt need upset its calm. On the 21st, however, a number of events took place which were to have a far-reaching effect on its future.

It will be remembered that on the 21st an officer of the 6th Royal Sussex had reported on the events which had taken place at Amiens; as a result a near panic took place at HQ. Urgent messages were sent to the CO of the local garrison battalion, the 12th Royal Warwickshire Regiment, ordering him to tighten up security and to construct all-round defences at HQ. At the same time General de Fonblanque sent an urgent signal to both Brigadier Beauman and Brigadier Shilstone (commanding 3rd AA Brigade) ordering them to withdraw all guns located north of the Seine behind the river. Any that could not be moved at once were to be destroyed.[4] Had Brigadier Shilstone, who was responsible for the air defence of all the ports in the district, complied with this order, they would have become quite untenable; the loss of guns on fixed mountings, such as at Le Havre, would have been irreparable.

During the week covered by the last chapter events occurred which were to have the greatest influence on the final outcome of the campaign in France and Flanders. Owing to the continuing advance of the enemy since the opening of their offensive on the 10th, the Allies were in serious danger of being cut off from their supplies. Also, there was the imminent prospect of the Germans wheeling southwards and capturing Paris before reinforcements could be brought north.

On the 16th Mr Churchill travelled to France to meet the new French Premier, M. Reynaud. It did not take Mr Churchill long to discover how deep the sense of defeat had penetrated into the very soul of the French administration. Though brave words were spoken, it was quite evident that little hope was entertained for a successful outcome of the struggle. It was during this meeting that the Prime Minister recorded that he had seen the burning of the archives at the Quai d'Orsay, evidence that the French Government was seriously considering the abandonment of the capital. So seriously was he affected by the situation that Mr Churchill sent his now famous telegram to the Cabinet giving for the first time a true picture of the state of affairs. A week had passed, therefore, before the Cabinet were aware of exactly how serious the situation had become.

Even as early as the 17th consideration was being given to the evacuation of the BEF. But for this operation the prospects were anything but bright. Should the enemy be able to reach the Channel coast, this would reduce the possible ports to Boulogne, Calais and Dunkirk; none of these were suitable for handling heavy equipment. The Army would then arrive home with nothing with which to continue the struggle. Indeed, it seemed that the salvation of the situation rested on such action as could be taken by the allied Air Forces in support of the ground troops. As we already know, the Air Forces were not geared to such support. The heavy bombers were totally unsuited for attacking troop targets and the mediums had had little training in this form of warfare. Though these latter made a commendable effort they were quite unable to affect the situation and were continually harried by enemy fighters and ground artillery. In fact, it was to the allied fighters that everyone looked for their salvation. If the German 'aerial artillery' could be silenced then the troops could make their presence felt on equal terms. Unfortunately, fighters were not available in sufficient numbers to achieve this, owing to it being considered essential to retain in England a large number of squadrons for defensive reasons. The German armoured columns were, therefore, able to advance virtually unaffected by anything that the Allies were able to bring against them.

General Gamelin, the Supreme Commander, soon realized that

the only way that the situation could be saved was by a joint, and massive, attack southwards in conjunction with a similar attack northwards from across the Somme. Plans were laid accordingly. Before, however, they could be implemented, M. Reynaud had recalled General Weygand from North Africa and placed him in supreme command in place of General Gamelin. On assuming his new command, General Weygand cancelled the original plan as he was anxious to make himself fully acquainted with the situation before deciding his future policy. It was three days after his assumption, on the 20th, that General Weygand came out with a plan similar, in most aspects, to that of his predecessor. By then, of course, more valuable time had been lost and the situation had deteriorated accordingly.

By 18 May the War Cabinet in London considered that urgent measures were now required if the whole of the BEF were not to be lost. It was quite evident that unless the Allies were able to maintain their communications it would not be long before their supplies failed, thereby rendering the Armies in the north incapable of further resistance. It was decided, therefore, that Lord Gort should be given instructions to disengage his forces from the Northern Front and to make a complete withdrawal in force to the south so as to regain touch with his communications. Though this meant sacrificing the Belgians, it seemed that there was no alternative. The French were to be asked to conform in an operation similar to the plan proposed by General Gamelin.

On the 19th, therefore, General Ironside was sent to France to discuss with the Commander-in-Chief the proposed operation. Lord Gort was not enthusiastic. He considered that, if he retired south, he would open a wide gap between himself and the Belgians through which the German armies in the north would pour, thereby cutting him off from the Channel ports. It was finally agreed that an attack with two reserve divisions, with a third in support, strengthened by the 1st Army Tank Brigade in conjunction with formations from the 1st French Army, should be mounted. The object was to reconnect the Lines of Communication between Arras and Amiens and to cut off the heads of the advancing German Armoured Divisions. In order to ensure the success of the projected operation General Ironside visited the Headquarters of the Northern Army Group. There he saw the Commander, General Billotte, who finally agreed to the operation. On his return to Lord Gort's Headquarters, General Ironside explained what had been arranged. Lord Gort was extremely sceptical about the French attacking; nevertheless, he agreed to go ahead with the operation. The two reserve divisions, the 5th and 50th, each of two brigades only, were moved into position near Arras, together with the 1st Army Tank Brigade. It had been proposed that the attack should take place on the 21st. General Billotte now stated that it would be quite impossible for his troops to be ready before the 23rd at the earliest. General Prioux, commanding the French Cavalry Corps, however, said that his formation would support the attack if Lord Gort decided to proceed, as he had planned, on the 21st.

Since the War many people have wondered why Lord Gort decided to go ahead with the operation, knowing, as he must, that the forces employed would be totally incapable of carrying out the projected mission. It must be assumed that Gort was motivated by his innate loyalty to both the British Government and his Allies.

On the 21st the attack was duly launched; not, however, by two divisions but with two mixed columns of tanks, one battalion of infantry and some artillery in each. At first the enemy were taken by surprise. The columns made good progress, capturing a number of prisoners and destroying a considerable quantity of enemy guns and tanks. But after about twelve miles the attacks petered out. For unexplained reasons the columns received no support. Three brigades remained stationary. The enemy quickly recovered from their surprise. They hurled in a massive counter-attack. Had it not been for the excellent work of the units of the French Cavalry Corps the columns would have been overwhelmed. As it was, the survivors struggled back to their start line having suffered a considerable number of casualties both in men and tanks. As is now known, the attack had a marked effect on the German High Command. They thought that a major threat existed to the flanks of the advancing tank columns and slowed down their advance. There, for the time being, the matter rested. The Germans had gained the Channel coast and were preparing for their advance northwards so as to encircle the Allied forces in the north. They had begun to establish bridgeheads across the Somme at both Amiens and Abbeville. On the British side, troops had been sent from England to reinforce the garrison at Boulogne. It is important for the reader to note the dates in the above account in order to appreciate what follows.

At this time a new 'performer' appeared on the stage, the 1st (and only) Armoured Division. The formation of the 1st Armoured Division requires examination, if only to discover why it came to such an ignominious end.

It was descended directly from the 'Experimental Force' initiated by the CIGS, Sir George Milne, in 1926. Though it was abolished in 1928 for financial reasons, it was resuscitated in a somewhat emasculated form in 1936, its new nomenclature being the 'Mobile Division'. As certain eminent military writers pointed out, 'What's in a name? All divisions are mobile!' In fact, the only difference between it and an ordinary division was that all the troops were carried in motor vehicles. Tanks were excluded as all its commanders, including Major-General A.F. Brooke, pointed out, 'They are not the sort of vehicle one wants around!' Also it was considered that Tank Corps personnel were little better than mechanics!

After the visits by General Ironside and the CIGS, Sir Cyril Deverell, to the German manoeuvres in 1937, reports were submitted to the Secretary of State recommending the organization of an Armoured division similar to those which had been on display in Germany. For some time this suggestion was resisted, mainly through representations by the cavalry. In 1938, however, it was, with the greatest reluctance, agreed to organize such a division. The leading cavalrymen insisted that it should follow the lines of a cavalry division. This consisted of a light and heavy brigade (shades of Balaklava!), the light brigade being equipped with tanks armed with a Besa machine-gun only. These vehicles being considered to be the nearest approach to a horse, the cavalry were prepared to man them. The heavy brigade, consisting of heavier vehicles armed with both a 2 pdr and a machine-gun, were handed over to Royal Tank Corps personnel. It should be pointed out that at no time during the Division's formation or training was the opinion of a tank man sought. Indeed, when the time came for selecting a commander, the most experienced officer in the British Army in handling tanks, Major-General Hobart, was passed over in favour of Major-General Roger Evans of the Royal Horse Guards.

The agreed establishment of the Armoured Division included, besides the two modified brigades mentioned above, a Support Group. This latter formation was very well 'found' on paper. It was to consist of two RHA Regiments (it was traditional for the RHA to accompany cavalry) and two battalions of infantry carried in armoured vehicles. These battalions were selected with the greatest care. They could not be mere infantry of the Line. The Guards were not available so the choice fell on a battalion each from the KRRC and the Rifle Brigade, both excellent fighting units. In addition, it was necessary to have one Field Squadron of Engineers.

With this organization the cavalrymen expressed themselves satisfied. Unfortunately, a spanner was thrown into the works by a Gunner. He pointed out, with truth, that under modern conditions, it was vital to have some anti-aircraft protection and guns which could be employed in an anti-tank role. So it was decided to convert two existing units into a Light AA and Anti-Tank Regiment. It was to be equipped with mobile Bofors anti-aircraft guns for two of its batteries and with 2 pdrs for the other two. The new unit received the name 'the 101st Light Anti-Aircraft and Anti-Tank Regiment RA'. This unit was, however, to be in place of, and not in addition to, one of the RHA Regiments.

As the Support Group and, in particular, the 101st Regiment, play such a prominent part in subsequent events, it is necessary to consider them in some detail. When first formed, the Support Group consisted of the 1st Battalion, the Rifle Brigade and the 2nd Battalion, the KRRC, together with the Royal Engineer unit referred to above. The artillery were represented by the 1st RHA Regiment, together with the new 101st LAA and Anti-Tank Regiment RA. This latter consisted of two LAA Batteries each of ten Bofors guns and two batteries of ten 2 pdr AT guns. The units selected to make up this regiment were, in the case of the AA portion, drawn from the 11th LAA Regiment TA (44th Finsbury Rifles). The anti-tank portion was formed from the 60th (Royal Welsh Fusiliers) Anti-Tank Regiment TA (237 and 239 anit-tank batteries). The whole was under the command of Lt-Colonel H. Sherriff Roberts RA.

It should be noted that while the anit-tank batteries were at full war establishment, both in arms and personnel, the LAA batteries had to leave both their guns and vehicles on their original gun-sites. It was not, therefore, a very balanced regiment that assembled at Aldershot in February, 1940.

The main body of the Armoured Division was, at this time, located in the area between Ringwood, Hants, and Bovington in mid-Dorset. The 101st left Aldershot for Puddletown in Dorset on 15 March for training with the other parts of the group and the Division as a whole. Though the CO and the battery commanders had attended a War Office exercise in January, owing to shortness of equipment the Regiment was prevented from taking part in any training with the other units of the Group. The batteries, however, were able to undertake some field-firing practice at various ranges during April. The members of the Regiment were not unduly disturbed, as they had been informed that they would be going to France in June for the purpose of training with the Division on the new divisional training ground; there was no likelihood of them being called upon to take any active role until after September that year. In any case, the Division itself would not be properly equipped until November, 1940.

The 1st RHA Regiment had gone to France with the BEF and had been placed in GHQ reserve. It was not, therefore, available for training with the rest of the Group. Lord Gort had insisted that every available Artillery regiment should be sent to France when the Expeditionary Force left England in 1939. On 1 May 1940, the two infantry regiments had been withdrawn for special training. It was thought, at the time, that this move was purely temporary. As subsequent events will show, this was not so and the infantry of the Support Group was lost to the Group for ever.

Also on 1 May, the CO left the Regiment and the second-in-command, Major Payne, assumed temporary command. A somewhat depressing event occurred at this time; the two LAA batteries were supplied with 96 Lewis guns in place of their missing Bofors. It will be seen, therefore, that when the advanced party left for France on 11 May the 1st Support Group consisted of a much under-equipped LAA and Anti-Tank Regiment, one Field Company RE and one Field Park Company RE. This latter unit had been added at the last minute, owing to the representations of the Divisional Commander. One can readily imagine the feelings of the Support Group

Commander, Brigadier F.E. Morgan, (a highly experienced Gunner) when he surveyed what was left of his command that had begun with such high hopes.

The move of the 1st Armoured Division to France was so unsatisfactory that it seems as if it was a case of 'forthcoming events casting their shadows before them'. The advanced party, on arrival in France, reported to GHQ on 15 May. Their reception was most casual. No one seemed to know anything about them or where they should go. No preparations had been made for their reception. The Divisional Commander himself arrived on the 16th and eventually managed to obtain agreement with the C-in-C as to the disposal of the Division. It was to be located between Arras and Amiens. However, by the 17th the enemy had made such progress that this arrangement was likely to be out of date before it was implemented.

The first part of the Armoured Division consisted of the remains of the Support Group. As Group HQ had not moved with the remainder of the formation, Major Payne, as senior officer, opened his sealed orders when the convoy reached the open sea. They gave the Group's destination as Ninove, after landing at Le Havre. Unfortunately, even as Major Payne was reading these orders, the Germans occupied Ninove. On arrival at Le Havre on the 17th fresh orders were issued for the Group to move to Blangy. The Group moved the first day to Fauville and went into billets. On the 20th the Group was ordered by HQ Armoured Division to proceed to the new Armoured Divisional training ground at Pacy-sur-Eure, south of the Seine, to the east of Evreux. Conditions were found to be chaotic on arrival, no provision having been made for the arrival of the troops. It was with the greatest difficulty that the Group was able to obtain any quarters or even rations.

Owing to the rapid deterioration north of the Somme, the second flight was disembarked at Cherbourg and moved direct to Pacy. This consisted of the 2nd Dragoon Guards (the Queen's Bays).

On 21 May, an instruction was received from GHQ for the employment of the Armoured Division, or as much of it as was then available. It read as follows:

> 1. The enemy has penetrated the forward defences of the Allied front and has pushed mobile formations forward in the directions of

Abbeville and Montreuil.

2. Communications between the BEF and L of C are temporarily severed on line R. Somme and it is vital to re-establish them.

3. You will employ 1st Armoured Division on following tasks:

(*a*) To seize and, hold crossings R. Somme between incl. Picquigny and Pont-Rémy. This task is most urgent and should be undertaken directly the following minimum force is available:-
One Armoured Regiment.
One Fd Sqn.
One Fd Pk Tp.
One Lt AA and Anti-tank Regiment.

(*b*) To concentrate the remainder of the leading brigade in the rear of R. Somme area Picquigny — Pont-Rémy.

(*c*) When this is done prepare to move either eastwards or northwards as the situation allows with a view to intervening in operations in the area of the BEF.

4. You will be supplied by L of C Northern District as far as R. Somme. Thereafter supplies will have to be arranged as circumstances dictate; arrangements are being made to place supplies, petrol and some ammunition in channel ports north of R. Somme, and you should arrange to keep in touch with the situation at these places.

5. You will use own discretion regarding use of wireless — frequencies herewith. You will communicate the location of your HQ by means of Liaison officers and will maintain one or more Liaison officers with these Headquarters.

Signed POWNALL
Chief of General Staff.
British Expeditionary Force.

One can readily appreciate the feelings of General Evans on receipt of such an over-optimistic order. Presumably because of the reaction which it was thought that this order might provoke, the GSO I (AFV) at GHQ was sent to reinforce the order, bringing a copy of it with him.

On receipt of the confirming order from Lt-Colonel Raymond Briggs, General Evans went to HQ Northern District to discuss the matter with Brigadier Beauman. As it was known that the Germans had penetrated south of the Somme at the very time the original order had been written and also that rumours stated that the enemy were moving on Rouen, it was agreed that certain action should be taken to ensure that there would be no interference with the arrival of the necessary troops at the place of assembly. It was decided to move up to an area which would enable the flank of the possible enemy advance to be threatened and thus safeguard the front of the defensive position held by Northern District. Accordingly the 101st was sent forward to hold the crossings between Pont de l'Arche and Vernon over the River Seine. The engineers were ordered to prepare a line of demolitions between Neufchâtel and Dieppe. (It will be remembered that Brigadier Beauman had already begun to take such measures). The Bays were instructed that, on arrival at Pacy, they were to move forward to the Fôret de Lyons. In fact they arrived in this position on the morning of 22 May.

It will be seen from the above that there was not the slightest chance of any attack being mounted before the 23rd at the earliest and probably later. It should be noted that, while all these other preparations for defence were going on, not the slightest effort was made to take any measures to discover whether the rumours emanating from refugees bore any resemblance to the truth. In any case, it is extremely difficult to understand why GHQ issued the Instruction in the first place. As the reader will have appreciated, no effort had been made to co-ordinate the attack from Arras with the proposed attack by the Armoured units nor was there the least likelihood of a further attack southwards before the 25th or 26th. But, as will be seen, worse was to follow. One can understand why no mention of these orders is made by General Pownall in his Diaries. In any case, GHQ must have known that such a trifling force could have made very little impression on what they must have known was a considerable enemy combination north of the Somme, in spite of the Intelligence Reports received from GQG.

General Ironside returned from France in the early morning of the 21st. On entering his office in Whitehall he was greeted by Colonel Macleod, his Personal Assistant. 'I think you should see this at once,' he said, handing the General a signal which had arrived a few minutes before. It was a copy of the order issued by General de Fonblanque to Brigadier Beauman regarding the guns north of the Seine.

'My God,' said the General, 'This must be stopped at once!'

'I have made out a signal to that effect,' replied Macleod.

'Send it priority,' ordered Ironside.

As a result of this signal, and the number of disturbing reports which had been filtering through from the L of C, General Ironside decided that something urgent had to be done to try and straighten out the situation which was obviously developing south of the Somme. He turned to Macleod.

'We must have a man out there who can handle a situation like this. Get Karslake; he is the best soldier in the British Army. If anyone can do it, he can. Get him on the telephone.' Macleod put the call through to Romsey. When the connection had been made the CIGS took the 'phone. 'Henry,' he said, 'I have a job for you. Come up here at once — even if you are in your birthday-suit!'

On arrival at the War Office General Karslake was shown up to the CIGS's room. Besides General Ironside were Mr Churchill, the Prime Minister, and Mr Anthony Eden, the Secretary of State for War. General Ironside explained the situation, adding, 'In any case, there is far too much stuff out there. If the worst comes to the worst we shall need everything we can lay our hands on. Here is a list of priorities. Get out all you can without alarming the French. If all we hear is true, it will be a close-run thing. You will just have to stave off the Boche with what troops you can scrape together. Of course, we will do all we can to help you.'

'But don't expect to get any guns,' rumbled Churchill. 'There just aren't any.'

General Karslake then asked about a staff. He was told that there was no time for that; he had to leave at once for France. However, efforts would be made to provide some officers on whom he could rely. They would meet him at Southampton the following day. With that, General Karslake had to be content. All present wished him luck; it was obvious though that none of them entertained much hope that he would achieve anything or even that he would return alive.

On the morning of the 22nd a staff car arrived at the General's house and drove him to Southampton. There, to his surprise and pleasure, he met Brigadier G. Bruce, of Everest fame, who was to be his Brigadier, General Staff. The third member of the party was Major E.L. Fanshawe, his GSO II. That evening the three men boarded the S.S. *Prague*. It already held a large number of troops of the 3rd Armoured Brigade. This Brigade was under strength, as one of its units, the 3rd Battalion, Royal Tank Regiment, had been removed from its command just before it had embarked. This battalion was going to Calais.

IV

23 May — 31 May

At ten minutes past one on the morning of the 23rd the signal giving the news of the appointment of General Karslake to the position of GOC L of C was handed to General de Fonblanque at his HQ at Le Mans. An officer who was present describes what happened after the General had read the contents: 'The General stared at the signal for some seconds, as if he could not grasp the contents. Then, with a shout of rage, he tore off his General's insignia and threw them to the floor. "If I am considered no good as a General," he shouted, "I will become a Private." He then stormed out of the War Room. It was the first time I had ever seen General de Fonblanque go off the handle. Luckily, by the time the new General arrived he had regained his normal equanimity.'[1]

The S.S. *Prague* docked at Cherbourg at 0600. The disembarkation of the 3rd Armoured Brigade, consisting of the 2nd and 5th Battalions only of the Royal Tank Regiment, began. All necessary arrangements had been made to entrain the tanks on five trains and to route the wheeled vehicles to the divisional assembly area at Pacy-sur-Eure.

General Karslake, accompanied by Brigadier Bruce, left Cherbourg by air at 0630 for Le Mans. Major Fanshawe brought on the baggage and batmen by car.

On arrival at the HQ of the L of C the General was met by General de Fonblanque who introduced him to the members of his staff. Not wanting to waste time, General Karslake told de Fonblanque the details of his mission over breakfast, enquiring also about the state of the defence force which was supposed to be covering the approaches to Rouen and acting as a protection for the large stores depots in the area.

General de Fonblanque explained the general disposition of the troops, adding that they were very vulnerable owing to the complete lack of supporting artillery. Karslake was not surprised as he had already been warned of the dearth of guns on the L of C. He asked, however, whether there were any sort of guns at Ordnance or in any of the reinforcement parks. It would seem that this question was not answered as the General then asked if, on the Staff, there was an Artillery officer who would be capable of undertaking the formation of an Artillery Regiment, should some guns be forthcoming. The name of Major Elliott was put forward; after all, he was doing nothing useful and had done nothing since his arrival.

General Karslake instructed Major Elliott to proceed at once to all possible sources of supply. He should also visit the reinforcement centres to discover what numbers of suitable Gunners there might be to man any guns that he might find. Having completed this survey, he was to report to the General. If it was at all possible he was to assemble, as quickly as he could, as many artillery units of all kinds; he was then to report to Brigadier Beauman at Rouen who would direct their deployment.[2] General de Fonblanque was extremely sceptical as to the outcome of these instructions.

After waiting just long enough to complete the initial arrangements and to acquire an ADC, Lord Inverclyde, the General, once again accompanied by Brigadier Bruce, set off for La Ferté-sous-Jouarre, the HQ of General Georges. General Georges was General Karslake's immediate superior; it was essential to report to him as soon as possible, also to obtain the most up-to-date information regarding the overall situation.

Passing near Pacy-sur-Eure the party met the advancing units of the Armoured Division. At this time they only consisted of the Queen's Bays and the surviving portions of the Support Group (less its Commander and HQ who were still in England). The General had a brief chat with General Evans, commanding the Armoured Division. General Evans explained the object of his move forward, showing General Karslake a copy of the original GHQ Instruction and the subsequent order which contained the sentences, 'It is vital to safeguard the right flank of the BEF during its southern advance to cut German communications between Cambrai and Peronne. Immediate advance of whatever elements of your Division are ready is essential. Action, at once, may be decisive; tomorrow may be too late.' This order had been received at ten minutes past twelve that day. As we have seen, the formations of the BEF which had been employed on the 21st for the attack south of Arras had already returned to their original positions; no further attack was contemplated before the 26th at the earliest. It is difficult to understand, therefore, the reason why this order was issued. Again, no mention of it is made by General Pownall in his records for the period.

General Evans then explained his weakness, owing to the removal of his infantry and artillery; also the fact that no reconnaissance had been made of the crossings of the Somme. The only piece of information which had come to hand was a report from HQ L of C to the effect that the bridge at Ailly was intact. (It will be remembered that an officer of the 6th Royal Sussex had stated that the bridge was intact but he was referring to Ailly-sur-*Noye* and not to Ailly-sur-*Somme*.) The RAF had received no request to carry out any aerial survey or to co-operate in any way with the operation, as far as is known. In fact, General Evans regarded the whole enterprise as most unsatisfactory, but as it was a direct order he had no option but to try and carry it out. Indeed, the only encouraging feature was the latest Intelligence report, obtained by Colonel Briggs from GQG. This read as follows:

(1) French 3 Army hold from Montmedy to Attigny to excl. Rethel. French 6 Army incl. Rethel — R. Aisne — Canal Oise — excl. R. Oise.
French 7 Army holds Oise and Canal Croazat as far East as Istrée (St Simon). 7 Army had last night six divisions complete and 2/3rds of two more divisions. Mobile troops of 7 Army gained contact with enemy on R. Somme last night between Péronne and Amiens.
7 Army has been ordered to cross R. Somme today.

(2) Belgians are holding from coast to Ghent — Halluin — B.E.F. Halluin — Maulde [their old line before the German offensive on 10 May]. BEF are holding Douay—Arras.
1st French Army were pushed back to Macforce.
Yesterday French attacked towards Cambrai and British towards Bapaume. Intercept about 12.30am 22 May indicated that enemy required assistance 9km north of Cambrai. Another intercept ordered an attack on Arras with all available resources.

[These latter details refer to the results of the British attack to the south of Arras on 21 May.]

The enemy is acting defensively on the southern front approximately on line of contact as far west as Péronne and possibly further west still.

Last two days he has been bombing intensively in 7 Army area. Of his ten Panzer divisions two seem to be facing southern flank, one south of Sedan and the other probably in St Quentin area. At least two are attacking north-west towards Valenciennes. This leaves the mangled remains of six Panzer divisions, which appear to have come through the gap between Cambrai and Péronne, to have carried out recces south of the Somme, found nothing and withdrawn to the R. Somme. The largest numbers ever reported south of the Somme were three separate parties of not more than 20 AFVs each. The main tank attack now taking place appears to be at St Omer from the south-west and on Arras from the north-west.

(3) The bombing resources of Great Britain have been concentrated on:

    (*a*) Crossings over R. Oise from La Fère — Landrecies.
    (*b*) Communications west of Brussels and Gemblous.
    (*c*) Crossings over R. Meuse between Namur and Charleville.
    (*d*) Marshalling yards on R. Rhine at Bonn, Cologne, Dusseldorf, Wessel and west of Rhine at Aachen.

[It will be noted that *nothing* was being done to aid the attacks, which were so vital, across the River Somme.]

If, indeed, there were only the 'mangled remains' of a number of German Armoured Divisions to oppose them, then prospects of success for the proposed British attack seemed slightly less dim. Nevertheless, even this prospect did not solve the real problem, namely that of crossing the Somme with the very small number, and total unsuitability, of the troops available.

General Karslake was inclined to agree with General Evans on the subject of the problematical value of the projected operation. He said nothing, however, of his fears. He tried to encourage him by repeating what he had heard before he left London, namely that the French were planning to attack across the Somme in strength. It was possible that Evans' effort was to be in conjunction with that. Then, wishing him good luck, General Karslake proceeded on his

7 (*above left*) Lieutenant-Colonel A. L. Cameron.

8 (*above*) Lieutenant-Colonel J. H. Roberts.

9 (*left*) Major A. G. Syme.

10 (*below left*) Major G. M. Elliot.

11 (*below*) CQMS J. S. Brown.

12 A 'Super-Heavy'—a 12″ Howitzer Mark IV in France, 1940.

way to La Ferté-sous-Jouarre. He arrived at the Swayne Mission (to General Georges) at 2000 hrs and discussed the whole matter with Brigadier Swayne, also telling him the details of the instructions he had received from the CIGS. Regarding Evans' attack Brigadier Swayne considered that it was highly unlikely that it was designed to coincide with anything that the French might be contemplating; in fact he was very pessimistic about the whole situation. Indeed, he went so far as to express the opinion that he did not think that the French would carry on much longer. He suggested, however, that General Karslake should remain at his HQ overnight so as to meet either General Georges or General Roton (General Georges' Chef de Cabinet), both of whom were expected back the following morning.

On the 24th, having learned that General Georges was not expected back until the evening, General Karslake discussed the situation with General Roton. General Roton said that, though the French had agreed to the Evans attack, it was entirely a British affair and must be considered as an independent exploit. This intelligence was most disconcerting. Before he left London General Karslake had been told that the Armoured Division was not to come under his command as it was under the command of GHQ. There was nothing, therefore, that he could do to prevent what was obviously likely to prove a valueless and expensive enterprise.

After his interview with General Roton, Karslake was inclined even more to agree with the forebodings expressed by Brigadier Swayne. He was determined, however, to do his utmost to ensure that his command should suffer as little as possible and, above all, to recover as much equipment as he could for the future continuance of the war, if necessary, from the British Isles alone. It seemed obvious that it was quite impossible for those in London to know the true nature of the situation in France. Orders received from there were likely to be based on false premises and, in any case, would be received far too late to prove effective in their objective. Indeed, orders from GHQ BEF were likely to be worth even less owing to its lack of knowledge through being cut off, also through the enormous delay occasioned by them having to be relayed via London. This had been proved beyond all shadow of doubt over the employment of the RAF from England rather than directed by those on the spot. Now that the BEF was effectively cut off from the forces south of the Somme it was vital that this latter area should be considered as a separate command.

On leaving La Ferté-sous-Jouarre Karslake made for Rouen. He felt that it was essential to make himself acquainted with the only force which existed between the Germans and his HQ.

On arrival at Rouen, he first drove to the HQ of the local sub-area. He informed the commander of the proposed programme as regards the evacuation of stores and instructed him to issue warning orders to all the Depots within his command. He then went to the L of C Operational HQ, which was situated in the outskirts of the town. There, for the first time, he met Brigadier Beauman, commander of Northern District L of C and now Force Commander of the troops defending the approaches to Rouen. He was impressed by the state of the morale both at sub-area HQ and Force HQ. It was very different to the uneasy atmosphere he had experienced at Le Mans.

At first Brigadier Beauman was very much on his guard. It was not until later that General Karslake was to discover the real reason for Beauman's attitude. The Brigadier had suffered in 1938 under the Belisha plan. Up to then he had had a most successful career. In fact, when he retired in 1938 he had been given the unusual distinction of being granted the rank of Brigadier-General, this rank having been abolished in the early twenties. The present situation was one, he felt, that would allow him to show his potential. Hitherto he had been given carte blanche by General de Fonblanque. With the arrival of such a senior General it seemed that this opportunity was likely to be removed from him.

General Karslake, who sympathized with him, having suffered in a similar fashion and having decided that he was undoubtedly capable of carrying out whatever was required, reassured him. However, he recommended that there should be some major alterations in the organization of the Force. He considered that, as it was, it was unwieldy; it should be formed on Divisional lines. Brigadier Beauman agreed but said that there were no officers who could really be counted on to act as Brigadiers with an independent staff. The General promised to take this up with the CIGS at the earliest possible moment. He also told Brigadier Beauman what he had done about trying to get him some artillery. The Brigadier mentioned that when he had provided the Royal West Kents with guns he had noticed that there were others in the workshops. At that time they were not in working condition.

It was during these talks that the General learned that Brigadier Beauman had had to part with one of his battalions, the 4th Border Regiment, less B Coy, that was guarding the ammunition dump at St Saens, which it was hoped would partly compensate for the loss of the infantry of the Support Group. This battalion, which had hitherto been employed on guard duties on the L of C, was at least one of the few that had had some form of military training.

One fact that emerged from the talks with both General Evans and Brigadier Beauman was the complete absence of any method of obtaining accurate information. Certainly a 'fog of war' hung over the whole area. Information from French sources was quite unreliable. The General determined that, as soon as possible after his return to his HQ, he would take the necessary steps to improve this situation. On arrival at Le Mans he gave orders that groups of motor-cyclists, each of three men, found by RTR officers, should be formed, these groups to be sent out to discover *exactly* where troops were stationed (both British and French) and as much as possible about the enemy.[3]

As he had no Staff other than the two officers he had brought with him, the General decided that it was essential to try and build up a 'G' department to handle operational matters. Supplied with a list of officers on the existing Staff, he soon discovered that, other than one officer, there was no one who was competent to act in that capacity. As Colonel Fanshawe has since stated, 'They were a poor lot.'* In fact it was almost a case of non-cooperation. For instance, when the General asked for a full return of all arms located in the Southern part of the Command, practically nothing was shown. As will be seen in due course, there were in fact huge stocks of Bren guns. These were lost to the enemy at the final evacuation.

It is now time to follow the fortunes of the 1st Armoured Division. Before, however, detailing the operations it is interesting to read

---

* The situation was further aggravated by the attitude of many of the Staff Officers. They regarded the new General as an interloper. They tended to 'work to rule'.[4]

from the Official History, the 'reasons' for the Armoured Division being ordered to undertake the attack on the Somme bridges.

'In the light of this information [the Intelligence Report received from GQG on 23 May], and believing that the British and French counter-attacks on the 21st/22nd were the beginning of a joint effort to close the gap, General Headquarters had sent an Operation Instruction [based on that sent on 21 May and quoted above].' It will be appreciated that the above statement is pure fiction. One can only assume that it was intended to excuse GHQ for sending the order.

GHQ were fully aware that the counter-attacks at Arras on the 21st were never designed for the purpose stated; in fact, the British Divisions had already been withdrawn to their starting point before the order was issued. Who was responsible for this fiction is difficult to discover.

General Evans realized that the whole operation was impracticable with the forces at his disposal but, as his orders were quite categorical, he ordered the advance. During the night of the 23rd-24th a troop of the Bays, which had been sent forward to reconnoitre the bridges near Longpré, became involved with the enemy. A brief action followed in which two tanks were knocked out. It was thus found out that all the bridges in this area were well guarded and protected by mines. There seemed little doubt that the other bridges, higher up the river, would be found to be in like state, if not destroyed. Nevertheless, the attack was ordered to continue. Three bridges had been selected for attack, those at Dreuil, Ailly-sur-Somme and Picquigny. Each bridge was to be assaulted by one troop of armour and one company of infantry. The 4th Border Regiment, consisting at that time of only three Companies, had joined the force at 0400 on the morning of the 24th. Even had any of the attacks proved successful, the size of each attacking unit would have been quite inadequate to take advantage of it. In fact, neither the troops at Picquigny nor at Dreuil were able to approach their objective owing to enemy resistance. Two little actions should be mentioned in the above connection, namely those of A and D Companies. A Company (Captain R.W. Hind) drove the enemy out of the village of Saveuse, capturing several prisoners, but was unable to approach the bridge at Dreuil. D. Company (Major J.F. Hopkinson) managed to clear the woods at the approach to the bridge at Picquigny. Increased enemy resistance brought this small detachment to a halt, the armoured units being prevented from rendering assistance by anti-tank fire. At Ailly, however, C Company of the Borders under Captain A.W. Thompson, advanced under increasing enemy machine-gun and mortar fire. Though the bridge was largely destroyed, two platoons succeeded in crossing it, another being left on the bridge. On arrival at the other side of the river the platoons drove into the village of St Sauveur. The enemy fled. The British set up defensive positions, assuming that reinforcements would shortly appear to support them. Though they held on all day, no one appeared. In the face of increasing artillery and mortar fire, the troops were forced to retire once more across the bridge which they had won at great sacrifice, having gained nothing. The reason for the lack of support was that there was none to be had. The Engineers, having no bridging equipment, were unable to restore the bridge so as to enable the tanks to cross and there was no artillery to give covering fire. The LAA and A/T Regiment, which was there, could do nothing. Its guns were far too light to be of service. It just had to watch the drama being played out.

It will be appreciated from this brief account of the action of the Somme bridges that the whole force behaved with the greatest gallantry. 'And then they rode back, but not the Six Hundred'. In fact the whole enterprise could be likened to that other Affair! That evening General Evans withdrew the whole force, which had now been joined by the other units of the 2nd Armoured Brigade. Leaving the infantry to observe the approach to the bridges, the remainder of the force concealed itself in the woods nearby.

It was not until the morning of the 25th that General Karslake heard the story of the abortive attack. However, what concerned him most was the fact that the enemy, having located the dispositions of the Force, were now launching aerial attacks upon it. Immediately he telephoned to Air-Marshal Barratt. He explained the position and begged him to send fighters to alleviate the situation. This was attended to at once. In this connection, there is a confirmatory entry in the diary of the LAA and A/T Regiment:

> German bombers flew over our position continually in squadrons

varying in size between 25 and 40. Bombs were dropped all round us without hitting any personnel or material of the Regiment. 44th Battery, who were in action round RHQ, armed with Lewis guns, were unable to engage enemy aircraft which were flying too high; three Spitfires appeared in the sky at about 1600 hrs. They were sighted by a German squadron of bombers, unescorted by fighters, who immediately released their bombs to lose weight and made off for home. These were the only Allied planes seen by the Regiment during our period in France, (until two Blenheims came over St Valéry on June 11th at 0930 hrs).'

It will be remembered that the 3rd Armoured Brigade, which had landed in France on the 23rd, had been ordered to proceed to Pacy. All arrangements had been made to this effect. The Brigade Commander had gone on ahead to report to General Evans. On arrival at Pacy he learned of the advance of the 2nd Armoured Brigade and that General Evans had set up his headquarters to the north of the Seine. On arrival at Divisional HQ Brigadier Crocker was ordered to divert his Brigade northwards. As a result he went to Rouen to make the necessary arrangements. Thanks to the excellence of the Movements Staff, all the trains were intercepted and reversed. The troops that had gone ahead were redirected to the new destination, Neufchâtel.

Owing to the disaster that had occurred on the railway line trains were delayed as clearance had not yet been completed. Instead, therefore, of the trains arriving during the night of the 24th-25th, they arrived on the 25th in broad daylight, thereby rendering themselves vulnerable to attack from the air. Luckily, as we know, arrangements had been made to provide fighter cover for the Armoured Division. The 3rd Armoured Brigade suffered no interference from enemy aircraft. Brigadier Crocker states in his report, 'Fortunately, the protecting fighter patrols had shot down an early enemy recce aircraft just before dawn. To this we can attribute the fact that during that long and anxious morning we suffered no interference from enemy aircraft while the Brigade was detraining and moving into cover of the woods.'

On the 25th General Evans received the news that his formation was now under the orders of 'A' Group of the 7th French Army, commanded by General Robert Altmayer.

By midday on the 25th General Karslake had completed his long and detailed report on the situation for the CIGS. Brigadier Bruce was, therefore, sent by plane to deliver this *most secret* document. Unfortunately, during the flight, Brigadier Bruce developed severe stomach pains through, it is believed, some form of poisoning. On arrival at Northolt it was decided that it was essential for him to go to hospital. He was transferred to the Royal Masonic Hospital at Hammersmith. From this time onwards he disappears from the story. As the details to be delivered to General Ironside were of such a secret nature it was considered essential that General Karslake himself should fly over. The plane returned to Le Mans to collect him. It was not until 2100, therefore, that the General reached Whitehall and entered General Ironside's room.

The two officers finally decided that the Beauman force should be constituted on divisional lines; that Beauman should command it [his sub-areas to come directly under HQ L of C (Howard Report)] and that every effort should be made to provide the necessary Brigade commanders. It was further agreed that, owing to the complete segregation of the L of C from the BEF, a separate Command should be instituted placing all units and formations under the command of General Karslake. Just before they parted, General Ironside remarked that he was leaving the War Office to assume command of all the troops in Great Britain, a job much more to his taste. His appointment would be from Monday, 27 May. The General concluded, 'Don't worry, Henry, I shall make damn sure everything is taken care of before I leave.' With that the two men parted, never to meet again. It will never be known what occurred on the 26th. Whether it was because of the pressure of the hand-over or from some other cause, certain matters received endorsement and were acted upon, while others were ignored or cancelled. These latter were to have serious consequences in the days to come.

On the 27th two Brigadiers arrived at Le Mans accompanied by a Major Brittorous. (This latter officer had landed from Singapore only the day before.)[5] Brigadier M.A. Green and Brigadier Kent-Lemon had recently been serving in Norway. All these officers were to prove their worth.

Meanwhile, as a result of General Karslake's decision to reconstitute Beauman's Force, great efforts were being made to ensure that it was provided with as much equipment as possible. The Chief Signal Officer of the L of C, Major W. Scott, had collected all the equipment and personnel necessary to provide the new formation with a complete Divisional Signals establishment. With the exception of Number 2 Company (unnecessary under the circumstances) the new Commander would find that he had all that he would need in this connection.[6]

The GSO I (AFV) GHQ, who now found himself completely cut off from his Headquarters, devoted himself to organizing a scratch Tank Company. This consisted of a few 'Infantry' tanks, intended as replacement for the 1st Army Tank Brigade. They were placed under the command of Captain Colan of the RTR. As the vehicles were new, all that was necessary was the fitting of guns in the Mark II versions (2 pdrs) and, of course, the assembling of personnel. Through the immense energy of Captain Colan and his Warrant Officer (they were only notified on the 25th) the Company was ready for action on 28 May.[7]

Finally, Major Elliott had scoured the whole area of the L of C for guns. He managed to assemble eight 18/25 pdrs (formerly of the 51st Division), and 20 anti-tank guns (both 2 pdrs and 20mm); these latter had been discovered spread over a wide area, as far south as Bordeaux. He reported that there were more but he was unable to raise sufficient gunners to man them. His last effort was the discovery of four abandoned mobile Bofors guns. These had been located on a deserted airfield. As a result of the above 'finds' Major Elliott had organized one Field Battery (X) and one anti-tank Regiment (E for Elliott).[8]

By the evening of the 28th the complete organization of the new 'Beauman' Division had been achieved. Though by no means a formidable fighting formation, at least it was something under British Command with which to protect the masses of stores on the L of C while they were being moved either out of the country or out of harm's way to the south.

On his return to his Headquarters on 26 May, General Karslake was met with a startling piece of intelligence. A completely new formation was going to appear in his area. This was the 51st Highland Division from the Saar. No advanced warning had been given of its pending arrival. It seemed that the Division was due to enter his command on the 27th. Tremendous efforts were, therefore, required to prepare for it, in addition to all the other multifarious duties which had to be carried out. Luckily the staff of the L of C, though not geared to operational duties, were quite adequate for dealing with such a situation. With their usual efficiency all arrangements as could be made in the time were made. On the 27th the advanced units began to arrive. As the arrival of this formation introduces an entirely new element into the story, it will be dealt with later.

It will be remembered that the Armoured Division had, at last, concentrated and had been placed under the command of the French. In fact, this was the only time that the Division was ever to concentrate as a formation. Its Support Group, being but a shadow of its intended self, though located nearby, was unable to play any active part as its was not equipped to do so. The Division's position on 25 May was as follows:

> The 2nd Armoured Brigade near Fresnoy.
> The 3rd Armoured Brigade on the line of the River Yeres.
> The Support Group, including the 4th Border Regiment, in the Fôret du Hellet.

The 3rd Armoured Brigade should have reached Haute Fôret d'Eu at this time but the amount of erroneous information that came filtering through caused the Brigade Commander to halt and deploy on the River as stated above.

While the above moves were taking place some of the hoped-for French reinforcements began to arrive. This was a great relief to General Evans who had been informed that he had to safeguard the line of the Somme from Picquigny in the east to St Valéry-sur-Somme in the west, an impossible task. By the 26th, the 2nd and 5th DCLs (*Divisions Cavalerie Légère*) had moved up. These Divisions consisted mainly of Armoured Cars and 'Cavalry' carried in armoured trucks. They were referred to as '*Dragons Portées*'. Most of their other transport was horse-drawn. These troops had been engaged in severe fighting in the east and the formations were not up to strength. Also they possessed little or no artillery.

On the 26th General Evans was called to the Headquarters of General Altmayer. He was informed that a major attack was scheduled to take place the following day for the purpose of driving in the enemy bridgehead at Abbeville. His Formation was expected to open the way for the two French Divisions. General Evans explained that his tanks were totally unfitted for this sort of work. They bore no resemblance to the heavy tanks of the French Armoured Divisions; in fact they were only suitable for employment against ground troops in the open, not against prepared positions. General Altmayer would have none of it. He told General Evans that those were his orders and it was up to him to carry them out.[9]

This was the first of many occasions when the absence of a British overall Commander was badly felt. General Evans had no one to whom he could appeal; his Division was not under General Karslake but still under GHQ (or was it the War Office? No one knew for certain); there was no hope of contacting them in time, even if he had had the right to do so. With considerable anxiety, therefore, he returned to his Headquarters to issue the necessary orders.

The general plan was for the 2nd Armoured Brigade to support the 2nd DCL, and the 3rd the 5th DCL to the south bank of the Somme from excluding Longpré-les-Corps-Saints.

When considering the design and execution of the attack on the Abbeville bridgehead, it should be remembered that the Germans had been in occupation of the area since the 20th. They had wasted no time in preparing the area for defence. In this context the following extract from the Report of the 3rd Armoured Brigade is illuminating.

'Information of the enemy was somewhat nebulous; the area between the River Bresle and the Somme was in the nature of a no-man's-land over which the enemy patrols had complete control, or at any rate, a distinct moral superiority. We found, later, that the German motorcycle and armoured car patrols were often in and through the villages. These enemy movements had given rise to exaggerated reports of German occupation and defences in various places. The only fairly definite information was that he was holding all the bridges across the Somme with more extended bridgehead positions at Abbeville and St Valéry-sur-Somme. The villages of

Toeufles and Moyenneville were believed to be defended.' With such paucity of intelligence, it was highly unlikely that any attack could prove a success.

Had the force employed been of a nature as would normally have been used for such an enterprise, it is *just* possible that some success might have been achieved. On paper, at least, every effort had been made to ensure the complete collaboration and co-operation between the Allied forces. 'French troops, mechanized cavalry consisting of lorried infantry, lorry-carried 'infantry', machine-guns, armoured cars etc., were to follow closely behind the advance of the tanks and, in order to ensure close liaison, a French Agent was to move [in a Scout car] with each [armoured] squadron HQ whose duty it would be to keep the following troops fully and quickly informed of the progress of the tanks so that they could take advantage without delay.'

Actually, the task facing the attacking force was a formidable one. The enemy had sited anti-tank guns on the forward slopes of all the hills towards which the Allies would have to approach. Each copse and village was fortified and covered by machine-guns and yet more anti-tank artillery. Heavier pieces covered the approaches from across the river. German infantry were concealed in the woods. As no aircraft were available none of these defences had been observed. Even when the attack was in progress, no help was received from the Air Forces of the Allies; the German Stukas and bombers were able to range at will over the battle area without interference.

The plan of attack was as follows:

'The 2nd Armoured Brigade, whose objective was from Bray to Mareuil, advanced with the Bays on the right and the Tenth Hussars on the left.' It was not long before both Regiments ran into a mine-field which caused serious casualties; but worse was to come. At Huppy there was a major concentration of anti-tank artillery. As the tanks passed over a ridge athwart the village they came under fire. An observer described the scene as similar to that of a Shooting Gallery where 'ducks' passing on a continuous band are shot at. As each tank breasted the slope so it was picked off by the anti-tank guns. It soon became obvious that no further progress could be made in this direction.

'The 3rd Armoured Brigade advanced on the axis Maisiniers — Aigneville — Chépy — Quesnoy — Le-Montant with 2nd RTR on right and the 5th RTR on the left.' Their attack can be best described in the words of the 3rd Brigade Report. Leading troops crossed the start line at 0430 hrs:

0500 2nd Bn reports right of first bound clear.
0525 2nd Bn reports first bound clear — contacted with French — going on to 2nd bound.
0610 5th Bn reports 1st bound clear, going on to 2nd bound.
0630 2nd Bn reports Chépy and Valines clear.
0725 2nd Bn reports 'C' Sqn at Miannay — one enemy armoured car met — 'C' Sqn all clear so far.
0740 5th Bn reports halting on 2nd bound for 20 minutes to establish liaison with the French.
0815 2nd Bn reports being shelled by mortars from Frireulle.
0830 French L.O. reported *French* tanks (there were none) had been fired at near Toeufles.
0830 5th Bn reports reconnoitering rly. crossing SW of St Valéry.
0855 French LO reports enemy tanks near St Mard.
0858 2nd Bn reports 'enemy' tanks are his which have been scattered by shell fire.
0920 2nd Bn reports 'A' Sqn removing AT guns in Toeufles and then proceeding on Moyenneville.
0940 2nd Bn reports HQ severely shelled near Frireulle.
0955 5th Bn reports patrols approaching St Valéry.
1005 2nd Bn reports held up 'generally' on 2nd bound.
1010 2nd Bn situation very confused. French were failing to take advantage or co-operate. OC 2nd Bn ordered to remain in observation on left and to continue to act to discover strength and extent of opposition in Moyenneville area.
1035 5th Bn report St Valéry strongly held — locals report 1,000 enemy — all entrances blocked and held with AT guns and mines — some artillery fire — French refuse to take on. OC 5th Bn ordered to observe St Valéry, not to incur casualties, and to patrol towards R. Somme on his front east of St Valéry.

In spite of repeated applications to French Divisional HQ for closer liaison and support from the French lorried infantry and for getting forward more quickly, no response was forthcoming.

At 1200 the situation, confirmed by subsequent events, seemd to be that 'A' Squadron, when attempting to advance on Moyenneville was badly shot up by A/T fire and lost four Cruisers and two light tanks. No further progress was made in this area where it was obvious that an organized attack by infantry and artillery would be needed to deal with the situation. Further to the left and north, 'C' Squadron (2nd Bn) which had reached Miannay without opposition, other than by artillery fire, had found the village unoccupied and had removed the road barricades there. Attempts to advance further east, however, met with resistance which might well have been overcome if immediate support had been forthcoming from the 'following' French. But the hours passed and, despite every effort to persuade the French to follow up quickly and take advantage of the initial success and surprise, nothing was done. Every excuse was offered. 'Were we sure that this village was clear?'; 'An enemy tank was reported in that wood'; 'We have very few soldiers'; 'Our troops have been fighting for three weeks'; etc, etc.

'On the 5th Bn front our patrols continued to act vigorously. One patrol actually broke through the enemy forward defences between Boismont and St Valéry.

'Between 1530 and 1830 a succession of different plans were made by French Divisional HQ. Eventually it was decided that the French *Dragons Portées* Regiments would establish a line of defended localities on the general line of the 2nd Bound.

'As practically no enemy had been met during the advance to this line, it meant that most of our efforts and casualties had been in vain. But, despite every argument, this plan was put into effect. We were asked to assist by holding, with our tanks, the centre of the "line" — the villages of Franleu and Arrest. This was not agreed to, but, to help, dismounted detachments armed with Bren guns and Boyes (anti-tank rifles) were brought up from the transport and were disposed to hold the entrances to these villages for the night. The Bns were to be withdrawn and located centrally in support of the whole front — this was agreed after some argument and after an order to dispose of the tanks in small posses along the front had been resisted.'

This latter order is of interest as it was by doing this very thing during the operations north of the Somme that the fine heavy

French Armoured Divisions had been rendered ineffective!

Thus these operations came to an end. Virtually nothing had been gained and the Germans held on to their bridgeheads in as strong a position as before.

That evening the 2nd Armoured Brigade had withdrawn a short distance, leaving the 9th Lancers, which had suffered least, at Ramburelles in support of the French. The 3rd Armoured Brigade, similarly, withdrew to the area of Feuquières.

As a result of these operations and through the lack of time for maintenance, the casualties in tanks were out of all proportion to the battle in which they were incurred. Due to enemy action 65 tanks were lost; from wear and tear and mechanical defects, 55 were no longer effective — a total of 120 out of 257 tanks of all kinds that had landed with such hopeful prospects less than a week previously. Though some of the tanks suffering mechanical trouble were able to be restored (though spares were negligible) nevertheless the 1st Armoured Division, as such, had more or less ceased to exist as a fighting formation.

While these operations were in progress the Beauman Division was taking shape and, by the 28th, had assumed the form which will be seen in Appendix B. The troops that had been in action at Amiens and Abbeville were being employed mainly on the original tasks on which they had been engaged before their advance. So much re-organization and re-equpping, to say nothing of rehabilitation, was required, that it was considered highly unlikely that they would be fit for any form of battle-usage for some time to come — if at all. Besides, the War Office was still sending in vast quantities of supplies via the southern ports of Nantes and St Nazaire. As yet no consideration had been given to a possible evacuation south of the Somme. It was a curious situation. While every effort was being made to evacuate essential stores, at the same time ships loaded with ammunition and petrol together with supplies for a force similar to that of the original BEF were arriving in France. Representations were made to the War Office but had no effect. Even General Karslake was becoming discouraged. He remarked to his GSO II, 'As time goes on I begin to feel a deep affinity with Sisyphus.'

It is now necessary to break off the narrative of the affairs south of the Somme and examine the situation north of the river. After the withdrawal of the British from Arras on 24 May General Weygand considered that the combined British and French offensive, scheduled to take place on the 26th, was now dead. A defence of a large perimeter round Dunkirk was the only alternative. Orders were therefore issued accordingly. At the conference held on the 25th General Weygand explained the situation to the War Committee of the French Government. He felt it his duty to give them the facts. These were extremely unpalatable, as they showed that, with the resources available, there was but the slenderest chance of holding the enemy on the line of the Somme or of saving any of the forces cut off in the north. It is important to note that it was at this conference that the word 'Armistice' made its first public appearance — public, that is to say, to the governing body of France. When, on the 26th, General Weygand learned that instructions had been issued to Lord Gort by the British Government to evacuate his troops, he was quite convinced that nothing remained but to explore the possibilities of obtaining an armistice. Though this opinion was discussed only with his immediate intimates, his feelings must have been observed by others. There is no doubt whatsoever that, when the head of an organization begins to lose confidence, this feeling will sooner or later permeate throughout the whole of his command.

It should not be thought that, because of their convictions, either General Weygand or his principal staff officers relaxed their efforts to stem what they considered to be the inevitable outcome. Troops were ordered forward from North Africa. The Maginot Line had every available field formation withdrawn from it. The only major formation which was barely touched was the Army of the Alps. This was left mainly intact, owing to the unknown attitude of Italy. All the rest were moved forward to the potentially dangerous areas as quickly as transport would allow. Unfortunately most of the troops were served by horses and were dependent on the railways for their speedy transportation, movement by road being far too slow, and even the comparative speed of rail movement became restricted as the enemy concentrated a large number of bombers on the system.

The Aisne and Somme Fronts were of considerable extent. To

defend them adequately at all points was quite beyond the available resources. It was hoped, however, that by concentrating the troops in depth in the form of strong points, the enemy would be cut off from his supplies and reinforcements. He could then be destroyed piecemeal.

At first it was considered that the main threat was likely to be towards Paris. Plans were made to concentrate the maximum number of troops to cover the approaches to the city and the vital manufacturing centres in the vicinity; subsequently, it was thought that Montmédy was the danger point. Finally, the Lower Somme appeared to be the weakest part of the proposed defence line.

In the early months of 1940 it had been considered that, in order to gain experience, British formations of brigade strength should be attached to French formations operating in front of the Maginot Line, in the Saar. In April this policy was modified. It was then decided that a British division should actually take over a portion of the line from the French. The division selected was the 51st Highland Division. Though this had been a Territorial division its composition had been altered by the replacement of three of its Territorial battalions by Regular battalions. When it was ordered to the Saar, its establishment was changed again. It received a considerable number of additional troops and artillery. In fact it became the strongest division in the whole of the BEF, equal to one and a half normal divisions.

From 1 May, after the Division arrived in the Saar, it took part in a number of small engagements. These proved of the utmost value in gaining experience and discovering the strength of their opponents. The troops were not dismayed by their antagonists. While not underrating them, nevertheless they felt that they were their equal, at least, and probably their superior, when fighting on equal terms.

Meanwhile the German offensive had begun. On 20 May, it's tour of duty in the Line having been completed, the 51st Division was ordered into reserve to cover Paris. On the 23rd the orders were changed and the Division was redirected to Varennes owing to the threat of a German break-through at Montmédy. On the 25th the orders were changed yet again. The Division was to proceed to Normandy owing to the threat to the Channel ports, particularly Le

Havre and Cherbourg. The rail parties covered an immense distance, having travelled southwards to Tours before going northwards again to Le Mans and thence to St Léger. They arrived at St Léger on the 28th and Headquarters was opened on that date. The enormous road column, consisting of over 3,000 vehicles, moved by a more direct route. Curiously enough, the road party found less obstruction than they had anticipated. Indeed, as far as Paris the roads were virtually clear. Even from there on they found the situation not too bad. The worst trouble they experienced was the vast cloud of dust which caused extreme discomfort to both drivers and passengers and, worst of all, to the motor-cyclists.

On arrival the Division concentrated in the Haute Fôret d'Eu. So successful had been the conduct of this major move that only six vehicles had become casualties and only one man had been killed, in an accident. They had had one other piece of good fortune; owing to the low cloud ceiling they had not been either observed, or attacked, by enemy aircraft. This was as well as no Allied aircraft were made available for their protection.

One can well imagine the delight of the Division when it found that it was, once more, back with its own people. General Karslake was very relieved at its advent. Though he had not learned of the Division's impending arrival while in London, nor indeed of its existence, the increase of force for defending the L of C was most encouraging.

Since the abortive attack on the 26th, the Armoured Division had done its best to restore itself. However, the 2nd Armoured Brigade was but a shadow of its former self. A composite regiment, made up from the remnants of the 9th Lancers and the 10th Hussars, was constituted, the HQ and the remains of the 2nd Dragoon Guards being brought into reserve. The 3rd Armoured Brigade, being still relatively strong, concentrated on repairs so as to make it, once more, into an effective force. Fortunately, as the result of representations made by both General Evans and Colonel Briggs, it was at last appreciated by the French that what the British classified as an Armoured Division was not in any way similar to what the French regarded as such. In fact it was totally unsuited to the work that the French had envisaged as its role. The Armoured Division, therefore, or rather what remained of it, was left in peace to lick its wounds for the time being.

From the 28th onwards the French continued to try and reduce the Abbeville bridgehead. Though reinforced by the 4th DCA (*Division Cavalerie Armoré*) of General de Brigade C. de Gaulle, the attacks faiied. This was due primarily to the lack of artillery and infantry support. As will be seen in due course, had these attacks not been carried out and the French substance wasted, it is *just* possible, when the full strength of the French Tenth Army had assembled, that a major assault could have been undertaken with a reasonable chance of success. Whether, however, this would have served any useful purpose, in view of the German plan, is very doubtful.

Meanwhile, the Cinderella of the Armoured Division, the 1st Support Group, was receiving encouragement. On the 25th, its Commander, Brigadier F.E. Morgan, and his staff, had arrived from England. In fact he was just in time to observe the débacle of the 2nd Armoured Brigade.

Having discovered that the promises which had been made to him about the equipping of his command had not been fulfilled, Brigadier Morgan met General Karslake at Rouen. He explained the situation to him and begged for his help. General Karslake had known Brigadier Morgan in India. He had regarded him as a most promising commander of the future. At first, Brigadier Morgan's representations seemed unlikely of fulfilment, certainly as far as Bofors guns for the AA batteries were concerned. The General remembered the surplus of anti-tank guns which were still available. He offered those as some form of compensation, and on the 28th 20 of these guns were allotted to the already equipped A/T batteries. This gave them a 100% reserve. Such a large number, however, became an embarrassment rather than a help. They required every spare man, including cooks and drivers, to man them.

By dint of considerable inquiry the General did manage to locate 10 Bofors guns which had been left on abandoned airfields. The RAF had evacuated these airfields when the Germans had crossed the Somme at Amiens and Abbeville. So hasty had been their departure that the gun-crews, imagining that they were going to be overwhelmed at any moment, had departed, leaving everything behind them. These guns were issued to 44th AA Battery, who were delighted to discard their hated Lewis guns. Now, at last, they felt they were AA gunners again.

When the battery was equipped it was 'borrowed' by the 1st Armoured Division to protect the entrainment of its tanks. Then it was 'loaned' to the Headquarters of the 51st Division. Thus, once again, the Support Group lost another of its units. There is no record of Brigadier Morgan's feelings on the matter. But this was not to be the end of his disappointment. It will be recalled that, when the first Support Group was formed, the 1st Regiment RHA was part of its establishment. This Regiment, on the insistence of Lord Gort, had proceeded to France with the remainder of the BEF and had been placed in reserve. When it was decided to move the 51st Division to the Saar, the 1st RHA was attached to it as part of its increase of strength. Now that the Division had moved west, it was only reasonable for Brigadier Morgan to expect that his missing unit would, at long last, be returned to his command, to which, of course, it would make a considerable difference. It would create a Support Group which could, to a reasonable extent, be capable of playing the role for which it had been designed. This was appreciated also by the Armoured Divisional Commander. However, when General Evans and Brigadier Morgan approached General Fortune on the subject of returning the 1st RHA to its proper command, General Fortune had to, reluctantly, decline the suggestion. He reasoned that it would upset his 'fire-plan'. As there was no one to whom an appeal could be made, this decision had to be accepted.

Soon after his arrival at his new HQ, General Fortune was approached by General de Gaulle for assistance in his new attack on the Abbeville bridgehead, which he was planning to carry out on the 29th. The General explained that it was mainly due to the lack of infantry that his previous efforts had failed. Somewhat reluctantly, General Fortune agreed to a small number of his troops being employed — the 1st Black Watch, 153rd Brigade, being designated for the operation. However, owing to a mass of contradictory orders which caused the Battalion to move forward to a variety of destinations, it took no part in the actual attack. It was not until dawn on the 30th that it relieved some French Cavalry at Bouillancourt and Toeufles; and at two o'clock in the afternoon 'B' Company was ordered to take the Grand Bois de Cambron at quarter past four. In the wood it met with little resistance and arrived at its objective on the north-eastern outskirts. But because the French attack on the village of Cambron was unsuccessful, the Black Watch was left with a flank in the air and had to retire so as to come into line with its neighbours.

Just before midnight on the 30th General de Gaulle informed Brigadier Stewart, commanding 152nd Brigade, that he was doubtful if, without help, he could hold the villages of Moyenneville and Bienfay, which he had succeeded in taking on the 29th. Brigadier Stewart readily agreed to provide the necessary assistance and sent forward the 2nd Seaforths. So speedily did this battalion move that the two villages were occupied by six o'clock the following morning. The remainder of the Brigade, the 4th Camerons and 4th Seaforths, were at Limeux and Béhen.

These movements were the first active engagements of the 51st Division in the forthcoming operations. So efficiently had the Division been brought to readiness after its long movement from the Saar that its troops were quite ready to be brought into action with little warning.

Brigadier Stewart had been one of the advance party of the Division and had arrived in the area on the 27th. In fact he had been in time to observe the action of the 1st Armoured Division on that day. He describes the activities of the 2nd Armoured Brigade most graphically in his diary: '... was reconnoitering in an area east of the battle and found myself, without intention, an intimate spectator of it. I was surrounded by its overflow. The tanks, moving hither and thither jerkily, with sudden rushes, were strangely reminiscent of insects darting across the surface of a pond — without, apparently, either rhyme or reason. In spite of gun-fire, the éclat of bursting shells, the spectacle appeared curiously unreal. War, which had once been a solid thing, had become almost entirely fluid.'

Before relating the activities which culminated in the 'Battle of France', it is essential for the reader to appreciate the curious Command system which existed at this time. From this he may be able to understand the reasons for the apparently contradictory orders which occurred.

The chain of Command that existed in that part of France in which the British Army was operating was as follows:

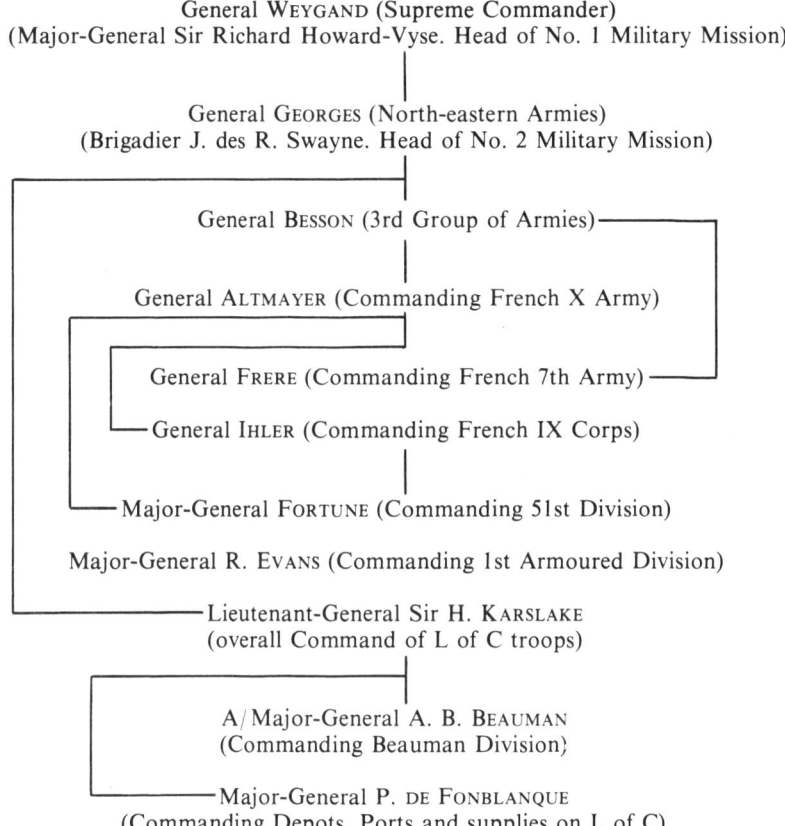

General WEYGAND (Supreme Commander)
(Major-General Sir Richard Howard-Vyse. Head of No. 1 Military Mission)

General GEORGES (North-eastern Armies)
(Brigadier J. des R. Swayne. Head of No. 2 Military Mission)

General BESSON (3rd Group of Armies)

General ALTMAYER (Commanding French X Army)

General FRERE (Commanding French 7th Army)

General IHLER (Commanding French IX Corps)

Major-General FORTUNE (Commanding 51st Division)

Major-General R. EVANS (Commanding 1st Armoured Division)

Lieutenant-General Sir H. KARSLAKE
(overall Command of L of C troops)

A/Major-General A. B. BEAUMAN
(Commanding Beauman Division)

Major-General P. DE FONBLANQUE
(Commanding Depots, Ports and supplies on L of C)

It will be seen from the above that the various British formation commanders were 'buried' beneath a massive French hierarchy and owed 'allegiance' to all and sundry from whom they could receive orders at any time, all quite independent of one another. In addition it was quite possible for them to receive orders from the War Office in London; these could be at variance with those received from their French Commanders. In this latter connection, it should be pointed out that *French* orders had priority. Also, there was no appeal against them. No one had received this authority as no over-all commander had been appointed. It is difficult to believe that the reader will be able to disentangle this situation any more than the British then in France.

As the general consensus of British opinion was one of lack of reliance on the French capability of withstanding a determined German assault across the Somme naturally precautions were taken to safeguard the British formations that were being employed.

Though no one held the post of Commander-in-Chief, nevertheless this did not prevent action being taken in case of a situation arising when the French would no longer be able to exercise effective control. General Karslake was determined that he would do all he could to ensure the safety of *all* the British troops irrespective of whether they were under his command or not. Accordingly, as soon as General Fortune had set up his HQ, he sent Brigadier Beauman to see him. His mission was to explain the situation and to arrange emergency measures for his Division's safety should the occasion arise. The following extract from the 51st Division's War Diary is of interest in this respect:

> During his visit the question of any arrangements in the event of a withdrawal were brought forward. The position then being taken bore a very close resemblance to that in which the BEF had found itself in Belgium. Enemy penetration at Amiens, where the enemy had a bridgehead, would automatically isolate all forces to the north whose only way of re-effecting junction with the Main Allied Army in case of withdrawal would be either through Rouen or embarkation in the north and thence to Cherbourg. It was learned that Dieppe was impractical for any embarkation, being heavily mined with magnetic mines, and the port and harbour had been seriously damaged by air attacks. Further, no lines of defence west of the River Béthune to Le Havre had been prepared, though Le Havre was the only real port left in the area if embarkation was decided upon.
>
> The grave danger of joining up through Rouen was that, not only would the few crossings of the Seine constitute serious bottle-necks but also the enemy might well anticipate the force at Rouen, since the Allied Forces were to execute a pivotal manoeuvre whilst the enemy would be operating on a more direct and shorter route. At this meeting Brigadier Beauman and Division Commander made an outline plan to fall back on Havre whereby 51st Division and BEAUFORCE [as

Brigadier Beauman's party was called] working together would leapfrog backwards. The dispositions of the Support Group were made with this in mind to cover the right flank of 51st Division and link back to the position held at the time by BEAUFORCE.[1]

The reference to the positioning of the Support Group requires clarification. After the abortive attack on the bridges across the Somme on the 24th, the Support Group, as represented by the 101st LAA and A/T Regiment only, was positioned in the neighbourhood of Camp L'Amenoirs. The Regiment had not been called upon to play any part in the attack and was now being used to protect the HQ of the 2nd Armoured Brigade against a possible counter-attack from the direction of the Amiens bridgehead. The 4th Border Regiment, which as yet had not come under command of the Support Group, was to form the infantry for this protection. During the evening of the 25th the 2nd Armoured Brigade withdrew and the 101st was ordered to move to the Forêt de Helles. On the 27th, for the first time since it had landed in France, it became officially part of the Support Group again. It will be remembered that Brigadier Morgan and his staff had arrived from England the day before, so, with its Commander present, the Group was re-constituted, the 4th Border Regiment being attached to the Support Group in place of the two infantry battalions that had gone to Calais. The two Royal Engineer units, the 1st Field Company and the 1st Field Park Company, were also included.

As a result of the conversations held at HQ of the 51st Division on the 28th, a reconnaissance was carried out by two companies of the Borders along the River Bresle between Senarpont and Aumale. It had been considered by Command that the River Bresle formed an obstacle to tanks along this section. Vulnerable points, where crossings might be attempted, were to be well covered by anti-tank artillery. Though it is true that the river was only crossable by vehicles at certain fords it was easily traversed by infantry at any point. Also, the hills on the east side gave the enemy a clear view of any positions taken up by the British on the west. This would have enabled the enemy to bring down fire wherever a post existed, thereby clearing the crossings.

As a result of the report submitted on the above, the scheme was abandoned and a new line substituted. This ran from Aumale to Forges-les-Eaux. As will be described in the next chapter, this formed a 'switch line' between the front, as represented by the French IX Corps and the Beauman line. This latter ran at approximately right angles through Forges-les-Eaux.

At the end of the period covered by this chapter, the enemy still retained his bridgeheads across the Somme at St Valéry-sur-Somme and Abbeville, the left wing of the French Tenth Army, consisting of the 51st Division on the left, then the two DCLs (or rather their remains) and finally the Support Group (such as it was) running at right angles to the town of Forges. The Beauman Division (it had been officially designated as a Division on the 31st) ran along its original line from the coast to the Seine. This formation was now far stronger, better organized and equipped than it had been when it first took up its positions during the second week in May. Of the 1st Armoured Division, the Composite Regiment had been loaned to the 51st Division, first to increase the striking power of the Lothian and Border Horse and, thereafter, to reinforce the Support Group to the south of Aumale. General Evans had also loaned Colonel Broomhill, his GSO I, to the Division to give guidance as to the employment of the Composite Regiment. The 3rd Armoured Brigade and Divisional HQ were withdrawing to the neighbourhood of Louviers where repairs and refitting could be carried out. Except for some desultory patrol activity the 3rd Armoured Brigade had not been engaged since the 27th.

Other than by aerial action, the Germans showed no inclination to attack.

V

31 May — 6 June

AT the time of General Ironside's appointment as Commander-in-Chief, Home Forces, Mr Churchill had stated that he was convinced that the Germans would attack Britain as soon as they had finished with the Allied Forces within the Dunkirk Perimeter. He had impressed on the General that it was vital to ensure the safety of Britain against a probable attack across the Channel in the very near future. General Ironside, however, considered that such action on the part of the enemy was unlikely at such a time. Knowing the German mentality, he felt that it was far more probable that the Germans would complete the subjection of France before undertaking a new and vast enterprise. Also, while he thought that the Germans would have planned for such a possibility, it would take some little time before they were able to mount a combined sea and aerial invasion. The assembly of the necessary craft for the crossing of the Channel presented a major problem. The General calculated that it would require at least fourteen days after the final fall of France before such an operation could be undertaken. He admitted that it would be possible for the Germans to launch an airborne attack, but without a quick follow-up by support troops coming by sea, it was doubtful if the enterprise held out much hope of success. The Germans were not the type of people who would engage in an operation before they were reasonably certain that there would be a satisfactory outcome. Indeed, their whole strategy was based on their idea of 'Economy of Force', meaning the minimum force necessary *to ensure success.*

The main problem that faced the General was the acute shortage of equipment. It was quite evident that, even if troops were brought back from Dunkirk, all equipment would be left behind. The stocks in the United Kingdom were minimal. So little effort had been made to increase output from the factories that production was little better than before the outbreak of war. The prospect, therefore, of being able to supply sufficient arms to the forces which were being raised in England *plus* re-equipping such troops that might be available from France, before 1941, was bleak. Even with the greatest optimism Ironside could not believe that Hitler would be so kind as to allow such a breathing space.

Though, to a lesser man, the prospects might have seemed hopeless, General Ironside threw himself into his new job with his accustomed energy, determined not to be beaten by apparently insuperable obstacles. Notwithstanding the fact that production was so poor, two Divisions, the 52nd Lowland and 1st Canadian, received their full complement of guns by 31 May. This was but a drop in the ocean; nevertheless it was a beginning; the General began to feel more hopeful.

Mr Churchill went to Paris on 31 May to attend a meeting of the Supreme War Council. The whole situation was discussed in detail. The reports from the senior French officers, including General Weygand, were anything but encouraging. In fact it seemed that the French considered that, unless Britain was able to contribute considerably more in the way of troops and aircraft, the situation was rapidly becoming hopeless. Though not recorded in the minutes of the meeting, it would seem that the matter of organizing some sort of resistance point near a major Atlantic port was discussed. It appears that somewhere in the Breton Peninsula was put forward for this purpose. This is confirmed by the Prime Minister's actions after he had returned to England. There is little doubt, however, that Mr Churchill had been affected by the meeting. General Spears recounts that, when he met him afterwards, Mr Churchill had said that he considered that the French were beaten. This did not imply that no further help should be given to our Allies; on the contrary, all efforts should be made to reconstitute the BEF. The main difficulties which presented themselves were the lack of equipment and the time factor.

On 2 June, Mr Churchill drafted one of his famous memos to the Chiefs of Staff. This memo is of considerable importance and has hitherto been omitted from every history of the period, other than that written by Mr Churchill himself. The relevant passages run as follows:

... (3) The BEF in France must immediately be reconstituted, otherwise the French will not continue in the war. Even if Paris is lost, they must be adjured to continue a gigantic guerrilla. A scheme should be considered for a bridgehead and area of disembarkation in Brittany, where a large army can be developed. We must have plans worked out which will show the French that there is a way through if they will only be steadfast.

(4) A soon as the BEF is reconstituted for Home Defence three Divisions should be sent to join our two Divisions south of the Somme, or wherever the French left may be by then ...

I close with a general observation. *As I have personally felt less afraid of a German attempt at invasion than of the piercing of the French line on the Somme or Aisne and the fall of Paris, I have naturally believed that the Germans would choose the latter.* (Author's italics)

It will be seen from the foregoing quotation that, as early as June, the formation of a 'Breton Redoubt' was being seriously contemplated. It would be interesting to know if General Dill made this fact known to General Brooke at their meeting on 2 June.

There is another point in connection with the Breton Redoubt; on the 31st also, General Weygand received from M. Reynaud a confirmatory order regarding the creation of the Redoubt. This, combined with the above memo, is sufficient proof that a tentative decision had been made, and agreed to, by both the British Government, represented by Mr Churchill, and the French Government. As will be seen in due course, this decision was to create serious misunderstandings between the two Governments.

The final paragraph of the memo is of peculiar interest. General Weygand states that he reiterated time and again that Mr Churchill always gave as an excuse for not providing additional assistance in the air his opinion that the Germans would be most likely to attempt an invasion of England immediately after the Dunkirk evacuation.

The content of the memo was passed to General Ironside on 3 June. It was decided that an expeditionary force should be assembled at the expense of the Home Defence Force. This was the firm decision of the Chiefs of Staff. One can readily appreciate the effect that it had on the Commander-in-Chief. By a stroke of the pen all his reserve forces were to be dissipated. The formations selected as representing the first flight were to consist of the 52nd Division, a Territorial formation, and the 1st Canadian Division. This latter formation was not of the highest quality. It had arrived in England in December virtually unequipped and untrained.

Though everything on General Karslake's priority list had been evacuated by 31 May, this material, though essential in itself, was of minor value for the purpose of equipping a Field Force. Vital equipment, such as guns, simply did not exist south of the Somme.

The lack of artillery requires examination. Brigadier Beauman, when trying to provide equipment for the labour divisions due to be engaged north of the Somme, had found that virtually no guns existed in his command. After further investigation he discovered that there was no reserve, *and never had been*, in France! One may well wonder what would have happened if the Germans had attacked from the north only. The BEF would have been seriously engaged. Unquestionably, losses would have been experienced by the artillery. Had this happened one wonders how long it would have been before the artillery would have ceased to exist! This is not all. In England the situation was no better. For example, in June, between Portsmouth and Southampton there were only two field guns. These had been brought back from India many years before. The guns were old Royal Field Artillery 18 pdrs Mark II with a pole trail and a traverse of only three degrees. They were still in their old Eastern colour and were mounted on the original artillery wheels. As a result they could only be moved at a speed of some ten miles per hour. These ancient cannon represented a 'Mobile Column'; its object was to engage E-boats which might penetrate into the Solent. As if the disadvantages enumerated above were not sufficient, the only ammunition available consisted of shrapnel shell, totally valueless against such targets, assuming that they could have been engaged. Luckily, these guns were never called upon to fire as it was discovered that one would not recoil and the other would not recover. Thus it can be seen how badly the British Army was equipped for war with a major power.

It will be remembered that General Karslake had been told by Mr Churchill, before he left for France, that he could count on no artillery. The General simply could not believe that these words were literally true. Only after he had received Major Elliott's Report was the awful truth revealed. There is no doubt whatsoever that the abolishing of the position of Master General of the Ordnance by Hore-Belisha was largely responsible for this shocking state of affairs. Nevertheless, it seems strange that the matter was never brought up by the Artillery Chief prior to 10 May. There had been ample time for the GHQ Staff to have discovered any deficiencies. Yet there is no trace of any request for the provision of reserves.

On 2 June Lieutenant-General Sir Alan Brooke (he had just been created KCB on his return to England) was called to the office of the CIGS. General Dill informed him that he had been selected to command the leading Corps of the new BEF. In due course, when additional formations arrived, the force would once more be commanded by General the Viscount Gort VC. General Brooke has stated that he was seriously upset at the news. He had no faith in the enterprise or in our Allies and, when he learned that the greater part of his command was to consist of Territorials, he considered that it was valueless from a military point of view. He had no faith in the fighting qualities of the Territorial units, as he considered that they would not stand up to bombing and attacks by tanks. How wrong he was in his appreciation of the qualities of the Territorial soldier will be shown in due course.

After his interview with the CIGS, General Brooke saw Mr Anthony Eden, the Secretary of State for War. He informed Mr Eden of his dissatisfaction. He urged that, at least, the 3rd Division should be re-equipped as soon as possible. Though this was agreed to, General Brooke remained anything but satisfied. In fact, when the 3rd Division was re-equipped, it only possessed one battery of Field Artillery!

General Brooke set up his Headquarters at Aldershot. There he began to assemble a Staff. It would seem that this took over a week. In view of the urgency of the situation this seems a very long time, particularly as all the officers he required were, by that time, in England. Only once during the whole period he was in England did General Brooke visit any part of his command. This visit was to the Canadian Division the day before the General left for France.

On 31 May a remarkable telegram was received at the HQ of the L of C. It was from General Dill and instructed General Karslake to disband the Beauman Division and to send its personnel, together with all other troops who were not essential for the maintenance of five divisions, back to England. On receipt of this message, General Karslake went to General Georges's HQ. He informed General Georges of his orders and requested that the necessary arrangements be made to have Beauman's Division relieved. General Georges was astounded at the request. He immediately telephoned to General Dill. He said that it was vital that the Division should remain, not only because of its physical value but because of the effect its departure would have on French morale. As a result, General Dill reluctantly agreed to its retention.

The date and contents of General Dill's telegram are of considerable interest. Though the organization of the Division had begun on 27 May, it was not until 31 May that the War Office gave the formation its official designation — and recognized its existence!

In view of General Dill's telegram, it would be as well to consider the effectiveness and composition of the Beauman Division. This is all the more desirable in view of the comments made in his Report by General Marshall-Cornwall[1]; he says:

'Meanwhile, owing to the threat developing in the British base at Rouen, General Sir Henry Karslake, GOC Lines of Communication, had scraped together an improvised force for its local defence. This force comprised nine infantry battalions of a sort; they consisted partly of second-line Territorial units sent out to France for pioneer duties and partly of composite units made up from miscellaneous reinforcements at the base. They had no war equipment except rifles and a few odd Bren guns and anti-tank weapons, which they had never fired before. They were without artillery, means of transport and signalling equipment. They were placed under the command of Brigadier Beauman, in charge of the Northern District Lines of Communication.

'Very unfortunately, this heterogeneous collection of untrained and ill-equipped units was given the title of a Division; the French were thus misled into thinking that it was a fighting formation, complete with artillery and ancillary services.

'Beauman's so-called division had been given the task of holding a back-line along the Rivers Béthune and Andelle covering Rouen, and had done good work in organizing defences of this position.'

As has already been related, the Beauman Division was organized from the various 'forces' which had been assembled by Brigadier Beauman prior to General Karslake's arrival. General Karslake considered that it was essential to possess a formation which would not only give him some sort of defence force, but also would provide a line on which, if necessary, the advanced troops could fall back. In order to achieve both objects it was essential to have a properly constituted formation, however weak, that could be successfully controlled and employed. He decided that, in view of the number of infantry battalions which had been made available, the ideal formation was that of a division. With this in mind, he obtained from General Ironside two experienced Brigadiers — all that were available — and one highly recommended Major. The actual Order of Battle is given in Appendix B.

While, at first, 'A' Brigade consisted of two Territorial battalions which had been employed on guard duties, and one 'Labour' battalion from a Territorial division, sent over for that purpose, this was soon modified. On 5 June the 4th Border Regiment, who were serving with the Support Group, exchanged with the 2/6th East Surreys, joining 'A' Brigade. Thus 'A' Brigade consisted once again of the original battalions that had formed the 25th Brigade in England in 1939. This Brigade was undoubtedly the strongest of the three, all the troops having had a fair amount of training.

'B' Brigade was, indeed, a miscellaneous collection of troops. Few of them belonged to the same battalion and none of the officers knew their men. They were raised from the reinforcement depots. However, they were *trained* soldiers ready to return to their units in the BEF. But being such an assortment, they did not have the cohesion of troops accustomed to operating together. Undoubtedly, this was the weakest formation.[2]

'C' Brigade consisted entirely of Auxiliary Military Pioneer Corps troops in their own battalions. Designed to act primarily as labour, nevertheless they included a number of erstwhile trained soldiers and were commanded by their own experienced officers.

Certainly, in the matter of equipment, as far as both 'B' and 'C' Brigades were concerned, at first this was weak. It improved, however, later. All the men were capable of handling their weapons. Indeed, other than the troops which had formed the three 'labour' divisions, all the men had had a reasonable amount of training.

The amount of artillery available was small. Major Elliott had been able to raise, and man, one battery of field guns. Unfortunately, so short was the reserve of vital equipment that there were no dial sights. This prevented the guns being used in their proper role; nevertheless they proved invaluable as heavy anti-tank weapons firing over open sights. Two complete batteries of anti-tank guns (20) were available, together with a reserve of 20mm guns from French sources. In due course a number of Bofors guns became available through the abandonment of various airfields by the RAF.

Owing to the main Base Depot being located near Rouen, an immense amount of transport was available. All brigades and ancilliary services were up to strength in this respect. In view of the fact that a very large number of vehicles were used to move stores from the north to the south of the Seine, it is remarkable that there was no shortage. Finally, General Marshall-Cornwall states that the Division was without signal equipment. Beauman Divisional Signals was formed on 27 May under A/Lt-Colonel Scott. Although it was without '2 Company', it was otherwise fully equipped. 2 Company was omitted as, that Company being responsible for serving the Divisional Artillery, and there being so little, it was considered unnecessary. All units and formations were connected both by radio and landlines. In fact Divisional Signals operated fully until the very day on which the Division embarked for England. It should be pointed out that this was the only operational Divisional Signals which consistently remained open throughout its career.[3]

Owing to the nature of the task for which it was designed, the Division had more than its establishment of Royal Engineer units. Every bridge and culvert was prepared for demolition and every road, as far as possible, was provided with road-blocks ready to be put in place when required.

Regarding the statement that the French were misled into thinking that the Beauman Division was a full-strength formation, this is sheer nonsense — that is unless the Divisional Commander himself had given that impression. Certainly General Karslake, in conversation with the various French commanders including Generals Altmayer and Georges, had explained in detail the reason for the organization of the Beauman Division and its limitations. As is clearly stated by General Karslake in his report, the Beauman Division was never intended as a proper fighting formation.

The Division was disposed so as to provide a thin covering line on which the advanced formations could withdraw. Considering that the major threat was constituted by the possible penetration by armour, a line was selected which, to a certain extent, would give some sort of anti-tank protection. The two rivers, Andelle and Béthune, seemed the only obstacle, however slight, that offered some sort of barrier. The area between the sources of these two rivers was considered to be the most vulnerable part of the front. On paper this was so. However, further east, near the upper reaches of the Andelle, the river was easily crossed. It was here that Major Elliott located the mass of his artillery. He considered that if it was too widely dispersed, by trying to cover too many points, its value would be dissipated. As will be seen in due course, he was right in this decision.

In the meantime, the 51st Division had taken up the following positions: The 152nd Brigade and the 154th Brigade were forward covering a front of some 16½ miles, north of the River Bresle from the sea eastwards; the 153rd Brigade were held in reserve on the River Bresle between Senarpont and Blangy. On their extreme right of the 154th Brigade was a company of Princess Louise's Kensington Regiment of machine gunners with the Composite Armoured Regiment behind them. On the extreme left was the 6th Royal Scots Fusiliers (Pioneer Battalion).

Though under the command of the 51st Division, the 1st Support Group was acting more or less as an independent formation, being widely separated from the division on its left. It had been placed in a position to act as a 'switch line' on the flank so as to connect the main front to Beauman's Division in the south. It was felt that if the enemy were able to make a serious penetration, this switch line would prevent them from cutting in behind the 51st Division. As the activities of the Support Group are a story in itself, one cannot do better than quote from the Group's diary covering this period. As the 101st LAA and A/T Regiment really represented the Group, the quotations are largely taken from the Regimental Diary. The sections in brackets are comments made by the Brigade Major at a later date.

The Regiment was ordered to recce line exclusive Forges (les Eaux) — exclusive Aumale with view to taking up defensive positions there; being a switch line connecting the right flank of the 51st Division on the Bresle with the right flank of Beauforce at Formerie. This line was 21 miles (?) in length.

31st. Recce of above positions which were to be occupied by 2 June by the Sp Gp which now consisted of 101 Regt RA (less 44 Bty), 1st Field Squadron RE, 1st Field Park Troop and 5th Bn East Surreys. (Actually this was incorrect. The 4th Borders remained with the Group until 5 June when it was relieved by the 2/6th East Surreys.) This unit was a Territorial unit (2/6th) whose personnel had never fired a rifle in their lives. (This was an exaggeration. About 50% had never fired a rifle and the great majority had never fired either a Bren or an anti-tank rifle. Being part of a 'Labour' division the unit's equipment and training was minimal.) It was heart-rending indeed for the Comd Sp Gp who now had under his command not one single unit that had been under his command at the beginning of the war — who now, with ill-equipped units, had to take the field against the full German might, in a role for which the Sp Gp had never been trained, attached to a Division that knew very little about the Sp Gp; and to this day is not aware of what it consisted.

2nd. Orders carefully planned by Brigade for outlet of vehicles from harbour ... The Bde was not spotted from the air in the move. RHQ established at La Mare aux Daims; Sp Gp HQ at Sausseuse-Mare. Signals got to work to fix up telephones between RHQ and Btys, and RHQ and Sp Gp HQ; each Bty took with it a No. 11 wireless set complete with staff ... Wireless silence was the order except in emergencies. 237 and 239 Btys established their HQs 1 mile N of RHQ and 1 mile SE of Aumale respectively. The role of 43 Bty was to supply one LMG per A/T gun for protection against low-flying aircraft and dive-bombing ... 44 Bty had come under command of 51 Div and so the Regt had lost the benefit of the 10 Bofors guns and arms which it had gone to such great lengths to 'scrounge' (see Chapter V); while 43 Bty, taken away from manning Bofors on sites for the Air Defence of Great Britain, were now in the fields of France clutching for dear life to that rather ineffective weapon for AA purposes, the LMG. Before any attack was made it was quite obvious that, with the guns manned by skeleton crews, an untrained Bn of infantry in support, not sufficient AA defence, no air support, no effective anti-tank obstacle, no defence in depth (the Composite Regiment had been withdrawn), in fact all elementary lessons of warfare thrown to the winds, I say again, it was quite obvious that we might just as well not be in the position at all for all the damage we could inflict on the enemy. This is borne out later when the notes on the attack and the subsequent events are read. (The writer's statement is only partially correct, as events will show.)

(On this day [3 June] a new CO was appointed to command the Regiment to the obvious dismay of certain officers.) Changes of plan and policy were inevitable with a new CO but they did not help when every minute meant the losing or saving of lives as the scene of battle was constantly shifting ... Considerable activity by German planes but we were not chosen as their objective; the planes flew too high for LMGs; never saw one plane shot down by French AA guns which were now dotted around us. Various French troops appeared in the area to add to the confusion, there being no liaison. 44 Bty report good work — 11 planes shot down — message from Cdr Sp Gp of congratulations.

There is one other reason why this extract has been given at length; it is to show, yet again, the shocking position in which the British found themselves through having no guiding hand in the form of a Commander-in-Chief.

It is now time to take a look at the over-all picture. The French intention, in theory, was to hold the line of the River Somme. In fact, of course, at no point did they have a position on that river. The enemy had retained bridgeheads all the way from Amiens to the sea in spite of Allied efforts to dislodge them. The organization of the Allied forces covering the 'Somme Line' was, again on paper, quite an impressive one. Army Group III, commanded by General Besson, was responsible for the line from the sea to the east of Amiens. This Group consisted of the 10th Army (General Robert Altmayer) from the sea to Picquigny; the 6th Army (General Touchon) and the 7th Army (General Frere) from Picquigny eastwards. It being the 10th Army under which the British served, it is that formation with which we are concerned. The two Corps, of which this Army consisted, were IX (General Ihler) from the sea to Abbeville inclusive, and X from exclusive Abbeville to Picquigny. On 31 May IX Corps had, besides the 51st Division, the 5th Colonial Division under command together with the remains of the 2nd and 5th DCL; also the 2nd French Armoured Division of some 160 tanks of all kinds. The artillery was in considerable strength, the 4th French Armoured Division having left its guns in that sector. Behind the 10th Army was the Reserve Group III (General Petiet). This had two divisions of infantry in preparation, the 31st (Alpine) and the 40th, together with a Light Cavalry division. Nevertheless, provided that sufficient respite was granted to them, these forces should have been able to form a fair defence in depth if the enemy decided to attack. In the meantime, it was decided that efforts should continue to be made to reduce the enemy-held bridgeheads.

It was not only the actual physical weakness of the various formations that was to influence the outcome of the engagements which were due to take place in the near future, but the very complicated chain of command.

The 1st Armoured Division came under command of Tenth Army *not* IX Corps Commander (except for the Composite Regiment and the Support Group which were in turn under General Fortune of the 51st Divison). At a later stage the Armoured Division came directly under General Weygand; this created a conflict of orders and caused the serious failure of an operation.

The Beauman Division, plus all the rest of the British troops, both fighting, administration and Services on the L of C, were still under General Karslake. He in turn remained under the direct command of General Georges. It will be seen that all British formations were under separate commanders, each acting independently of one another. It was, indeed, only by unofficial liaison that they were able to keep in touch with one another; by this means some sort of idea was obtained as to what might be likely to occur and what their requirements might be.

This thoroughly undesirable situation, it will be remembered, had been discussed by General Karslake and General Ironside on the former's visit to London on 25 May. General Ironside, fully appreciating the situation, agreed to make the necessary arrangements for General Karslake to assume the position of 'Corps Commander' over *all* the British troops serving in France. However, when General Dill assumed the appointment of CIGS, he decided that that was not desirable. As an alternative he sent out Lieut-General J.H. Marshall-Cornwall, an officer of vast experience in liaison duties, to head Number 17 Military Mission at General Altmayer's

HQ. It would seem that among the normal liaison duties that the General was called upon to perform, he had to 'coordinate and supervise the employment of the British troops under French command'. What precisely this implied is not clear. General Marshall-Cornwall had no executive authority. He held no command and was in no way responsible for the well-being or employment of the troops in France. He was unable to ensure that the troops were safeguarded against undesirable employment nor was he able to look after their safety. Without the authority invested in Lord Gort or, latterly, in General Brooke, he was quite powerless to influence any decision that the French Commanders might make (but see Chapter XI). Indeed, his appointment only made matters worse. Many officers were under the mistaken impression that he possessed the requisite powers and applied to him for help, only to be disappointed when they found that he was, apparently, unable to render them assistance. This caused considerable ill-feeling which in fact was unjustified in the circumstances. From 31 May, when General Marshall-Cornwall arrived in France, he tended to give the impression that he was a 'Corps Commander'. Unfortunately, he had had no experience of commanding troops in the field and his staff was only that of a Mission and quite valueless for a Command structure. The only thing that can be said of this appointment is that it was better than nothing (though some people have questioned even this!). It can well be appreciated that confusion was inevitable.

Though from 2 June General Brooke was technically commanding all the troops designated for the new BEF which were still in England, he was also theoretically commanding all those that were in France. Actually, of course, he seems to have had no control over any of them. There is no doubt whatsoever that, once it was decided that General Brooke was to be the new Corps Commander, he should have been sent to France at once, even with a limited Staff. He would have brought with him the powers that he was subsequently to receive. Had this decision been taken it seems more than probable that, in spite of his complete lack of faith in the projected enterprise, he would have been able to exercise his undoubted talents to ensure that the British Forces in France were properly employed. In spite of intensive research, the writer has been unable to discover why the CIGS did not take this action. In the event, as will be seen, when one General issued an order which fitted the occasion another Commander, out of touch with the situation, would countermand it. This necessarily led to confusion, unnecessary movements and finally the loss of opportunities — to say nothing of misunderstandings. Probably one of the best examples of this is when, with the authority of General Altmayer, the 51st Division withdrew behind the River Bresle on 6 June. General Weygand, who was completely out of touch with events, accused General Fortune of treachery, as he had issued orders that the line of the Bresle should 'be held at all costs'. There is no doubt whatsoever that, had there been a British Corps Commander, no Frenchman would have dared levy such a charge!

On 3 June General Karslake surveyed the position north of the River Seine. The withdrawal of all the items on his Priority List had been completed. The medical supplies from Dieppe had gone and all the depots had been emptied with the exception of the huge depot at Le Havre which contained the food supply of the BEF. However, this had been run down by the simple expedient of directing the supply ships to the south and using the contents of the depot for the benefit of the troops actually 'in the line'.[4] The great problem of the disposal of the main ammunition dumps contained in the vast area between St Saens and Buchy remained insoluble. The enormous quantity which had been placed there during the past nine months proved far too great to be moved with the resources which were available. Only ammunition that was in short supply in England could be lifted. The dumps containing the great shells for the super-heavy batteries and the thousands of tons of 25 pdr rounds would have required the total resources of the L of C to dissipate. However, the large dump of chemical warfare ammunition at Fécamp was shifted either direct to England or else dumped at sea. It was considered most undesirable that this material should be abandoned so as to fall into the hands of the enemy — if only for political reasons. As it was, it took D Company, 2/6th East Surreys, one Battalion of the AMPC and a Docks Operating Company over a week to empty the depot.

As a matter of policy it was decided that the port of Le Havre should no longer be used. Instead, the ports of Nantes and St Nazaire should be developed. Le Havre had become too close to the enemy for its continuance as a supply entry, being vulnerable to air attack. Cherbourg continued to be the main reception port for personnel and was capable of handling most types of other cargo when necessary. For some time General Karslake had been concerned for the safety of the southern ports. Though Cherbourg was well defended by AA, neither Nantes nor St Nazaire possessed any form of defence against aerial attack. Now that Le Havre had been closed, he decided to remove the guns and other aerial defence provided by the 3rd AA Brigade and transfer it south. He therefore instructed Brigadier Shilstone, the Brigade Commander, to make the necessary arrangements to move the guns to the southern ports. Only the mobile battery was to be left. It was felt that this unit would present no difficulty in shifting should the enemy appear to be approaching Le Havre. In any case, a mobile battery could be employed in an anti-tank role if necessary. The remainder of the guns at Le Havre were static or semi-static and required dismantling before they could be moved and it would, therefore, be some time before they could assume their new positions. The War Office was informed accordingly on 4 June that such action was being taken.

At 0930 on 5 June, the Port Admiral at Le Havre advised GQG that the British were withdrawing the anti-aircraft defences from that port. As a result General Weygand telephoned to M. Reynaud with the request that the British Government be asked to abandon the project and to 'maintain in Le Havre the anti-aircraft batteries as well as the barrage balloons that it had installed there'. He followed this call with a note which read, 'The Commander-in-Chief is obliged to point out that appeals to the British Government have continued to no avail. We are being subjected to the German attack without having benefited from any further assistance from Britain, neither fighter planes nor new Divisions.'

In fact, M. Reynaud had been in touch with Mr Eden on the subject of the AA defence of Le Havre. Eden had given an assurance that no guns or other equipment would be removed from the port. No orders, however, to this effect were given by the War Office to General Karslake. It was not until he received the information from French sources that he discovered that his plans had not only been questioned but were likely to be upset. He therefore wrote the following letter to the CIGS on the subject:

> To   Under Secretary of State for War, War Office, M.O.4.
> FROM Lieut-General Sir Henry Karslake.
> SUBJECT Air Defence — Active.
>
> In this HQs 486/G/S dated 4 June, 1940 we informed you of the steps we proposed to take to give a modicum of AA protection to those ports which are the main channels of transit for both personnel and stores for the BEF. I regard it of very great importance and consequently, in consultation with the Commander of the 3rd AA Brigade, drew up proposals for the most effective and economical use of the British resources in AA.
>
> I have now received a copy from French sources, the Admiral of Havre, that the British AA protection will not be weakened. Although I have received no orders myself this puts me in the awkward position of being unable to take such steps as the rapidly changing situation may require of adjusting the deployment of available AA. It even seems to prevent me from removing the mobile AA in the event of the loss of Havre becoming imminent.
>
> I consider that either I should be given the latitude to take such means as I consider necessary or that an officer be deputed from the War Office to report to my HQs with full powers. The rate of military operations makes control through the War Office most dangerous.
>   Signed,
>   H. KARSLAKE.
>   Lt. General Commanding the L of C.[5]

As the result of this letter no further insistence by the War Minister arose; on 8 June General Weygand himself agreed to the removal of the remainder of the guns (the mobile battery) from Le Havre.

The above event has been given in some detail as it provides an excellent example of the absurd situation that had developed in France owing to the absence of an overall Commander and the utter futility of the War Office in trying to conduct operations from England. Luckily in this instance reason prevailed. The guns from Le Havre were saved — only to be lost during the final evacuation.[6]

When day dawned on 4 June, it was to herald the last combined attack on the part of the Allies during the campaign in France and Flanders. On 31 May, after the failure to reduce the German bridgeheads along the Somme, General Weygand decided that it was essential to make a final effort to achieve this. He considered that it was particularly important that the bridgeheads at Abbeville and at St Valéry-sur-Somme should be eliminated owing to the vulnerability of the western sector of the 'Weygand Line'. It was thought that if the enemy were able to achieve a break-through along the coast it would effectively prevent any reinforcements being received from Britain. This segregation of France from her Allies would ensure that the campaign in France would end abruptly. General Weygand, therefore, instructed General Georges to mount a major assault on these bridgeheads at the earliest possible opportunity, and to use the strongest available force for the purpose. General Georges considered that three clear days would be quite sufficient for plans to be formulated and the necessary troops assembled. Owing to the lack of reconnaissance and the paucity of intelligence, the actual enemy strength was quite unknown. It could have been reasonably supposed that the enemy would have made every effort to strengthen his hold and to increase his defences against any likely attack from the south, particularly in view of the previous attacks that had been made by the Allies.

General Georges considered that, with the troops already in position, namely the 51st Division and the 2nd Armoured Division (this latter had relieved General de Gaulle's 4th Armoured Division), one additional infantry division should be quite adequate for the purpose. Further, the artillery situation was far above the average for the numbers involved. Not only was the 51st Division possessed of a greater quantity of cannon, many of larger calibre than a standard division, but the artillery of the 4th Armoured had also remained in the area. With the addition of a further division's artillery, plus the guns of IX Corps, at least 250 guns of all field calibres could be brought into action to support the attack. As far as armour was concerned, though, the 2nd Armoured had been engaged previously. Nevertheless, it still possessed some sixty heavy tanks and about one hundred light ones. The British armoured force in the area consisted of only the Composite Regiment. On paper, therefore, the force to undertake the attack should have proved sufficient. Unfortunately, as will be seen, it was not so in fact. Many factors had not been taken into consideration. The first of these was the complete lack of air support. The RAF had not been approached and, in any case, was not in a position to undertake work of this kind. The French Air Force was fully committed elsewhere. Secondly, as has been mentioned, little was known of the enemy's strength and dispositions. Thirdly, the time to bring the scheduled force into position prior to the opening of the attack had been grossly underestimated. It would seem that no account had been taken of the state of the roads over which the additional infantry division would have to travel. This latter miscalculation was particularly serious in its consequences. The 31st Alpine Division, though situated just north of the River Seine, was still in the process of reformation after its experiences elsewhere. When the warning orders to move were received on 2 June, it took some time to arrange for the various regiments and ancillary troops to be in a position to march. Even the efforts to clear the roads northward did little to help. Another point which had been overlooked was its situation regarding artillery. Being an Alpine Division, though equipped with 75mm guns, the ammunition for these guns was quite different to that required by standard formations. Little of the 'Mountain' type was available in the western sector. Much time was taken up trying to locate sufficient for the work envisaged. Even when the guns did arrive and ammunition had started to 'dribble' in, it was found that these guns could not be 'netted in' with the standard pieces owing to their curious trajectory.*

General Fortune had been placed in charge of the operation, with both the French divisions under his command.

On the same day (2 June) the French had only the 2nd Armoured Division and the 2nd and 5th DCL representing IX Corps. Both the 31st and 40th Divisions had been scheduled to come forward, the latter to be in reserve. The 5th Colonial Division was on the extreme right and not required for the attack.

The plan for the attack was that the two French divisions (31st and 2nd Armoured) should assault and capture two main ridges — the long Mont de Caubert spur on the west, which runs northward from Mareuil-Caubert, and a ridge of high ground west of Rouvroy. On the right of the 2nd Armoured Division the 152nd Brigade

---

* The Alpine 75 was the 'mountain' model, Schneider M1928. It had a much shorter barrel and fired a lighter shell. This combination would produce a very different trajectory to that of the standard 75 (M1897).

of the 51st Division was to capture the village of Caubert and the woods which border the road from there to Bray. The 153rd Brigade, operating on the left of the 31st Division, was ordered to take the high ground to the south of Gouy. The 154th Brigade was to engage the enemy at St Valéry-sur-Somme and prevent the Abbeville front being reinforced from there. The British tanks of the Composite Regiment were to be held in reserve as it was now appreciated by the French High Command that they were unsuitable for assault work.

In order to appreciate why these dispositions were not as satisfactory as they appeared to the French Command it is necessary to examine the situation immediately preceeding the attack. Of the 31st Division only one regiment had arrived before midnight 3-4 June. A second Regiment appeared at 0130 on the 4th. Neither of these regiments, therefore, were able to make any form of reconnaissance of their points of attack. Neither petrol nor ammunition for the 2nd Armoured Division had arrived at the time the attack was scheduled to begin; delay was inevitable. The artillery, which promised to provide an excellent support, was only partially ready at the time for opening the barrage. Though the British L of C had sent forward all the necessary ammunition (in fact an enormous amount was stacked by the guns) it was quite impossible for the whole of the artillery intended to be employed to be linked together and the necessary preparatory ranging carried out. Not only were there no spotter aircraft but there was no indication as to exactly where the enemy's defences were located. Also many of the French guns, particularly those of the 31st Division, had only just arrived in position before being required to open fire. It should be noted that the final regiment of the 31st Division did not arrive until after the attack had failed.

It has already been mentioned that neither Allied airforce took any part in the attack. In fact, no request had been made by either French or British commanders for such help to be given. General Karslake, who had been informed of the projected attack on 3 June, by courtesy only, (he had to arrange for the necessary supplies) was horrified at the situation. Though, as he states in his Report, 'it savoured of interference on my part', he telephoned Air-Marshal Barratt and asked for his help. Unfortunately, owing to the shortness of notice and the fact that the control of aerial operations was being conducted from London, the Air-Marshal could not participate in the attack; he was, however, able to send aircraft to try and make an aerial photographic reconnaissance of the area. Owing to the short notice and the very bad flying conditions, the results were not satisfactory — but at least some effort had been made to improve the situation. One is at a loss to understand why no one, particularly the French, made any representations to London for aerial help in what was obviously a major and vital operation. As no aircraft were available for either air-spotting for the artillery or support for the troops, this was to have a very serious effect on the whole enterprise.

The German forces had not wasted their time since they had first entered the area on 20 May. Every possible vantage point had been covered by anti-tank guns and mines; numbers of machine-gun nests had been installed in the sides of hills and the edges of woods: all were carefully camouflaged. It has been admitted subsequently that these positions could have been spotted from the air. The German artillery had been so sited that it covered every avenue of approach, all ranges having been taken and marked. The Allied artillery, on the other hand, through lack of spotting, was able only to range on points in which it was *thought* that the enemy might be gathered. To the outside observer it must have appeared obvious that the attack was doomed to failure even before it was 'off the ground'. Unfortunately, owing to his position, General Marshall-Cornwall's representations to the French Command for a postponement proved ineffective. Likewise, General Fortune was unable to request a delay. Being under the direct command of the French IX Corps, he had no one to whom he could appeal.

The attack was scheduled to take place at 0300 on 4 June. At 0250 the massed artillery opened fire. Though stated to be a barrage, it was certainly quite unlike any which would have been recognized by an artilleryman. The guns fired at various targets in the hope that they were the right ones. Even after the 'barrage' lifted it was not known if it had proved effective, no observation being possible. In any case a barrage of a mere ten minutes was quite inadequate. There was ample ammunition to ensure that, if the guns had been properly employed, saturation point could have been reached on primary targets. Here again the direction was bad. Even though the number of guns was considerable, the vague area which they were supposed to cover was excessive. In 1918 a frontage of some 2,000 yards would have been considered proper for the amount of artillery involved. This attack was spread over five miles!

At precisely 0300 the attack was set in motion. But here disaster struck. The heavy French tanks, which were supposed to lead the advance, had not even arrived at their starting point. They had been waiting till the last moment in the hope that more fuel would arrive. As it was, they had to move forward with their tanks only half full.

The 2nd Seaforths did not wait for the tanks but advanced at once and made short work of the enemy positions in the woods immediately in front of them. When the tanks did arrive and began their advance they had missed the protection of the 'barrage' and ran, first, into an undetected mine-field and then intense anti-tank fire. The German gunners had had time to recover from the initial shock. As a result of this unfortunate beginning, the tanks suffered severe casualties. Nevertheless, some of them reached the base of Mont de Caubert ridge from whence they drove the enemy. The 4th Seaforths, who were supposed to follow the heavy tank attack supported by the light tanks, waited until three of the latter arrived and then went forward to the south-eastern side of the Villers woods. However, they were soon decimated by machine-gun fire from the Mont de Caubert. Nevertheless, they pressed forward in spite of mounting casualties in an attempt to reach the heavy tanks, but the situation was now past redemption. In spite of the gallantry displayed by all those who had taken part, it was essential for the troops to withdraw to their original positions. The casualties suffered by the 152nd Brigade alone amounted to 20 officers and 543 other ranks.

The French, on the left centre, had been able to make no progress as they were completely blocked by the dug-in machine-guns on their front. Indeed, the only part of the 'Grand Attack' which made any headway was that of the 153rd Brigade on the left flank. There the battalions engaged achieved all their objectives but, without success elsewhere, there was no point in trying to maintain their newly won positions; therefore, with the utmost disappointment, they had to return to their starting points.

The whole enterprise had provided an excellent example of the results produced by a hastily conceived and badly coordinated attack. In theory there existed all the makings of a successful affair; yet almost everything that could go wrong did so. Though the force on paper was quite adequate in strength, in fact it was not so. Of the French infantry only the equivalent of one brigade was available and ready to advance. The lack of petrol for the tanks forced them to attack with quite inadequate supplies; as a result, they had to retire to refuel in the middle of the engagement. Indeed, some actually ran out of petrol during their movement, and had to be abandoned.

Cyril Falls, in a footnote to the affair as recounted by Benoist-Méchin in *60 Days Which Shook The West*, states that throughout the action Anglo-French cooperation was exemplary. One is at a loss to understand how he reached this conclusion; every detail was mistimed or miscarried. There appears to have been a complete lack of liaison between the units engaged where those units were of a different nationality. Basically, however, the failure of the attack must be placed firmly on the shoulders of those who ordered the operation to proceed without having ensured that adequate preparation had been made. Even after the lessons which must have been provided by the failure, it was seriously contemplated re-mounting the attack on the 5th! One can readily imagine what the result would have been if the Germans had not intervened, providentially, to prevent it!

As a result of the casualties received by his command during the attack, General Altmayer ordered the 40th French Infantry Division forward to reinforce his line. With the departure of this Division from the Group Petiet, which had been designed to act as a mobile reserve and intended to be used to counter-attack any possible break-through by the enemy and to provide a defence in depth, the 10th Army was left on its own.

The 3rd DCL was General Petiet's own command. It was now sent back across the Seine to form the nucleus of yet another reserve which was being hastily gathered together. This reserve was designed to consist of French formations that were being returned to France after their evacuation from Dunkirk. These formations not only lacked cohesion, but also possessed very few weapons.

Luckily the French were in a much better position to supply the latter than the British. Reserves of artillery still existed south of the Seine. The morale of these troops was a very different matter. Nevertheless, again the French were fortunate; General de la Laurencie had returned to France. He was a very able commander and possessed considerable driving force and great personality. Though engaged in a seemingly impossible task, he was able, in a surprisingly short time, to produce a force which gave promise that all was not lost. In addition to the French troops, numbers of Poles and Belgians, who had managed to escape to France, were being quickly formed into divisions. Given time, these men would be able to give a good account of themselves but, of course, it was all a question of time. With this in mind, it was planned to employ them as part of the garrison of the Breton Redoubt under General Réné Altmayer.

At 0400 on 5th June, the whole front from Montmédy to the sea burst into flame. Ever since the last embers of Allied resistance in the north had been stamped out, the German armies had been regrouping for the carrying out of 'Plan Red', the operation that was finally intended to destroy the remainder of the Allied Forces in France.

The section of the front which directly concerned the British was that between Amiens and the sea, and in particular from Picquigny westwards. The German forces lining the Somme in this sector consisted of the bulk of von Kluge's 4th Army. This was composed of two Panzer divisions (5th, von Hartlieb and 7th, Rommel), one motorized division, one motorized brigade, one cavalry division and six infantry divisions. On the Allied side facing them, reading from left to right, were the 51st Division, the 31st French Infantry Division, supported by the remains of the French 2nd Armoured Division and the 2nd and 5th DCLs from Petiet's reserve. On their right was the X French Corps of the 10th Army, consisting of the 5th Colonial Division and the 17th Infantry Division.

It will be seen that, after the causalties suffered on 4th June, even with the prospect of reinforcement by the 40th Division, the Allied line was in no position to repel a determined attack. The Allies suffered from yet another disadvantage, a disadvantage so serious that it was to influence the whole course of events from the moment the Germans opened their offensive. This was, once again, the lack of air support. Whereas the enemy were provided with a complete airfleet, its members having been trained in ground support, the Allies had virtually none. Even the air-arm which it did possess was quite inexperienced in direct cooperation with ground troops. Communications were lacking and, what was worse, it had been decreed that all aerial operations over the front should be conducted from England. Indeed, there were practically no suitable British aeroplanes in France at that time. Those there were were also under the Air Ministry, not under the RAF Commander in France. This continued for some time in spite of repeated representations made by Air-Marshal Barratt. The results were inevitable. When aerial support was asked for, by the time it arrived, such as it was, the time had passed for that particular intervention. More often than not, the RAF arrived to find no hostile aircraft; they had departed long before, having completed their tasks.

To obtain a clear picture of the aerial situation it is only necessary to study the 'Administrative position in BAFF (British Air Force, France) at 1800 hours, 2 June'. (see Appendix B) This 'position' existed for some time after the start of the new German offensive. The 'Air Component' had been withdrawn before the evacuation from Dunkirk, its airfields having become untenable, all sorties thereafter being directed from England. In its place, after Dunkirk, a new organization known as 'South Component' had been set up. This proved to be thoroughly unsatisfactory. It was not designed to function in the same way as its predecessor, namely to be at the disposal of the Commander-in-Chief. This was understandable as, of course, there was no Commander-in-Chief south of the Somme. What was worse, there was no Authority which could direct the efforts of the Component in support of the ground forces.

Though the original AASF (Advanced Air Striking Force) continued to exist in its original form, this formation had no connection with the ground forces; it acted independently in a strategic role as directed by the Air Ministry. Indeed, the attitude of the RAF towards the Army was such, and their contribution to the Army's support so small, that it was only after a direct representation to Air-Marshal Barratt by General Karslake that information was forthcoming from that source regarding the disposition of the RAF in France. To say the least, this was most curious, as a complete Brigade of AA Artillery, together with Royal Engineer units, was operating with the various RAF formations and units. It would seem, according to the existing records, that virtually no information had been provided by the RAF to the HQ of the L of C prior to 3 June. As the L of C was responsible for providing all the necessary supplies for these attached Army units, it is extraordinary that the GOC of the L of C had not insisted on such a provision being made regularly, RAF dispositions being constantly changed. Fortunately the relationship between Air-Marshal Barratt and General Karslake was most cordial. The Air-Marshal, when a Wing Commander, had commanded the RAF Wing in Quetta when General Karslake had been appointed District Commander in 1933. Owing to the role that the RAF had been required to play in the defence of the extreme North-West Frontier of India, Air-Marshal Barratt was fully alive to the necessity of close co-operation. Both senior officers did their best to achieve these desirable ends but were thwarted by their relative positions and the decision by the Air Ministry to direct operations from England.

The Germans' opening gambit was a thrust by three infantry Divisions between Abbeville and the sea, the main attack coming from the bridgehead at St Valéry-sur-Somme. This was the sector for which the 51st Division was responsible. After intensive artillery and mortar fire combined with aerial action, the German Divisions launched a furious attack. With a frontage of sixteen miles to protect, the British Division was spread very thinly on the ground. The 154th Brigade was holding, or more correctly, occupying, a number of widely spaced villages. They fought with dogged courage against unequal odds and it was not until 1800 that the enemy were able to make any headway. Even then it was because it was found impossible to maintain the defenders' ammunition and other supplies that the Brigade was forced to withdraw to a line between Woincourt and Eu. The 153rd Brigade, on the right of the 154th, was also assaulted with great violence and, in due course, was compelled to pull back but not before it had inflicted considerable casualties on the enemy. This Brigade had had the support of a large part of the Divisional artillery and machine guns. After their withdrawal, they assumed a line from Toeufles through Zoteux to Frières. At this point the 31st Division was in position, separating the rest of the

51st Division from the 152nd Brigade and the flank guard provided by the Lothian and Border Horse.

By the evening both the 31st Division and the 152nd Brigade had been forced to fall back; at the end of the day the line ran from Oisemont to the sea near Eu. One major success had been gained by the Germans; at some points they had reached the 'gun-line' of the 51st Division. Many guns including some four medium and four field pieces had been destroyed.

During this period the Composite Regiment was refitting at Beauchamps. The 1st Support Group with its infantry was still in position between Aumale and Forges-les-Eaux. The 4th Border Regiment having returned to 'A' Brigade on the left of the Beauman line, its place had been taken by the 2/6th East Surrey Regiment. The Support Group was not to have its baptism of fire until 7 June.

Meanwhile, of Hoth's Armoured Group, Schmidt's XXXIX Corps, consisting of the 5th and 7th Panzer Divisions, together with the 2nd Motorized Division, had crossed the River Somme by several bridges to the west of Hangest which the French had, one presumes, inadvertently left intact. This force, though exceedingly powerful, ran into serious opposition from the 5th Colonial Division. It was not until the evening of 6 June that they were able to break out into the plains, which were admirably suited for tank deployment. It was only then that they were able to begin their dash for the River Seine.

The British had by now had a foretaste of what was to come. It was quite evident to General Fortune that his Division was being employed far in excess of its capabilities. Not only had the formation been reduced through serious casualties but the front which it was supposed to hold was excessive. Believing that General Marshall-Cornwall was acting in the capacity of Corps Commander, General Fortune wrote to him on the night of the 5th-6th, explaining his position and asking that his Division should either be relieved or, at least, part of his front taken over by another formation. Unfortunately General Marshall-Cornwall was in no position to arrange for the carrying out of such requests. He could only refer the matter to General Altmayer, who pointed out that he had no reserves to enable him to replace the 51st Division in the line.

However, with the arrival of the 40th Infantry Division, a certain reorganization took place. The 152nd Brigade rejoined the 51st Division by moving round the 31st Infantry Divison. This brought it over to the westward flank of this Division. Also, the 31st Division itself had side-stepped westward so as to allow room for the 40th Division on its eastern flank. After these manoeuvres had been completed, the frontage of the 51st Division had been reduced to 12½ miles, not much of a reduction but better than nothing. However, the Support Group on the eastern flank was now separated more widely than ever from the 51st Division. Furthermore, as the enemy were applying pressure on the extreme west of the line, the Composite Regiment of the 1st Armoured Division was moved from the rear of the Support Group to the threatened flank. This meant that, should a serious attack develop on the Support Group's front, there were no troops to support it. Also the original plan on which the lay-out of the defences of the Group was based had now to be abandoned. As will be seen shortly, Brigadier Morgan was seriously affected by these developments.

The German offensive was much less violent on 6 June as far as the sector held by IX Corps was concerned. Other than the pressure mentioned above, little of note occurred. On the extreme right of IX Corps, at the junction between it and X Corps, the situation was very different. The full weight of the Panzer advance was directed at the sector held by the 5th Colonial Division. It is noteworthy that, in spite of the fact that such powerful forces were used, the enemy were unable to make any great progress. Nevertheless, it was becoming obvious that it would not be long before this thrust southwards would have serious consequences if reinforcements were not forthcoming. As is known, there were no reinforcements available to support the threatened left wing of X Corps.

General Fortune wrote once again to General Marshall-Cornwall requesting that the 51st Division, together with the French 31st Division, should be allowed to withdraw behind the line of the River Bresle. This was a far better defensive position than the open country to the north. General Altmayer agreed to this proposal and, at the end of the day, the two formations assumed their new positions: the 31st Division from Senarpont to Gamaches and the 51st Division from Gamaches to the sea, the reformed 40th Division continuing the line from Senarpont to Aumale. In this latter area were also located the remains of the 2nd and 5th DCLs. As far as IX Corps was concerned, its line then continued southwards, manned by the Support Group and the 2/6th East Surreys, to Forges-les-Eaux, where as before it connected up at right angles with the Beauman Division's 'B' and 'C' Brigades.

Realizing that the situation of the 51st Division might be doubtful after the fierce fighting of the 5th, General Karslake, though in no way responsible for the activities or direction of this formation, decided to visit its HQ with a view to discovering if there was any way in which he could be of help. He took General Beauman with him, as this officer's command was not far distant. Also, as the reports of casualties which had been received at the HQ of the L of C had been so serious, the General felt that some help from General Beauman's force might prove welcome.

The two Generals motored forward to the site of the 51st Divisional HQ north of the Bresle only to find that it had been evacuated. No one had seen fit to inform HQ L of C of the move. There appeared to be only a weak rearguard in the vicinity and, what was more, information was received that German troops had been seen crossing the River Bresle on either side of the position. Hurriedly the car was turned round and made across the bridge once more, fortunately without encountering the enemy. They appeared just behind the car after it had passed.

Eventually the new HQ was found. General Fortune explained the position and told them that, as a result of the very severe casualties received both in the attack of the 4th and the subsequent fighting on the 5th, two of his Brigades had been seriously reduced in numbers, some of the battalions being less than three hundred men. General Karslake suggested, after consultation with General Beauman, that 'A' Brigade of the Beauman Division, at present situated on the River Béthune some miles to the rear, should be brought forward and used to reinforce the Division. It was also suggested that the brigade which had suffered most should be withdrawn and placed under the command of General Beauman for service in the Beauman line. General Fortune agreed to these suggestions with gratitude. (Actually, no brigade from the 51st Division was withdrawn.) It was further agreed that, should the 51st Division have to withdraw to the Dieppe area, the 2/7th Duke of Wellington's should also come under General Fortune's command.

The conversation then ranged over the whole aspect of the campaign. One particular subject, however, was discussed at length; this was the problem of the Division's withdrawal should the enemy be able to out-flank the defending force on the extreme right of the Corps. General Fortune told the other two of the correspondence which he had had with General Marshall-Cornwall. It was then explained to him exactly the position this officer held and that he was quite powerless to initiate orders or to cancel orders issued by the French. Fortune was astonished at this as he was under the impression that General Marshall-Cornwall had been sent out as Corps Commander. General Fortune then said that if he was forced to withdraw, it would have to be on Le Havre if the Division was to be saved. From the news that the other two Generals had received that morning it seemed that the out-flanking movement was more than a possibility; but, as General Karslake explained, there was no British Commander in France who could issue the order to move even if it meant the saving of the 51st Division from destruction. Nevertheless, he would do all he could to persuade the British Government to provide the necessary authority for him to withdraw the Division before the situation became too dangerous.

The two Generals then left for the HQ of 'A' Brigade. Brigadier Green was given orders to move as soon as possible. He took immediate action. 'A' Brigade moved to its new position south of the Bresle before dark that same evening. Once back at his HQ at Le Mans, General Karslake ordered Colonel Vicary to arrange for reinforcements to be sent forward to the 51st Division so as to enable the battalions to be brought up to strength. As a result, a total of nine hundred men from the depots moved northwards. By the evening of the 6th, therefore, the 51st Division had been reinforced by some 3,000 men, not just 900 as stated in the Official History.

In the meantime Colonel Vicary had been busy raising yet another battalion out of the troops still located in the reinforcement depots. This battalion, (to be known as the 4th Provisional) under Lieutenant-Colonel Syme (Royal Scots), arrived in Rouen during the evening of the 6th. General Beauman, after the discussion he had had during the day, decided that it was essential to strengthen the area to the immediate north of Rouen. If, as appeared likely, the enemy broke through, Rouen would be their most obvious objective. Colonel Syme was, therefore, instructed to put the village of Isneauville in a state of defence. This village lies about five miles north of Rouen and is a road junction of some importance. Two roads, the Amiens — Rouen road via Aumale and Neufchâtel and a road between Rouen and Dieppe, join at the northern end of the village. Both had road-blocks constructed by the Royal Engineers, ready to be closed at any time. In view of the importance of the position, Colonel Syme had been reinforced by four two-pounder antitank guns and a machine gun platoon, lent to him by 'C' Brigade. Immediately on his arrival at the village, Colonel Syme set everyone to work to prepare for a protracted defence. Every possible site was exploited. In due course, Colonel Syme was to prove a particularly galling burr in the side of von Hartlieb.

Also on the 6th, two battalions, which had suffered in the tragic affair of 20 May at Abbeville, were sent forward to reinforce General Beauman. These battalions, the 2/4th KOYLI and the 2/6th Duke of Wellington's Regiment, had been rested and re-equipped as far as possible. With the advent of these three battalions, General Beauman was partially compensated for the loss of his 'A' Brigade. Also his excessive frontage had been much reduced as he was no longer responsible for most of the Béthune sector. General Beauman posted the 2/4th KOYLI to defend the Pont de l'Arche just above Rouen, the 2/6th Duke of Wellington's Regiment being detailed to prevent the enemy from crossing the Seine by the railway bridges some way up-stream.

At 1800 on this same day, General Beauman received a message from General Marshall-Cornwall asking him to come to 10th Army HQ at Lyons-la-Forêt where the latter had set up his HQ. At the conference was also General Evans, commanding the 1st Armoured Division. A notable absentee was General Karslake. As Senior British Officer in France this is surprising to say the least; in fact he was never apprised of the conference.

The reason for this particular conference was the acquisition of an Operation Order from the body of a dead German Officer. This clearly showed the enemy objectives for 7 and 8 June. The objective for the 7th was the approximate line of the Beauman Division in the area of Forges-lex-Eaux; indeed, in part, it was beyond that point.

On the 8th Rouen itself was included. A discussion followed as to how these threats could best be met. General Evans said that, though his tanks were in a bad state, he would arrange for as many as possible to be available in the rear of the Beauman line to render such assistance as they could when the time came.

When the 1st Armoured Division, less the Composite Regiment with the 51st Division, was withdrawn south of the Seine to Louviers to refit, it was the first time since it had landed in France that it was possible for the stores which had been brought over to be unpacked. At last it was possible to refurbish the tanks after their seemingly unending movements. However, even then it was found that much that was needed to refit them was absent. Nevertheless, by the evening of the 6th some 30 Light Tanks and 40 Cruisers were available for action. While but a shadow of its war establishment, at least it provided a useful force.

It was at this meeting that General Beauman raised the question of the withdrawal of the 51st Division and the conversation which had been held at its Headquarters that morning. He was told that a withdrawal at this stage was quite unnecessary; in fact, the French were about to launch an attack to close the gap in the neighbourhood of Poix. General Evans retorted that this operation had been tried before without success; in fact, the French troops, instead of advancing, had at once retreated. The conference broke up; the two Commanders returned to their formations much disturbed at what they had learned. They both agreed that the 51st Division was doomed. General Karslake's representation to the CIGS had likewise proved abortive.

The events of the past three days should have convinced Sir John Dill of the vital necessity of having a British Commander in France. However, on 6 June, he wrote to Brigadier Swayne, of No 2 Military Mission at General Georges' Headquarters, that General Brooke would be coming out to France in about a week; also that the 52nd Division was on its way. Unfortunately General Dill's decision was to prove too late for the men of the 51st Division.

VI

7 June — 13 June

OWING to the rapid deterioration of the situation on the Bresle front and the impending arrival of the 52nd Division, General Karslake sent a telegram to the CIGS on 7 June urging the despatch of the new Corps Commander. He emphasized that this was necessary as, unless an overall commander was on the scene, the chances of the survival of the 51st Division were unlikely. In reply General Dill said that General Brooke could not arrive before the 11th at the earliest, also that the 52nd Division was to come under Karslake's orders, *but was not to be employed piecemeal.*

On 6 June, Lt-General Pownall, the erstwhile Chief of Staff to the BEF, received orders from the CIGS to proceed to France. His mission was to assure the French High Command of the determination of the British to reconstitute a BEF for their support; also to obtain information as to the French situation and intentions. His visits were to include the Headquarters of Generals Weygand and Georges and also to discuss matters with Generals Marshall-Cornwall and Karslake.

General Pownall was able to give Weygand the programme for the arrival of the new divisions in France. The 52nd would sail on 7 June; the Canadians on the 11th and the 3rd Division about 22 June. General Weygand expressed his appreciation of the efforts that were being made but added that speed was the all important factor. Curiously enough, the most important matter which he brought up was the vital role to be played by the Beauman Division, which he considered to be a slender but invaluable asset.

General Georges appeared to be in the gloomiest frame of mind and Brigadier Swayne considered that little hope of assistance could be expected from that quarter.

General Marshall-Cornwall gave a 'run-down' on the present situation on the Tenth French Army front. He considered that the 51st

Division was not 'too badly off'; the French 31st Division had come up and reduced the frontage held by the 51st. (This, it will be remembered, had occurred some appreciable time before. The 31st Division had had considerable casualties since then.) Also, with the advent of Beauman's 'A' Brigade and substantial reinforcements from the depots, the strength of the Division had increased considerably. This notwithstanding the fact that the Division's Brigades had lost some 80%, 60% and 25% respectively.

As far as the 1st Armoured Division was concerned, its total strength in tanks, capable of taking part in operations, was 141. Spares and replacements were minimal and supplies were urgently required.

General Pownall's report on his visit to General Karslake's HQ at Le Mans is of sufficient interest to be quoted verbatim:

> I then went to Le Mans, arriving at 1800 hours, and saw General Karslake. He informed me that Beauman's Force, holding River Béthune south-eastwards from Dieppe, consisted of nine battalions, with a certain number of A/T rifles, A/T mines and 24 A/T guns. A good deal of good work had been done on the river line and demolitions prepared; although it could only be held by small posts, they could give a good account of themselves. He had also collected two battalions of the 46th Division from Rennes (2/4th KOYLI and 2/6th Duke of Wellington's Regiment) and was putting them on the south bank of the River Seine, available for Beauman if required. General Fortune and Brigadier (A/Major-General) Beauman would work in together if a general retreat became necessary, using bridges east of Rouen. Additional arrangements had also been made by the collection of 26 motor barges, for use as ferries, and six ferry boats capable of taking vehicles.
>
> It should be noted that this joint withdrawal by 51st Division and Beauman Force across the Seine is at variance with General Weygand's desire that the Beauman Force should hold out to the last to protect Havre. But General Karslake pointed out, with no little truth, that if the Germans reached the Seine, it was immaterial to the French whether they retain Havre or not.
>
> General Karslake has arranged for the 52nd Division to concentrate, as it arrives, at Evreux where it will be under his orders until it is committed by him to support General Fortune. He urged, very strongly, the need for General Brooke to come out and take over com-

mand of the whole, even if only a reduced staff and signals had to be accepted. He also questioned whether it was desirable for General Brooke to be placed under General Altmayer's command.

According to General Pownall's report, the following telephone conversation between General Marshall-Cornwall and the War Office took place on *8 June*. Giving details of the serious developments which were taking place on the Tenth Army front and the breakdown of the Army HQ, he added:

'Karslake should prepare all possible temporary bridges, boats and ferries over the lower Seine above and below Rouen.' (Of course this had long since been anticipated and done, as we know.) He goes on: 'I have sent up 11 infantry tanks from the south of the Seine to help Crocker hold the Andelle.'[1] These troops were not under his command. By taking such action he had removed the one armoured support force (small though it was) on which General Beauman could rely to help his badly equipped infantry.

Perhaps the most interesting detail contained in the interview between Generals Pownall and Karslake is that referring to the 52nd Division. The proposed concentration area at Evreux clearly shows that, at that time, there was no question of the Division being only employed as part of the projected Breton Redoubt. It would seem that the change of venue to Le Mans must have been decided by the War Office on about 9 June. Though it is stated in the War Diary of the 157th Brigade that, prior to their leaving Southampton on the 7th, there had been rumours that the Brigade was going to Brest. As we will see in due course, this rumour had some foundation.

The River Bresle forms a good obstacle, particularly along its lower reaches where flooding was produced by artificial means. The most dangerous part of the 51st Divisional front was where the enemy had made slight penetrations at Eu and Ponts-et-Marais. Two Battalions of 'A' Brigade, the 1/5th Sherwood Foresters and the 4th Border Regt, made great efforts to eliminate the pockets.

On 5 June the Composite Regiment had been withdrawn from its position behind the Support Group. General Fortune had decided that the 1st Lothian and Border Horse needed support in its efforts to prevent the enemy from penetrating into the Haute Forêt d'Eu.

However, these movements had left the Support Group, such as it was, on its own. It had no prospect of receiving reinforcements nor, indeed, any help from other British troops. It was far removed from the rest of the 51st Division; by this time there were four French Divisions separating them, namely the 31st, 40th Infantry and 2nd and 5th DCL.[2] With the conditions prevailing, Brigadier Morgan could see little merit in his command remaining in such a disadvantageous position. He determined to represent the matter to General Fortune and to suggest that his command should either be withdrawn to the Division or that it should revert to the 1st Armoured Division. It appeared obvious to him that, situated as he was and given the weakness of his troops, he could do little to influence any serious attack by the enemy; he was in imminent danger of having his command cut off and destroyed, having achieved nothing.

It seems that Brigadier Morgan had little sleep during the night of the 6-7th; he was constantly turning over in his mind what was best to be done. By 0630 he had decided that he must go at once to Divisional Headquarters. He also decided that he could not leave his command in such an untenable position.

Before leaving his HQ at Sausseuse-Mare (popularly known as 'Sausage and Mash' by the troops) he issued firm orders that the HQ of the Group should move to a rendezvous at the southern tip of the Basse Forêt d'Eu by 2000 hrs that evening, the remainder of the Group to move off at dusk. At 0800 the Brigadier left for Divisional HQ, leaving Colonel Cameron in temporary command of the Group.

During the 7th the enemy made determined attacks on a number of positions held by the Group, employing both armour and motorised infantry. The situation had been complicated by the fact that French troops were withdrawing through the Group's line before the German advance. Nevertheless, the Group put up a spirited resistance. At length, 'A' Company of the East Surreys was overrun and a number of AT guns were destroyed just south of Aumale. Further south still, other infantry detachments and their accompanying guns received severe casualties. The Germans, were, however, prevented from crossing the Bresle at any point, and even from the places where they had crossed the railway embankment they were forced to withdraw. After this action it was not known by the

Group that the Germans had decided that they were too hard a nut to crack; that they had decided that they would not try and press westwards, but would direct all their energies towards the capture of Rouen.

In the meantime, General Evans, accompanied by Major Dunphie (to act as interpreter) had arrived at French 10th Army Headquarters, in the Forêt de Lyons. With General Marshall-Cornwall, they discussed the situation with the Army Commander, General Altmayer. While they were talking, the sound of a trumpet was heard. General Weygand always travelled with one staff officer and a trumpeter; the latter would sound a long blast announcing the approach of the Commander-in-Chief. This proved extremely useful when roads became congested.

When General Weygand entered, the three British officers withdrew. However, a short time later they were recalled to the conference room. General Weygand then disclosed the situation as far as it was known. Turning to General Evans, he told him that the outcome of the impending battle depended on him and his command. The Armoured Division would be responsible for the defence of the River Andelle and the area as far west as Serqueux. In reply, General Evans explained the weakness of his force. The only concession that General Weygand would grant was that, if it became necessary to withdraw, owing to the impossibility of holding the line, he could cross the River Seine but not, on any account, move towards Le Havre.[3]

On returning to his Headquarters, General Evans issued the necessary orders to his Brigade commanders. He was pleased to find that his GSO I, Colonel Broomhall, had arrived from 51st Division. Colonel Broomhall had been allotted to the 51st Division to advise on the employment of the Composite Regiment.

General Evans considered that, in view of the new situation, it was essential for the whole of his Division to be concentrated once more. It was evident that it was likely to be engaged in a severe battle in the very near future. He decided, therefore, to send Colonel Broomhall back to the 51st Division to explain matters to General Fortune. He was to request that both the Composite Regiment and the Support Group should be released and sent back as quickly as possible to the Armoured Division. (See reference to this matter in

General Karslake's report.)

Immediately after lunch Colonel Broomhall set out on his return journey to 51st Divisional HQ at Château La Grande Vallée, arriving at 1700. He discussed the matter with Colonel Swinburne, GSO I of the Division. Then the two officers, accompanied by Brigadier Morgan, laid the facts, together with General Evans' request, before General Fortune. General Fortune immediately, and generously, agreed. Though he was fully aware of what might arise from the withdrawal of such important units, indeed, how seriously such a move would weaken his position, orders were at once drawn up for the move. In view of the position of the HQ of the Armoured Division when he had left it that afternoon, Colonel Broomhall gave the rendezvous at Les Hogues in the Forêt de Lyons. As the Composite Regiment was Colonel Broomhall's prime responsibility, he despatched a signal at once giving details of the rendezvous. Brigadier Morgan said that he would take the orders personally to his command which he would then accompany to the rendezvous. He placed his copy of the orders in his pocket. As it was getting late, Brigadier Morgan said that he intended to spend the night at Divisional HQ, adding the somewhat cryptic statement that he thought it would be unlikely that he would be able to rejoin his Command.

According to instructions, the Headquarters of the Support Group moved to the rendezvous in the Basse Forêt d'Eu, arriving just after 2000 hrs. The Group Intelligence Officer, with a Section, was left at Sausseuse-Mare to guide the Group Commander should he return there. At dusk the remainder of the Group moved into its new location, taking up defensive positions facing southeast and east. Patrols were sent forward towards Aumale to try and maintain contact with the enemy and also a Company of the Kensington Regiment which had been posted to the north of Aumale in support of the French.

Not long after the Group had moved it was approached by officers from the two DCLs. It seemed that the Group's position ran right athwart the rear of these Divisions. It was felt that this area should be left clear in case it was necessary for these formations to withdraw. Colonel Cameron was in no position to accede to the request that his formation should move. His orders had been quite explicit; he was to remain at the rendezvous until the return of Brigadier Morgan. As he explained to the French, he did not anticipate that it would be very long before the Brigadier returned. Brigadier Morgan not having returned and the importuning of the French increasing, at 0200 on the 8th, Colonel Cameron contacted the HQ of the 51st Division by wireless. He said that the Group had moved to its new position and urgently required orders. The reply was to the effect that orders had been issued and he was to await the return of his Commander. At 0800, as orders had still not been received and there was no sign of Brigadier Morgan, Colonel Cameron, accompanied by his Brigade Major, reported in person at 51st Divisional HQ.

General Fortune was, at first, extremely annoyed that the Group had not carried out his orders of the previous day. On being informed, however, that Brigadier Morgan had not returned, he was astounded. He was aware that the Brigadier had left his HQ at 0500 that morning, ostensibly to return to his command. As he now considered it too late for the Group to carry out the original plan owing to the rapid progress of the enemy, he instructed Colonel Cameron to liaise with the Commander of the French 31st Division, under whose command he would act.

On his return to his HQ, Colonel Cameron found a full return of his strength awaiting him. Of the East Surreys, some 500 all ranks had reported in. The Artillery Regiment still had twenty-three guns out of the thirty-four which had survived the engagement of the previous day. While not a formidable force, nevertheless it was still capable of giving a good account of itself.

That night, on the orders of the 31st Division, the Group moved with the greatest difficulty to the Forêt d'Eawy, once again assuming defensive positions. Some desultory fighting occurred on the 9th. On the 10th, having received orders to revert to the 51st Division, it started on what was to prove a most desperate venture. By this time the Germans had cut right across their rear, and indeed, covered every route by which they could withdraw. Nevertheless, by using every ruse and concealment, the remains of the force, consisting of three hundred all ranks with four guns of the 101st, together with about two hundred all ranks of the East Surreys, arrived in the vicinity of St Valéry-en-Caux. On the morning of the

12th it fought its last action. At 1030 it received orders to surrender.

It is now time to follow the fortunes of the Composite Regiment and of the missing Commander of the Support Group. At 0120 on the 8th a signal had been sent from HQ 51st Division to HQ Armoured Division, stating that both parts of the Armoured Division had reverted to Armoured Division's command. The Composite Regiment had already moved to Fresnoy on its way south. This signal was not received until 0500 at Armoured Divisional HQ. General Evans immediately decided to send orders for the Composite Regiment to link up with the 3rd Armoured Brigade at Vieux-Manoir and for the Support Group to extend the line to Serqueux in support of Beauman's infantry. A signal to this effect was sent at once to HQ 51st Division for onward transmission.

Back at 51st Division HQ, Colonel Broomhall had decided, at 0400, to move to the rendezvous at Les Hogues. At 0500 he left, accompanied, in a separate car, by Brigadier Morgan. An hour later the signal from Armoured Division arrived at 51st Divisional HQ. Colonel Swinburne immediately despatched Major Vere-Laurie with the new orders. He was to locate both the Composite Regiment and the Support Group and ensure that both knew their new positions. The roads were much congested and it was not until midday that Major Vere-Laurie caught up with the Composite Regiment and Brigadier Morgan (who was still accompanying Colonel Broomhall). Having delivered the orders to Major Macdonnel, commanding the Composite Regiment, and to Brigadier Morgan, commanding the Support Group, Major Vere-Laurie rightly considered that he had completed his task. He therefore remained with the Composite Regiment.[4]

Colonel Broomhall, still accompanied by Brigadier Morgan, decided to continue his journey southwards to the new rendezvous, so as to give advance notice of the Regiment's pending arrival to the 3rd Armoured Brigade. Passing through Vieux-Manoir without seeing any signs of the Brigade, he continued southward for a further two miles to the crossroads at Préaux, there to await the Regiment's arrival.

Just north of Vieux-Manoir the Composite Regiment was attacked by an enemy force of tanks from the direction of Serqueux. A brief but severe skirmish took place; the enemy, receiving some casualties, broke off the engagement. The Regiment then went on its way to Préaux. There being no sign of the 3rd Armoured Brigade, it was decided that, in view of the close proximity of increasing enemy strength, the Regiment should continue southwards and cross the Seine at the Pont de l'Arche. Major Macdonnel, however, was very anxious over his petrol position. Even though the engagement had been brief, he had had to consume additional fuel which had reduced his stock to a dangerously low level. Colonel Broomhall volunteered to go forward to Rouen to try and locate some petrol. It was arranged that the Regiment would move from north to south through Martainville. It was reckoned that it would have reached the centre of this town by the time the Colonel returned. Colonel Broomhall and Brigadier Morgan then set off for Darnétal, just north-east of Rouen. There they ran into a small petrol convoy, which Brigadier Morgan identified as one belonging to the Support Group. With Brigadier Morgan's consent, Colonel Broomhall decided to guide it back to Martainville. Mounting the leading lorry, he gave instructions to the driver of his scout car to carry on to Armoured Divisional HQ and explain the position. Meanwhile the Regiment had made better progress than had been anticipated. It had cleared Martainville by the time the convoy arrived. As the convoy turned the corner in the centre of the town, with the object of following up the Regiment, it was intercepted by a German Armoured Force and Colonel Broomhall was captured. He was made to ride on the front of the leading tank which was heading for Rouen. When the column entered Darnétal, Colonel Broomhall was relieved to see that Brigadier Morgan's car was no longer there. Brigadier Morgan arrived at 1st Armoured Divisional HQ during the early hours of 9 June.

In view of the above story, it is as well to examine the details as supplied to the War Office by the Headquarters of the Armoured Division, as given by Brigadier Morgan.

> Meanwhile, Brigadier Morgan had been experiencing a harrassing time. Summoned to a conference at HQ 51st Division, he had left his Headquarters on the previous afternoon (7th). The conference was a protracted one, and he was still at HQ 51st Division when he got news of the German advance and at 0200 hrs on 8 June, the single

13 Troops of the 51st Division on the River Bresle, 8 June, 1940.

14 Conference at Neuborg, 9 June, 1940. *Left to right*—Major E. L. Fanshawe, ADC, Lieutenant-General Marshall-Cornwall, Lieutenant-General Sir Henry Karslake, Major-General R. Evans.

15 The Surrender of the 51st Division at St Valéry-en-Caux, 12 June, 1940. In the foreground—Major-General Erwin Rommel and Major-General Victor Fortune.

16 Arkforce leaving Le Havre, 12/13 June, 1940.

code-word from his own HQ which signified to him that they were moving *but which did not convey to him destination or direction of their movement.*

He set out with Colonel Broomhall hoping to intercept them in what he expected to be a westerly movement. Actually the Support Group and Divisional Engineers had been heavily attacked and either overrun or forced north-westwards, though not before they had inflicted considerable casualties on the enemy by minefields and anti-tank fire. [This action refers to that of the 7th.]

Brigadier Morgan was unable to find his HQ or regain touch with any of his troops, by this time overrun by the German advance, and after much time spent in searching an area full of the enemy's armoured columns, he was forced to abandon his quest, and ultimately to make his way across the Seine with the Composite Regiment.[5]

Actually, the Composite Regiment crossed the Seine at Elboeuf at 1830 on 8 June.[6]

After the departure of Colonel Broomhall, General Evans discussed with his Brigadiers the task which had been set the Division. Owing to the extreme weakness of the 2nd Armoured Brigade, through having had its main strength loaned to the 51st Division, it was decided to produce one brigade of maximum strength until such time as the Composite Regiment returned to command. This was done by the simple expedient of reinforcing the 3rd Armoured Brigade with the surviving squadron of the Bays. Subsequently, Colan's squadron which, it will be remembered, was raised to support Beauman's Division, was put under Brigadier Crocker's command. It should be noted that this was done without reference to either General Karslake or General Beauman.

The original orders were for the 3rd Armoured Brigade to advance to the Gournay area but at about 2000 hrs a message was received from Divisional HQ which at long last threw some light on the hitherto 'very foggy' situation. It was now learned for the first time that two German Armoured Divisions had thrust south and interposed themselves between the French 17th and 31st Divisions, the latter being to the westward and operating with the 51st Division. In view of this development, it had been decided to withdraw the Brigade so as to cover a rough line, including the railway and river crossings between Neufchâtel and Serqueux. This would have had the advantage of prolonging the line designed to be held by the Support Group when it returned from the north. Indeed, for the first time this part of the Armoured Division would come under direct operational command of its parent formation. Unfortunately, this was not to be. As we know, the Support Group never returned to the south and, also, the Germans were moving at alarming speed. The Armoured Brigade had to fall back and, at the same time, cover the rear of the retreating French Infantry. It was at this time that firm orders were issued that the Brigade was not, under any circumstances, to move westwards (so as to avoid being bottled up in the Le Havre area) but, if forced to retreat, was to pass over the Seine by the bridges east of Rouen.

By 2330 the Brigade, with its reinforcing units, had established itself on the river/railway line. This line had, until then, been the responsibility of the right battalion of 'B' Brigade and the left battalion of 'C' Brigade of Beauman's Division. These battalions had the advantage of being supported by a troop of anti-tank guns belonging to Elliott's regiment. Nevertheless, this garrison was very weak and quite unable to prevent the massive oncoming wave of the enemy from crossing the River Andelle. All dispositions had been taken up by dawn on the 8th. It is interesting to note that while the 3rd Armoured Brigade HQ was at Bois Heroult, the HQ of the French 17th Division was at Bosc Edeline; in other words, both HQs were in close proximity to one another, yet there was no liaison between them.

It was not until 1115 that enemy activity became manifest. It was evident that the Germans were advancing in strength and crossing the river at various points. It was quite impossible for the British Armour and Beauman's Infantry to hold the front on their own. Therefore, having ensured that the infantry had safely withdrawn across the river, Brigadier Crocker gave orders for his command to withdraw also. As soon as everyone was safely across, the bridges were blown. The French 17th Division, though fully equipped, had made no effort to hold the line; in fact it never even deployed. As soon as it was evident that the Germans were crossing the river, the whole Division withdrew in a southerly direction.

At 1500 Brigadier Crocker received the news from HQ

Armoured Division that the Composite Regiment (previously with the 51st Division) was to come under his command. Unfortunately, no information was given as to its present whereabouts. It was impossible, therefore, to contact it. Also, at this time, Brigadier Crocker received some discouraging news. This was that the 3 DCL (General Petiet), which was supposed to be acting in support of the 3rd Armoured Brigade, had already crossed the Seine. It was now imperative that Crocker's command should cross the Seine itself with the utmost expedition if it was not to be cut off by the advancing enemy. Orders were therefore issued to begin the withdrawal at 1630. Just as the Brigade was moving off, a liaison officer from Armoured Divisional HQ arrived to say that the Composite Regiment was then some ten miles north-east of Rouen. Officers were sent off to try and intercept the Regiment and instruct it to cross the Seine at Les Andelys. Unfortunately, the officers failed to make contact with the Regiment and, by 0330 on 9 June, the whole of the 3rd Armoured Brigade, together with 'B' and 'C' Brigades of Beauman's Division, were across the Seine.

The French announced that they were sending up reinforcements to cover the Seine crossings which, at that time, were only covered by two battalions of British infantry (2/4 KOYLI and 2/6 Duke of Wellington's Regt). It was suggested that, until these reinforcements arrived, the Armoured Brigade should support these battalions. Fortunately in this instance the French carried out their intentions, thereby releasing the Armour for maintenance purposes.

The three additional battalions which General Karslake had sent forward had been disposed of by General Beauman on the following sites: Syme's 4th Provisional Battalion, with 4 anti-tank guns, covered the main approach roads from the north to Rouen at Isneauville; the 2/4th KOYLI covered the Pont de L'Arche to the south of Rouen, while further east still, covering the river crossings, was the 2/6th Duke of Wellington's Regiment. The complete lack of coordination of the British troops in France at that time was demonstrating, if never before, how essential it was for there to be an overall commander. None of the British commanders had much idea of the actions of each other.

As mentioned above, when the German thrust at Forges and Sigy took place, it was faced by only the lightly equipped brigade of Kent-Lemon. Nevertheless, by the judicious use of his field battery and the arrival of the tanks of the 3rd Armoured Brigade, the Germans were held for a time. The left battalion of 'C' Brigade had also been involved and had suffered severe casualties. Colonel Brittorous, however, was able to withdraw the remainder of his brigade in comparative safety towards the Seine.

The 5th Panzer Division (von Hartlieb) then thrust towards Rouen and, finding little resistance, assumed that all it had to do was to capture the Rouen bridges. The Division took few precautions in its advance, such was its contempt of the French forces which it had so far encountered.

Colonel Syme had had some two days to reconnoitre his position and put it in a state of defence. He realized that, if he was not to be encircled, it was necessary to conduct his defence in depth. He therefore disposed of his force with two companies on either side of the main road just north of Isneauville. He also placed his two platoons of machine guns and his four anti-tank guns in a commanding position, from whence the approach to the village and his flanks could be covered. His two other companies were posted some 1,000 yards to the rear. Under normal circumstances his dispositions were ideal, but he had one major snag with which to contend. This was the continuous flow of both refugees and retreating French troops, who formed an unending stream through his position. Owing to the nature of the terrain some of the troops' positions had been observed from the air. As a result they received considerable attention from enemy aircraft. Fortunately precautions had been taken against such an eventuality and casualties were very light. As soon as the head of the German column was seen approaching Colonel Syme ordered that the road-blocks which he had organized should be closed. This was more easily said than done, as the pressure of the refugees was intense. Curiously enough, it was the Germans themselves who solved the problem. Their leading tank machine-gunned the column of flying people who thereupon dived off the road. Nevertheless, it was almost too late to close the block. However, an officer and two other ranks rushed forward pulling danna-ert wire across the gap and then strewed a number of anti-tank mines in the path of the oncoming tank. All this was done under heavy fire. It should be noted that where the road enters Isneauville it runs between high banks. As a result it was impossible for the approaching tanks to leave the road. The leading tank, having tried to charge the wire barrier, became entangled and was blown up. The second tank, following close behind the first, was unable to turn, and was duly despatched with a round from an anti-tank gun. The third tank suffered the same fate. The enemy, seeing that this approach was impossible, tried to advance on the flank. Here again the anti-tank guns proved their value. Three more tanks were put out of action. This complete hold-up of their plans caused the enemy to deploy infantry on both flanks. For a time the machine guns of the garrison took care of them, causing the enemy to desist. So desperate did the Germans become that they are said to have dropped parachute troops behind the position. (Though this was reported officially, it has never been confirmed by other sources.) The rearward companies, however, were ready for them. Not one survived. It now became obvious to the battalion commander that his forward companies must soon be encircled. He therefore gave orders for them to fall back through those in the rear. Both machine and anti-tank guns then took up similar positions with the rear companies. When the enemy tried their next attack, they found that they met with no opposition. Thinking that the British had withdrawn completely, the column advanced as it had done at first. The second line of the battalion being completely hidden, the Germans never saw the trap until it was too late. Once more the tanks were held up and the guns started their slaughter. This time the casualties inflicted on the enemy were even more severe — nine further tanks were put out of action. In addition an aeroplane which was dive-bombing the position was brought down by a shot from an anti-tank gun.

By this time the Germans had decided that they had had enough. Not unreasonably they considered that until the position had been blasted by artillery, it was too expensive to continue the frontal assault. As soon as the attacks ceased, Colonel Syme, seeing that the road to Rouen was now clear, formed up his command under some trees and marched them quietly back to Rouen in column of threes. At the bridge over the Seine, which the French were preparing to blow, they met with little obstruction other than from refugees. Soon they arrived at their designated rendezvous at Bernay. Rouen sub-area had, in the meantime, closed, to reopen at Lisieux.

As a result of the outstanding action by Colonel Syme and his men the Germans were prevented from entering Rouen until the 9th.

During the afternoon and night of 8-9th the remains of 'B' Brigade crossed the Seine by the ferries at Caudebec, Duclair and Quilleboeuf. In this connection it will be remembered that, just in case of such an eventuality arising, General Karslake had instructed Colonel Alms, the C.R.E. Rouen sub-area, to prepare plans for maintaining the ferries and to provide alternative methods for crossing the river. It was largely thanks to Colonel Alms and his staff that the whole movement was carried out so successfully and without casualties.[7] Having arrived in the Forêt de Brittone the Brigade bivouacked for the remainder of the night. Then Brigadier Kent-Lemon received an order to bring his command to Le Mans. Having adequate transport the move was carried out with little difficulty. On reporting to HQ L of C the Brigadier, to his surprise, discovered that no orders for him to move to Le Mans had been issued. He was ordered to return to the north at once and take up a position to the left of the Beauman Division along the River Risle. The Brigade left for the front on 12 June and arrived in position on the 13th.[8]

In the meantime, the remainder of C Brigade had crossed the Seine and proceeded to the line of the River Risle. The only British troops to the north of the Seine other than the 51st Division and the garrison of Le Havre were the two Territorial battalions guarding the bridges to the east of Rouen in conjunction with the French.

On the 8th General Weygand had, at last, agreed to the removal of the remainder of the AA artillery from Le Havre. Fortunately, owing to the action which had been taken by Brigadier Shilstone on the original orders, many of the guns were ready for immediate movement.

While Colonel Syme's battalion was holding up Von Hartliebs' attack on Rouen Rommel was attempting to capture the bridge at Elbeuf by a coup de main. Racing through the night, he reached Elbeuf in the early hours of the 9th. His attack had been quite unexpected by the French and his formation had met with no resistance after it had passed through Sigy; in fact, many people thought that his formation was British. However, in Elbeuf itself the French troops recognized the formation for what it was and instantly blew the bridges. When Rommel's assault force arrived at 0300 it was too late. There was nothing for it but to withdraw. Rommel realized that, once the attack had failed, his force was in a very dangerous position. He had driven into a pocket formed by the Seine. Had there been sufficient allied troops available, the whole column could have been cut off. Luckily, as Rommel remarks, the Seine valley was swathed in mist, thereby hiding his men from the artillery on the far bank. As a result he was able to withdraw his force largely unscathed.

By the end of the 9th, the situation of the Allied forces in the 10th Army sector was as follows: The 51st Division with the French IX Corps on its right was still on the Bresle line, completely cut off from the remainder of the 10th Army. Below the Seine, from west to east, were the remains of French X Corps. Along the Risle stood the Beauman Division, and loose parts of French Light Cavalry Divisions. The 2/4th KOYLI was at Pont de l'Arche. The 2/6th Duke of Wellington's, supporting the French, were further east, and finally, General de la Laurencie's III Corps.

In the Cherbourg peninsula were the French Dunkirk troops more or less formed into four divisions, though largely unequipped. In addition there were the French fortress troops of Cherbourg. On the British side the second flight of the 52nd Division was landing. Further south additional French formations were being hastily assembled and in the Brittany peninsula the 1st Canadian Division was about to land.

Rommel was now racing towards the Channel in order to cut off the British and French from Le Havre. Von Hartlieb with the 5th Panzers was consolidating his position in Rouen, while, further east, von Manstein's Corps was approaching the Seine at Les Andelys and Vernon.

Having described the gallant action of Colonel Syme's Battalion, it is now time to recount the actions of the other two battalions that General Karslake had sent forward to help in the defence of the Seine crossings.

It was not until 1730 on the 8th that the KOYLI arrived at their destination. Orders from General Beauman specified that they were to hold the far bank of the Seine from Pont de l'Arche to Le Manoir Bridge so as to cover the approaches to both bridges. To the CO's relief, he found that the 23rd AA Battery had already taken up position at Pont de l'Arche. 'A' Company (Captain Wilford) was on the right covering Le Manoir Bridge. Half a mile further north was 'D' Company (Captain Haughton) with a number of Military Police. In the centre at Alizay was 'C' Company (2/Lt Jones) and on the left, covering the Pont de L'Arche at Igoville was 'B' Company (Viscount Gormanston). The remaining companies were on the south bank in reserve. There were many French troops in the area, particularly at Igoville, when the KOYLIs arrived, but at about midnight the French departed, leaving, however, two anti-tank guns in position (with their crews) covering the bridge and approach roads. Action started at about 0445 on the 9th. Some light tanks and lorried infantry appeared from the direction of Rouen. The anti-tank guns made short work of the leading tank and the remainder of the force withdrew to higher ground and carried on a desultory fusillade. In due course the Germans fanned out and became engaged with 'B' Company. At 0600 both bridges were blown and the forward companies were ordered back across the river to join HQ on the south bank. 'A' and 'D' Companies were able to cross the river without interference, near the wreck of Le Manoir Bridge, by means of an improvised ferry service organized by 2/Lt Appleyard. 'B' Company had considerable trouble in crossing, being closely engaged by the enemy. The Company Commander was killed while trying to obtain a boat. 'C' Company was also engaged by the enemy and had to withdraw by platoons. The right-hand platoons crossed with comparative ease but the left platoons had to run the gauntlet of the enemy's fire; they eventually managed to cross by a small bridge some way upstream. In the meantime Lt-Colonel Hodgkinson had received orders from HQ Beauman Division to withdraw and concentrate at Bernay. By the night of the 9th the battalion went into bivouac at Bernay; it was then found that there were some 160 men missing. The 23rd AA Battery was not so fortunate. German dive-bombers had concentrated on its transport, completely destroying all the towing vehicles. The guns, therefore, had to be abandoned.

The 2/6th Duke of Wellington's arrived at Louviers at 1400 on the 8th. The battalion had been ordered to take up positions at two bridges over the Seine, one at Les Andelys and the other at St Pierre-du-Vauvray, about twelve miles distant. There was also a railway bridge about a mile south of St Pierre. The disposition of the troops was as follows:

    'B' Company at Les Andelys
    'C' Company at St Pierre-du-Vauvray
    Stores and transport near Acquigny
    Battalion HQ at Fontaine Bellenger

During reconnaissance the French were found to be holding Gaillon in strength and small detachments were scattered around within the battalion's area. The bridges had been prepared by the French for demolition, the approach to the main bridge at St Pierre-du-Vauvray being covered by a French field gun. The river between the two bridges, however, offered many opportunities for crossing other than by the bridges, owing to the large number of islands and of light craft on the river. The Commanding Officer regarded the task as likely to prove exceedingly difficult unless the French were prepared to cooperate to the full.

In the early morning of the 9th the CO received an order, prefixed with the codename NORA, instructing him to withdraw his troops to Bernay. Not knowing what the name signified, the Colonel decided to ignore it, suspecting that it might be of Fifth Column origin. (Actually it was the code for HQ Beauman Division.)

As a result of the action in which the KOYLI had been engaged the two advanced companies were ordered to withdraw to the south bank of the Seine. The CO then contacted the French commander of his sector and informed him of what had occurred and stated that he would remain in his present position until he had other orders and help the French to deny the river crossings to the enemy. In return the French commander told him that artillery and reinforcements were being brought forward. On his return to his Headquarters the CO found, to his relief, an order from Beauman Division to remain in his present position and take his orders from the French.

It was not until noon on the 9th that reports began to come through that there was enemy activity on the battalion's front. 'C' Company reported that the Germans had crossed the river to their north and were making their way in a westerly direction. Tanks had appeared opposite the bridge at Les Andelys but the bridge had been blown at 1100. 'B' Company, which had taken up new positions to the south of the river, was severely bombarded by mortars. So intense was the barrage that all the LMGs were knocked out and the Company itself, together with the French, had to withdraw to Bernières. At the bridge at Les Andelys 2/Lt Reynolds and six men with a machine gun defended the bridge to the last, firing at close range on the Germans crossing the river. He was eventually wounded and captured. The front of the battalion was now 'contracted' to about two and a half miles, and took up good defensive positions in front of the village of Venables. The actual companies involved were 'A' and 'B', with 'D' in reserve. 'C' was still covering the bridge at St Pierre-du-Vauvray and was supported by HQ Company. As a result of intense bombardment both from artillery and from the air, the French Light Artillery was put out of action completely, and the heavier artillery had to be withdrawn to the south. As the enemy was penetrating on both flanks of 'C' Company, the Commanding Officer went to find Colonel Watteau, the French commander of the part of the line, to obtain reinforcements. Near Louviers he ran into the emergency tank company under Captain Colan and asked for his help. It was as well that he did so, as Colonel Watteau proved to be a broken reed and was completely out of touch with the situation. On his return from the French Headquarters, the Commanding Officer found 'C' Company fighting a rearguard action in the direction of Louviers. The Germans had crossed the main road between HQ Company and 'C' Company and the latter was fighting desperately to maintain its position. Suddenly the tanks arrived and a brisk engagement ensued in which the tanks, in spite of being such a motley collection, behaved with great gallantry. The enemy were forced to break off the engagement.

Fighting in the Venables area continued throughout the morning of the 10th. At 1330 'D' Company reported that they were being outflanked by tanks and that the village of Venables was being severely bombed. 'A' Company reported that the French troops were withdrawing to the rear. The local French commander ordered the Dukes to take up a position near Ailly to reorganize. The 10th Hussars (part of the Composite Regiment), who were now located at Louviers, were asked to cover the withdrawal of the battalion. Three troops immediately advanced and remained with the battalion until General Maillard ordered it to rejoin the remainder of the British troops west of the River Eure. Covered by the 10th Hussars, the battalion successfully broke off the engagement and arrived at Bernay in the early hours of 11 June. The whole of the Beauman Division was now concentrated along the River Risle.

Considering that the 2/6th had been one of the 'labour' battalions, they fought in a manner that did them the utmost credit. If anything should have convinced General Brooke that his attitude towards the Territorial Army was wrong, the action of the 2/6th Duke of Wellington's Regiment should have done so.

On the 9th a conference was held at Armoured Divisional HQ. Present, besides the Divisional Commander, were General Marshall-Cornwall and General Karslake. The state of the Division was discussed. General Evans stated that, unless his tanks underwent a major overhaul, it would soon be impossible to take part in operations. In fact, only about 50 tanks from both brigades could be employed at that time, and then for a short period only. General Karslake considered that it was vital that as many tanks as possible should be sent to the base workshops near Le Mans. If this was thought practicable, he would at once make all necessary arrangements for the tanks' reception. General Marshall-Cornwall expressed his agreement. He said that he would try and persuade General Altmayer, under whom the Division was operating, to release the tanks. As the French had more or less stabilized their front at this time, and as it was agreed that the few surviving tanks of the 2nd Armoured Brigade should remain, General Altmayer agreed.

By 0900 on the 10th, all the tanks of the 3rd Armoured Brigade were on the move southwards. By 1930 the whole body had settled in the Forêt de Perseign. As soon as they arrived, the fitters descended on the tanks and the work of repair and maintenance was begun.

Though it had been hoped that a period of some five or six days might be allowed for the repair work, steps had been taken to ensure that a fighting unit would be available in case of emergencies. Events were moving at such speed that it was quite possible that a situation would arise when an armoured force, however small, could be of the utmost value. A composite Brigade HQ, from the 3rd Armoured Brigade, had been organized, both battalions of which had formed a composite squadron, each complete with transport for immediate action.[9]

It is now time to consider in detail the activities of the advanced part of the 52nd Division. The 157th Brigade, with the 213th Anti-Tank Battery and the 157th Anti-Tank Company, arrived at La Hutte at 1930 on the evening of the 9th. Brigadier Sir John Laurie, the commanding officer, visited L of C Headquarters and reported his arrival to General de Fonblanque. He was told to billet his Brigade locally, pending the arrival of the remainder of the Division. General Karslake had been out all day trying to arrange for further equipment to be supplied to the various units of the Beauman Division, which had lost a number of small arms in their withdrawal south of the Seine. On his return to Le Mans late that evening he learnt of the disposition of the 157th Brigade. In view of the seriousness of the situation in the forward areas, he decided that the Brigade could be put to better use by providing a defensive position in the locality. In the morning, therefore, he sent for Brigadier Laurie and instructed him to put the village of Beaumont into a state of defence. He pointed out that, as his orders were that the various formations of the Division were not to be used until the whole Division was assembled, it was most unlikely that any move would be made for at least four days. During his conversation with the Brigadier the General learnt, to his utter astonishment, that the Brigade had never fired its anti-tank guns or anti-tank rifles; in fact, very few of the personnel had ever seen a tank! In view of this, the General decided to try to make good these deficiencies by arranging firing practice soon after the Brigade had taken up its positions and, at the same time, for the tanks of the rear HQ of the Armoured Division to provide a demonstration.[10]

During the afternoon the Brigadier made the necessary plans for the all-round defence of Beaumont. The following day the various units made recces of their designated positions and arranged details for their firing practise on 12 June.[11]

On 11 June Mr Churchill, accompanied by Mr Eden and the CIGS, Sir John Dill, arrived at the Château de Muguet near Briare for a meeting of the Supreme War Council. On the French side were Pétain, de Gaulle, de Margerie, Colonel de Villelume and their Prime Minister, Paul Reynaud. Mr Churchill told the French that, with the 1st Canadian Division landing in France that night, there would be four British divisions ready for immediate use and yet another division would be arriving within a week. While the French were pleased to hear this news, they were particularly depressed by the actual situation on the various fronts. General Weygand was called in to give a situation report. What he told the assembled company was singularly discouraging. He regularly emphasized the fact that he had no reserves left; that those French troops who had escaped from Dunkirk were largely disarmed and it would take some time before they could be utilized again. Mr Churchill tried to encourage them by saying that every day the fighting forces held out the stronger they would become, while the Germans would be exhausting themselves by their efforts and their very long Lines of Communication. These latter were becoming more and more vulnerable to air attack. But Weygand was not to be convinced; he replied that it was not a question of days or weeks, but of hours. It was at this point that General Dill interjected with an astonishing offer. He informed General Weygand that, in view of circumstances, he was at liberty to use the British troops in France as he saw fit, *even to the extent of not being bound to use them as complete formations.* Such an astounding statement made the whole of the British delegation gasp. Once it had been made, however, there was no drawing back, though all knew that they were condemning, once again, small and incomplete formations to fight without proper command or support.

Weygand was not slow to take advantage of the offer. A telephone call was put through to General Karslake at Le Mans, instructing him to arrange for the '52nd Division under General Laurie' to advance and place itself under the command of General de la Laurencie commanding III Corps. When the call came through, General Karslake was out and it was not until the evening that he learned of it. Not being able to credit the genuineness of the order, in view of the strict instructions he had received on the subject, he himself put through a call to Briare. The order was confirmed by a French staff officer who added that General Dill was present. General Karslake then requested that General Dill should come to the telephone to confirm the order personally. He was informed that Dill was engaged. The General then said that, while he was prepared to implement the order to the extent of arranging for the move of the 157th Brigade, he required a confirmation of the order in writing. At 0830 on the morning of the 12th General Dill wrote out the order.

As agreed General Karslake wasted no time after he had made his call to Briare. He first telephoned to General Drew, GOC 52nd Division, at Cherbourg, informing him of the situation and asking him to issue the necessary orders to the 157th Brigade. He then arranged with the staff to plan the move which he had now learned was to be made to Conches. General Drew arrived at Le Mans at 0200 accompanied by, among others, his CRA, Brigadier Kennedy. As no artillery, other than the 213th anti-tank Battery, was to accompany the Brigade, Brigadier Kennedy was co-opted to help in the movement. By 0300 most arrangements had been made, and the GOC of the Division visited the Brigade to ensure that all orders were clear and understood. The schedule provided that the Brigade should move out by 0630. The whole organization for the move had taken five hours.[12]

In view of the fact that the Brigade was to operate under orders of III Corps, the Brigade Commander proceeded to HQ of the French 10th Army at Orbec, where it had been arranged for him to meet General de la Laurencie. The General would issue instructions as to the role the Brigade was to play.

At 0630 the leading unit, the 6th Bn The Highland Light Infantry, crossed the starting line. Though the whole move started well, the timings were nearly ruined by the closing of a railway crossing and heavy refugee traffic. By 1300 the whole column had arrived at St Maurice-les-Charencey where orders were received from the Brigadier that the Brigade was to take up positions west of Breteuil. Instructions were issued accordingly. This was but the beginning of the series of conflicting orders that were to be issued by the French command. At 1600 the Brigadier rejoined the Brigade and said that the orders had been changed, that the Brigade should move forward to a position three miles west of Conches. The Brigade moved again and arrived at its new position at 2200. At 2330 yet another order arrived from French HQ to the effect that defensive positions should be taken up along the railway from Évreux to Bacquepuis and, if possible, to advance to the next railway line *that day*. Notwithstanding that this order had been timed at 1700, but a short time after the Brigadier had left French HQ, it had taken over six hours to reach the Brigade. Obviously it was impossible to execute when it was received as there had been no time for reconnaissance or liaison with the French troops in the vicinity. Also, though it was not known at the time, the nearest French troops on the right were some twelve miles distant. It was finally decided that the Brigade should advance by bounds from Conches, particularly as constant rumours were coming in as to the location of the enemy.[13]

During the morning of the 13th the Brigade assumed the following positions:

> South Sector, from Conches to where railway crossed the line west of Glissoles—6 HLI.
> Centre Sector, to la Bonneville (including La Bretonnière) — 1st Glasgow Highlanders.
> North Sector, Ferrière-Ht-Clocher—Portes thence refusing left to Faverolles — 5 HLI.
> One troop of the anti-tank Battery was with each Battalion.

At 1500 Colonel Thomas and some officers of the French 72nd Artillery Regiment arrived at Brigade HQ. It will be remembered that the Brigade had moved forward without any artillery. The French had agreed to supply the deficiency. The Brigadier explained the situation and indicated the tasks which he wished to be carried out. At 1700 the Brigade HQ moved to Burey and the HQ of the French Artillery Regiment set up adjacent to it.

For the remainder of the 13th the troops prepared their positions and the Brigadier made all arrangements possible with the French Artillery for supporting fire to be given for the engagement which was likely to take place the following day. Liaison had been established with the French 3rd D.L.M. who provided them with the 127th Groupe de Reconnaissance to safeguard the Brigade's right flank. This unit was placed under the command of the 157th Brigade. As far as possible all had been done to prepare for any eventuality that was likely to arise. But there was something with which the Brigadier would be unable to contend, the behaviour of the French.[14]

Soon after the departure of the 157th Brigade, General Karslake held a conference at his HQ. It was generally agreed that the prospects for the Brigade were, to say the least, bleak. Brigadier Kennedy stated that it would be some days before any of the divisional artillery would be ready for action. All felt that the promise of artillery support by the French was extremely problematical. Intelligence reports and aerial surveys had shown that the enemy were making swift progress after their crossing of the Seine at Vernon and Les Andelys. Though the number of French appeared to be considerable, at least on paper, it was obvious that they were trying to hold too wide a front. Also their morale was anything but high.

Perhaps the two most important factors which were to influence the General's final decision were, first, that the only British troops in the 157th Brigade's area were the very small and weak armoured force represented by the few tanks of the 2nd Armoured Brigade and the right-hand brigade of Beauman's Division. Indeed, this latter formation had been considerably reduced in numbers since the actions north of the Seine; their equipment was in very short supply and they were spread very thinly on the ground. It should also be remembered that, in any event, this formation had been removed from the General's command on the 11th and placed under the French 10th Army.

Secondly, though the whole of both the 52nd Division, less, of course, the 157th Brigade, and the 1st Canadian Division were under General Karlsake's command, neither of these formations were likely to be ready for employment for some considerable time. This left only the armoured units being refitted near Le Mans, which could be used to give, at least, some support to the 157th Brigade. Yet another factor was the inexperience and lack of training of the 157th Brigade. While the enthusiasm and quality of its personnel were beyond question, these assets could not hope to match the massive and highly trained forces of the enemy. It was finally agreed that, though the ordering of the 157th Brigade to advance was a military error and should never have taken place, every effort should be made to give it a chance for survival.

At the conclusion of the conference, General Karslake telephoned to the rear HQ of the Armoured Division at La Hutte to ask for the position of tanks available if called upon to return to the front. The reply was reasonably reassuring. However, when it was suggested that the Divisional Commander should be contacted, it was said that this was impossible, the rear HQ being completely out of touch with General Evans. The General then tried to contact 17 Military Mission, again without success.

While this was going on, further information was coming in regarding the progress of the enemy. Indeed, the situation had now become so serious that General Karlsake realized that desperate measures must be taken. He also realized that if he tried to contact either General Evans or General Marshall-Cornwall by despatch rider, the reply would take so long to reach him that the delay might prove fatal.

The General then telephoned once again to rear HQ Armoured Division. He spoke to Brigadier Crocker, to whom he explained the whole situation. While sympathetic, Brigadier Crocker said that, as he was not under General Karslake's orders and, as he knew that it was against his Divisional Commander's policy, he regretted that he was unable to comply with the General's request to provide help for the 157th Brigade. This was not to be the only time that Brigadier Crocker 'regretted' his inability to help the 157th Brigade. The General, for his part, while appreciating the Brigadier's attitude, considered that he could not accept his refusal. He first gave Brigadier Crocker a direct order to move with every available tank to Conches, with a view to supporting the 157th Brigade. On arrival at Conches he was to report to Sir John Laurie and, as soon after that as possible, to inform General Evans of the reasons for the action. Unfortunately even this order was insufficient to move Brigadier Crocker. It was not until the order was given in writing, over the General's own signature, that Brigadier Crocker gave orders for his composite 3rd Armoured Brigade to advance. This order read, 'Proceed at once to Conches with any tanks available and fit, reporting to your Adv. HQ even if some drop out on the way. There must be no delay. Situation critical.' Much valuable time had been lost.[15]

Even before his command had started on its way towards Conches, Brigadier Crocker had left by car to inform his Commander of what was happening. In his report, Brigadier Crocker states that he hoped to intercept the Brigade at Aigle (presumably with the object of withdrawing it on the orders of his Divisional Commander). On arrival at the place where Brigadier Crocker believed the HQ of his Division was situated, he was informed that it was thought that the General had gone to 10th Army HQ at Orbec. Brigadier Crocker eventually caught up with General Evans at Orbec, where the latter had now set up his new HQ.

General Evans states that up to the time he finally left France he never received any explanation as to why the 3rd Armoured Brigade had been sent back to the line. This is strange as Brigadier Crocker had been given explicit instructions, orally, to inform General Evans. Furthermore Brigadier Laurie was also in Orbec at this time when he saw both General Altmayer and General Marshall-Cornwall. General Evans continues: 'No one, either in the Military Mission or at 10th Army HQ, could understand why the Brigade should have been ordered to Conches'.[16] However, in view of Brigadier Laurie's presence, together with the orders received by General Marshall-Cornwall from the CIGS, plus the information received by General Altmayer from General Weygand's HQ, this statement seems open to question.

As General Evans had decided before the arrival of the 3rd Armoured Brigade that it was essential for the remains of the 2nd Armoured Brigade to be relieved, the 3rd should be used for this purpose, and he instructed Brigadier Crocker accordingly.[17] Brigadier Crocker returned to his command and the whole harboured for the night at Le Chete. Brigadier Crocker says: 'During the evening I discovered that the 157th Brigade of the 52nd Division was arriving at Conches'.[18]

At 0700 on the 13th Brigadier Crocker received orders to proceed northwards to Thibouville to relieve the 2nd Armoured Brigade: he was to come under the Command of the 3rd DCL (General Petiet). Barely had the Brigade arrived when new orders were received that it was now to come under the command of General François, commanding the 237th French Division. General François told Brigadier Crocker that, as there was a gap of some five miles between his right flank and the newly-arrived 157th Brigade, his Brigade was required to cover that gap until reinforcements arrived. The Brigade was to position itself *so as to be able to support either the right flank of the 237th Division or the 157th Brigade.*

At about 1530 the 3rd Armoured Brigade had taken up its positions — HQ and the 2nd RTR at Barc and the 5th RTR at Barquet. That evening the promised reinforcements arrived. These consisted of the 236th Demi-Brigade and a medium machine gun battalion. The gap, at least in theory, was now filled, but the original instructions regarding support were not cancelled. In due course it will be seen how the ordering of the tanks forward was to benefit the 157th Brigade.

It is now time, once again, to return to the 51st Division. It will be remembered that it had take up defensive positions along the River Bresle. 'A' Brigade, some 2,000 strong, was on the left, then the 153rd Brigade. When orders were at last received for all the troops, both French and British, to retire from the Bresle line, General Fortune planned that the two forward Brigades should leap-frog back through those in the rear. These two Brigades, the 154th and the 152nd, were to occupy the line of the River Béthune. The withdrawal took place during the night of the 8-9th and, though much impeded by refugees and other traffic, was carried through successfully. The enemy failed to interfere owing largely to the action of 'D' Company (Major Hopkinson) of the 4th Border Regiment, which held the crossing at Incheville, and 'A' Company of the 1/5th Foresters, which held a crossing further up river. Owing to these companies being cut off when the orders came to retire, they never received them. As a result they continued to hold these crossings for another four days until they found that they were the last British in action north of the Seine. The greatest credit must be given to these two units, as not only were they completely unsupported during the whole period, but also they consisted of second-line Territorial troops.

On the 9th General Fortune received a message from the French Admiral at Le Havre, confirmed by a despatch rider who had been sent by Colonel R.B. Butler, who was commanding the small British garrison, that the enemy had occupied Rouen and were making, it appeared, for the coast. General Fortune, in consultation with General Ihler, decided that the projected move to Rouen was now a thing of the past. If their formations were to be saved it was now only possible to make for Le Havre and hope that the Navy would be able to evacuate them from there.

The French Admiral at Le Havre fully appreciated the way the situation was developing and sent a message asking for shipping to be arranged for lifting some 85,000 Allied troops from Le Havre to Trouville. General Dill questioned whether this was in accordance with General Weygand's plans. He understood that the idea was for the force to withdraw either side of Rouen; this he considered to be the correct procedure. Unfortunately Dill was not to know that this plan was long since dead, owing to the delay by Weygand in giving the necessary orders for the force's withdrawal. General Karslake had reiterated on several occasions that the withdrawal should be speeded up but, owing to the position in which the CIGS had placed him, he was in no position to insist on such action being taken. General Dill, however, considered that his was the right plan and should be adhered to. He informed the No. 1 Mission at General Weygand's HQ to this effect. However, he was to be disillusioned, as General Fortune was able to send a message through to Le Havre to the effect that he was withdrawing on Havre and added in a subsequent message:

> Ninth Corps including 31st and 40th French Divisions and two weak Cavalry Divisions moving west to Le Havre. 51st Division on sea. Sending rear-guard to reinforce French on line Fécamp — Lillebonne.
>
> My speed depends on French movement about 20 Kilos a day. [It should be remembered that whilst the British were a mechanized Division, the French were largely horse-drawn.] Tomorrow morning, line should be Dieppe. Essential that air delay enemy movement mostly AFV to south on Saint Saëns — Bolbec Road, also his infantry advance from the east. Air support requested to prevent unrestrained bombing. Naval support along the coast also of great moral support. If enemy break through French or cut me off from Le Havre will attempt on one of northern ports or in hope of evacuating

a few men from behind bridgehead. My rearguard assisting French Fécamp — Lillebonne has orders to drive on Le Havre to attempt embarkation as many men as possible.

Thus it was not until the night of the 9th that General Dill at last appreciated the situation, though Weygand still clung to the idea that the force could cross the Seine at Rouen.

General Fortune's statement that 'my rearguard assisting French' requires expanding. Having decided that the only hope his Division had of extricating itself from the envelopment by ten German Divisions was by withdrawing on Le Havre, the General, in consultation with the Commander of the French IX Corps, gave orders for a force to be assembled to safeguard Le Havre prior to the Division's arrival. This force consisted of both 154th Brigade and 'A' Brigade of Beauman's Division, together with two regiments of Field Artillery and Engineers with appropriate supply units. It was intended to combine with two French Battalions and some artillery already understood to be in position between Fécamp and Lillebonne. This small British force started off promptly during the night 9-10th and made good progress towards Fécamp. Luckily, the greater part of the Force had passed through Fécamp before the leading elements of Rommel's command arrived. Nevertheless part of 'A' Brigade became engaged. After a sharp encounter the Brigade managed to force its way through with a minimum of casualties, only one wireless lorry being lost. This vehicle had been intended to maintain communications between Arkforce, as the above formation was called, after Arques-la-Bataille where it was formed, and the 51st Division.

It soon became obvious to the Commander of Arkforce, Brigadier Stanley-Clarke, that there was little hope of maintaining a line along the front which had been designated, the French having made little or no effort to provide any form of defences. He therefore determined to withdraw to Le Havre. Further, it was obvious that, the enemy having reached the sea in strength south of the divisional position, there was no likelihood of the Division joining them at Le Havre. As part of his instructions the Brigadier had been told that, if the situation warranted it, he was to evacuate all British personnel. This was, of course, a wise thing to do. Unfortunately the orders contained an additional instruction to the effect that, if such an evacuation became necessary, all artillery was to be destroyed. Le Havre had undergone severe bombing attacks and all power had been cut off. This meant that all cranes had been rendered useless. Efforts were made to load certain vehicles by means of ramps but this proved extremely difficult and had to be abandoned. It was decided, though, that an attempt should be made to save valuable vehicles by means of crossing the Seine either by the ferries at Caudebec, if they could be reached in time, or by vessels at Quillebeuf nearer the mouth. It will be remembered that the 14th Royal Fusiliers had been stationed, as the British part of the garrison, at Le Havre. Lt-Colonel Heselton decided, when he was informed that evacuation was inevitable, to try and send his transport and heavy baggage by the river crossings. In this he was completely successful. The whole of the transport, under the command of the Quartermaster, made the journey successfully. In the meantime the troops were embarked and sailed for their appropriate destinations — the 154th Brigade to England via Cherbourg and 'A' Brigade to Cherbourg.

There are two points of interest about this evacuation. First, while it is admitted that the power was no longer available to work the shore cranes, the ships' derricks were, apparently, never brought into play. There is, however, one bright spot. It would seem that a junior officer of the 17th Field Regiment arranged for the derricks to be rigged on one ship, thereby saving several guns.[19] Secondly, there is little doubt that if orders had not been given to destroy the guns, many of them could have been saved in a way similar to that which saved the Fusiliers transport. So far, no explanation has been forthcoming as to why this latter course was not adopted. It has been suggested that it was the direct result of orders that left the Commander no discretion.

As the 51st Medium Regiment RA was a somewhat slow-moving unit General Fortune issued orders that it should precede the Division. On 7 June, therefore, it moved southwards with a view to crossing the Seine at Rouen. Unfortunately it arrived at the Rouen bridge after the 4th Provisional Battalion had arrived and the bridge had been blown. The CO therefore reported back to 51st Divisional HQ. He was told to try the ferries west of Rouen. In this he was fortunate as the ferry at Caudebec was still operating. The remains of the Regiment was able to cross and was eventually evacuated through Cherbourg.

After the debacle at Abbeville on 20 May, it will be remembered that the 2/7th Duke of Wellington's Regiment had been posted by Brigadier Beauman as a garrison for Dieppe. There it had remained until absorbed by the 51st Division during its withdrawal. It provided yet another 700 reinforcements which were to prove their value during the last days of the Division before its capitulation. Like the Territorial regiments of 'A' Brigade and, notwithstanding the fact that it was one of the 'labour' battalions, it showed the fighting spirit of a first line battalion. On arrival at Veules-les-Roses it combined with a French battalion, presenting a staunch front to the attacking enemy. The remainder of the Allied forces withdrew on St Valéry-en-Caux. Meanwhile, the Royal Navy had taken measures to evacuate the troops from their almost hopeless position. The Commanding Officer of the 2/7th Duke of Wellington's noticed the signals from a destroyer lying off-shore, so when the time came for him to withdraw, he was able to contact the ship, thereby obtaining passage for himself and his men. Other troops also were able to take advantage of the ships which, though under heavy gunfire from the German batteries, remained as long as possible in the hope of rescue.

Through a series of misunderstandings and, of course, the weather, few other troops could be taken off as the enemy had complete command of the approaches both to the beaches and the harbour of St Valéry. At 1100 on the morning of 12 June the Allied force capitulated. It had destroyed all its guns and transport, thereby ensuring that little of value had been left for the enemy. Of the 51st Division, only 2,137 men were saved but, in addition, 2,222 men, representing the 154th Brigade, had been evacuated to England and a further 8,837 men of 'A' Brigade and other units had been brought round to Cherbourg — a total of 13,196 out of about 25,000 when the Division left the Saar. The 51st Division had fought to the last and there was no alternative but surrender. A further considerable loss of lives would have gained nothing.

It must be pointed out that, though the 51st Division was particularly strong and had been well reinforced after the Abbeville affair, neither it nor the French IX Corps were capable on their own of staving off the attack of nine enemy divisions, two of them Armoured. The French movements were far too slow to allow the Force to escape from the trap that was closing round it. General Weygand simply refused to face facts and his orders, sound as they may have been under different circumstances, were issued far too late to be acted on. The operations were being carried out at such a speed that orders had to be issued, and carried out, with equal celerity. Those officers who were on the spot, or who were in a position to see for themselves the way that the battle was developing, realized that nothing short of a miracle could save the left wing of the French Tenth Army once the enemy had cut in between it and its right wing. No one had the authority to alter or modify the orders of the Generalissimo, though it was known that the orders, when received, were out of date. The British had no one to whom to appeal. No right of appeal had been given to any British Commander in France after the departure of Lord Gort (though see Chapter X). In fact it was not until the arrival of General Brooke, with similar instructions as had been issued to Lord Gort, that the British forces in France could feel themselves in any degree safe from the failure of the Allied Commander to take action in time.

On 11 June the state of affairs at British Headquarters was most confusing. It will be remembered that General Karslake had been instructed to put the 157th Brigade and the Beauman Division under French command. This left his defensive troops reduced to a minimum. The 52nd Division was by no means complete. The 35th Brigade had been ordered back to England. 'A' Brigade of Beauman's Division was not yet back in his area. The 2/7th Duke of Wellington's and the 2/6th East Surreys were with the 51st Division. But in the meantime the first flight of the 1st Canadian Division had embarked at Plymouth.

The 1st Canadian Division had landed in England during December, 1940. It consisted of some 16,000 troops and was commanded by Major-General A.G.L. McNaughton. Though strong in numbers, the men had had little previous training and possessed little in the way of arms other than rifles. As soon as possible after arrival every effort was made to remedy these shortcomings. However, though the three regiments of artillery were soon equipped with a full complement of the most up-to-date 25 pounder guns, there was a serious shortage of both LMGs and mortars. Also, anti-tank weapons were in very short supply.

By the end of May much progress had been made in training but even this was seriously interrupted by various alarms. For example, there was a projected move to Norway which required the complete abandonment of exercises and cancelling of firing practice. Then again, urgent appeals were made by Lord Gort, when at Dunkirk, for sending over the Division in order to ease the situation of his troops on the perimeter. Luckily for the Division none of these enterprises came to anything.

It was after the decision not to send the Division to France to reinforce the BEF that General McNaughton heard on 26 May that it was intended to use the Division as part of the new BEF. But it was not until 9 June that firm orders were issued for the movement of the troops to their port of embarkation. Indeed, it was not until 11 June that the Divisional Commander was actually provided with the final details of the projected expedition. On this day the new Corps Commander, Lieutenant-General Sir Alan Brooke, visited the Division for the first time. He arrived while a briefing conference was being held and 'chaired' the final part of it. After the conference was over, General Brooke and General McNaughton moved off together for a private discussion. It was during this discussion that General Brooke handed to General McNaughton a draft copy of the operational instruction for the employment of the new Corps.[20] As this Instruction is of the greatest importance, it is quoted below in toto:

(1) The Political object of the re-constituted BEF is to give moral support to the French Government by showing the determination of the British Empire to assist her Ally with all available forces.

(2) The Military object of 1 Canadian Division is, in conjunction with other formations of II Corps, to threaten from the general line NAZAIRE ... RENNES ... PONTORSON the flank of a German advance towards LE MANS ... ANGERS-NANTES and relieve pressure on the French Army by drawing German forces westwards.

(3) The coasts of the Peninsula projecting westwards about 150 miles from the line NAZAIRE ... PONTORSON have deep water close to the shores and there are many good harbours. The average width

from North to South is about 70 miles. The flanks of a force operating in this area can be supported by the Navy. The country is hilly, and intersected by many rivers and well-wooded. From a study of the map it does not appear to be suited to the employment of large armoured formations. Apart from its extent, it is thus a favourable theatre for the operations visualized by the British forces available.

(4) II Corps of the BEF consists of the following formations:
52 Division: Landing at NAZAIRE and assembling North of the Port.
1 Canadian Division and ancillary troops: Landing at BREST and assembling N.E. of the Port.
Remnants of 51 Division.
Remnants of 1 Armoured Division.
II Corps Troops.

(5) It is the intention of the Corps Commander to concentrate the whole of II Corps in the area North and South of RENNES as soon as formations are assembled.

(6) Thus there are two divisions, part of a third, part of an armoured division and II Corps troops available for operations within the area defined above. A division may have to hold 50 miles of the front . . .

Though this Instruction was due to be issued to the various formations after their arrival in France, this was not done. In fact, had it not been for the action of General McNaughton in attaching it to his Divisional War Diary, it is highly unlikely that a copy would be available today. As it was, the War Diary was made up to date before the first flight of the Division left for France and was deposited with the Canadian Military Headquarters in London for safekeeping.

This Instruction provides one with a number of interesting points:

(1) The date of the Instruction, prepared by Divisional HQ from that given to McNaughton by Brooke, is 13 June.

(2) The line to be taken up by the new BEF was identical to that designed for the 'Breton Redoubt'.

(3) A War Office Instruction issued on 6 June clearly gives the Ports of Disembarkation as Cherbourg for the 52nd Division and Brest for the Canadian Division. Also, the procedure for assembly was to be the same as for Plan 'W' issued to the original BEF before their departure for France in 1939. It must be assumed that the War

Office Instruction of the 6th (See Appendix E) was based on the decision of the Chiefs of Staff. General Dill, as CIGS, was, of course, a member. Mr Churchill had, on 2 June, issued a memo to the Chiefs of Staff with M. Reynaud on 31 May, at which the question of organizing the 'Breton Redoubt' was raised and the promises given to send troops to France as soon as possible. As is already known, these promises were duly confirmed by General Pownall during his visit to France.*

Bearing in mind the details of the War Office Instruction issued on the 6th, it is interesting to speculate why it was changed, as far as ports were concerned, to that in possession of General Brooke on the 11th. From the evidence, it would seem that General Brooke's Instruction was an even *earlier* one, issued between 2 and 6 June. If this is so then it is difficult to understand why General Brooke retained the earlier one as he must have been aware that it was out of date, owing to the movements of the 52nd Division. One must assume that he was issued subsequently with the revised version. If not, then it certainly seems incredible as a copy had been sent to both General Karslake and General Marshall-Cornwall. It would have been essential for the overall Commander to have the same information. General McNaughton states that he was considerably upset at finding that his command was being sent forward to the area near Le Mans instead of the district scheduled in the Instruction that he had received from General Brooke. Yet, as we know, the Instruction of 6 June clearly stated that the assembly areas were to be similar to those utilised by the BEF in 1939. In spite of considerable research, it has not been possible to discover whether General Brooke had the Instruction of the 6th in his possession.

The leading part of the first flight of the Canadian Division consisted of all the 1st Brigade transport, together with the guns and transport of the 1st Field Regiment, RCHA. This latter unit was under the command of Lieutenant-Colonel J.H. Roberts, who, as Major-General Roberts, commanded the Dieppe raid in 1942. It disembarked at Brest on the 12th and left immediately by road for the assembly area at Sablé-sur-Sarthe.

The second part of the flight, consisting of 1st Brigade HQ,

---

* See p. 152.

together with its Commander, Brigadier A.A. Smith, and the main body of infantry of the Brigade landed on the 13th. These troops left Brest by rail in three trains. Train number one carried the HQ and the 48th Highlanders; number two, the Royal Canadian Regiment and number three, the Hastings and Prince Edward Regiment. As will be seen, only train number one was destined to arrive at its destination. The artillery and transport arrived at Sablé-sur-Sarthe safely and were duly billeted in their quarters.[21]

Owing to the projected arrival of the new Corps, the 6th Royal Sussex were at Blain busily acting as labour for all the supplies which still kept pouring into France through Nantes and St Nazaire. The only reserves, if such they could be called, were the 12th Royal Warwicks undertaking guard duties at Le Mans and other local vulnerable points. It was quite obvious, therefore, that if the line failed to hold on the Risle, there was nothing to prevent the enemy driving through into the very heart of the L of C. The morale at Headquarters had been low on his arrival, but General Karslake had made a considerable impression on all with whom he had come into contact by his enthusiasm and example. With this final blow, however, all that good work was undone. Everyone realized that, having no force under British command on whom they could rely, the prospects were anything but bright. There is no doubt that, from that moment, everyone began to look to his safety. The small spark which had been kindled with so much effort began to die. At 1400 on the 13th it was finally extinguished. It was at that time that General Brooke arrived at Le Mans to assume command of the British forces in France.

General Brooke's arrival off the coast of France on 12 June was unfortunate. Owing to it being after dark, the Admiral at Cherbourg refused to allow his ship to enter. As a result it had to anchor outside till dawn. Eventually the General was able to obtain a launch to take him and General Eastwood ashore. Owing to the upset over his arrival, the RAF had not been able to provide an aeroplane to take him to Le Mans. It was necessary therefore for him to travel by car. One can imagine that, on arrival at Headquarters, he was not in the best of tempers. He was greeted by General Karslake and General de Fonblanque. Accompanied by General Eastwood, the three men proceeded to the War Room. General Karslake gave

General Brooke a complete summary of the situation as it then was, from the point of view of the British command. Unfortunately there exists no record of what transpired at the end of this meeting. All that is known for a fact is that General Brooke exercised his authority by curtly dismissing General Karslake having, as he said, no further use for him and suggesting that once he had put General Brooke's staff 'in the picture' he should return to England without delay. At 1500 General Brooke left by car for the Château de Muguet to see General Weygand. At 1600 General Karslake, accompanied by his GSO 2, left by aeroplane for England. The RAF did all they could to make his departure comfortable. It is related that so quietly did General Karslake leave that practically no one in the Headquarters building was aware of his departure. Likewise, so quickly had General Brooke proceeded southwards that he failed to notify anyone of the change in command.

On arrival at Briare General Brooke went to see General Howard-Vyse, head of No. 1. Military Mission to General Weygand, in order to arrange a meeting with the Commander-in-Chief. Unfortunately General Weygand found that it would not be possible to see General Brooke that day, saying that he was at a Cabinet meeting. He would see him, however, at 0830 the following morning.

Even as late as 13 June the War Office was still seriously considering the re-formation of the new BEF. During the morning of the 13th, on instructions from the War Office, there gathered together at the Headquarters at Le Mans the leading Engineers of the L of C under the direction of the Chief Engineer, General Cave-Brown. In view of the loss of Le Havre and the fact that the port of Cherbourg was virtually in the front line, it was considered that another port, farther south, should be developed for use as an alternative inlet for personnel. The port selected was La Pallice, the port for La Rochelle. It was necessary, therefore, for a survey to be made for the purpose of planning the Transit Camps and Reception Centres for the new formations and also the general development of the port. The officer selected to command the survey team was Brigadier McMullen, the Director of Transportation. After the conference, the survey party left Le Mans for La Rochelle. From then until 16 June the appropriate examination was undertaken. They received no further orders from Headquarters until the 17th, when they were warned of Marshal Pétain's request for an armistice. As a result, it was deemed essential to abandon the project and return to England. This decision was confirmed by a message from GHQ to the effect that they were to expect a large party from Marseilles, consisting of both military and RAF personnel, who were to be evacuated. The survey team waited for these people to arrive but no one appeared. It has since transpired that the Commandant at Marseilles had wisely decided to embark all those requiring passage to England on a British ship available at that port and that they arrived home safely.

In the port of La Pallice were two British colliers, loaded with coal. The head of the survey team decided, therefore, to embark his party on them. This was done successfully on the evening of the 17th. The ships set sail at once and, passing the wreck of the French ship *Champlain*, which had been bombed on the 16th, approached the boom across the harbour mouth. This boom was patrolled at regular intervals by a single French sailor in a rowing boat. On being requested to open the boom, he refused, saying that no one other than the Port Authorities could give the necessary instructions. After much persuasion, he at last agreed to row ashore and try to obtain the requisite permission. This was finally granted and the two ships docked at Newport on the 18th. 2,303 men had been safely brought home.

VII

14 June — 20 June

UNDOUBTEDLY 14 June was destined to rank in importance with 10 May, the date of the start of the German offensive. Not only was the future of the new BEF decided, but also the future relationship between Britain and France.

At 0830 on the 14th General Brooke met the Generalissimo at the Château de Muguet. He presented his credentials and immediately the two men began to discuss the situation. In the afternoon both Generals went over to General Georges' HQ. This was most necessary as General Brooke would be acting under the orders of the Commander of the North-Eastern Armies.

Among the subjects discussed were the employment of the newly arriving British troops and the protection of the proposed Breton Redoubt. While both French Generals expressed the view that this latter enterprise was unlikely to be of value, nevertheless orders had been issued by both the British and French Governments for such action to be taken. (As has already been seen, preparations for this had been made by the War Office.)

Owing to the fact that Major Ellis, the author of the *Official History of the War in France and Flanders*, has made certain important statements as regards this matter, it is essential to examine these before proceeding with the narrative of events.

Major Ellis's first remark deals with the 'Terms of Reference' given to General Brooke by the Secretary of State before he left for France. The Terms are similar to those issued to Lord Gort in the equivalent circumstances. They read:

> ... 2. The role of the Force under your command is to cooperate in the defeat of the common enemy under the Supreme Command of the French Commandant-in-Chief de l'Ensemble des Theatres d'Operations. His Majesty's Government have agreed that the latter may delegate the immediate command of your force to a subordinate

French commander, of the rank not below the commander of a group of armies, as he considers necessary. You will, however, at all times have the right of access to the French Commandant-in-Chief.

3. In the pursuit of the common object, the defeat of the enemy, you will carry out loyally any instructions issued by the French commander under whose command you may be serving. At the same time, if any order given by him appears to imperil the British Expeditionary Force, it is agreed between the British and French Governments that you are to be at liberty *to appeal to the British Government before executing the order.*

4. It is the desire of His Majesty's Government to keep the British Forces under your command, as far as possible, together. If, at any time, the French High Command finds it essential to transfer any British troops outside the area of your main force, it should be distinctly understood that this is only a temporary arrangement.

Major Ellis then adds: 'There was nothing at all about a Breton Redoubt.' But on the day after General Brooke's arrival in France, he received the following message from the War Office: 'At a meeting of Ministers, 11 June, CIGS was informed that a study was being made for organizing a bridgehead to secure Brittany in the event of co-ordinated defence of France becoming impossible, due to the present line breaking.' The message went on to suggest that General Marshall-Cornwall might be associated in this study, though it was to meet an eventuality which, the CIGS hoped, would never occur.

The statement that the Breton Redoubt had been omitted from the Terms of Reference seems curious. As in the case of Lord Gort, there was no question of any specific manoeuvre being included in such Terms. Any details of this nature would have been given to General Brooke by the CIGS, as the leading Military Authority. As we know, General Brooke had received such orders.

Regarding the 'Message' received from the CIGS on the day following Brooke's arrival in France, it is first necessary to decide what that day was. Major Ellis has stated that Brooke arrived in France on the 12th; in fact it was the 13th. If such a message had been received *before* General Brooke saw General Weygand, it would be natural to suppose that the matter would have been raised. There is no record that it was. Nor, incidently, is there any sign of the 'Mes-

From CIGS
To Generals Karslake and Marshall-Cornwall
                        Repeated VCIGS

In the present emergency I have agreed that General WEYGAND may delegate Command of all British troops South of SEINE to Commander X Army and that 52 Div may be Employed by brigades without awaiting complete concentration of division. Temporarily detachments of British troops may have to act under French divisional Commanders.
Inform EASTWOOD

J. G. Dill General
C.I.G.S

08.30 hrs
12.6.40

17 The CIG's final Instruction to General Karslake.

3ème CORPS D'ARMEE
ETAT - MAJOR
3ème Bureau
n° 38/3

P.C., le 14 Juin 1940

NOTE DE SERVICE

I - Je m'étonne d'après les compte-rendus qui me sont faits que l'artillerie aux ordres de la 157e Brigade Britannique soit en voie de repli alors que la situation ne l'impose pas.

II - Le Commandant de cette artillerie ne doit se replier que sur ordre du Général LAURIE. (1)

Le Général de FORNEL de la LAURENCIE
Commandant le 3ème Corps d'Armée

[signed]

(1) L'honneur militaire du Comm' de l'artillerie est en jeu. L'artillerie doit appuyer son Infanterie et partager ses sacrifices .... et ses risques.

[signed]

P.d.
A.t. du général Laurie
157° Brig Brit

18 General Laurencie's Rebuke.

sage' in the Command files. It is certainly true that the name of General Marshall-Cornwall had been put forward on the 11th, but the suggestion had been rejected by the French. If, on the other hand, the message had been received *after* Brooke had met Weygand, then there would have been no necessity, as will be seen, for Brooke to try and persuade the British government to change its mind over the establishment of a Redoubt in Brittany.

To return once more to General Georges's HQ at Briare, after the discussions had been concluded the three Generals signed an undertaking, the details of which are set out below:

> General Brooke, commanding the British Expeditionary Force, got in touch on the morning of 14 June with General Weygand commanding all the theatres of operations, and General Georges, commanding N.E. front, to determine how the British troops in France should be employed.

Under the arrangements agreed to by the French and British Governments to organize a Redoubt in Brittany, the following decisions were taken:

> 1. That the British troops now disembarking (the Brooke Corps, the last of the 52nd Division and the Canadian Division) should be concentrated at Rennes.
> 2. That the British troops with the Tenth Army (Evans Division, Beauman Division and the 52nd Division, less those elements not yet disembarked) should continue in their present task under the orders of the General commanding the Tenth Army.
> *Their employment in the over-all operations of this army should bring them, as far as possible, into action in the Le Mans area*, so as to facilitate their eventual re-grouping with General Brooke's forces.

The signing of an agreement of this kind was unique. One can only imagine that the French, considering that they had been let down on previous occasions through 'misunderstandings', were determined, in this case, that nothing of the kind should arise. General Brooke has stated that he signed the document under the impression that the British Government had agreed to the Brittany project (as indeed he had every reason to believe).

As soon as the meeting was over General Brooke went to General Howard-Vyse's HQ. There he drafted a message for the CIGS. It read:

> Weygand stated organized resistance has come to an end. French Army disintegrating disconnected groups. He told me of decision taken by Governments yesterday [the private meeting between Churchill, Reynaud and Weygand at Briare] to attempt to hold Brittany. He, Georges and I are in complete agreement as to military impossibility of this with troops which can be made available. Strongly recommend that decision should be reconsidered as it can only lead to further losses of British troops without hope of result. Present plan is to hold back drafts and Corps troops at Rennes and that others should reassemble in that area after falling back fighting with 10th Army on Le Mans. Recommend that Nos 1 and 2 Mission should be withdrawn as Weygand and Georges will have no effective control.

General Brooke, having sent General Howard-Vyse back to London with this message and a copy of the agreement, returned to Le Mans. Immediately on arrival he telephoned to General Dill so as to reinforce the message he had sent by hand. Dill informed him that no 'decision' had been taken over the Breton Redoubt, only that the project should be 'examined'. Further, that Mr Churchill had said that he knew nothing of such a project. It should be emphasized that General Dill *said* that Mr Churchill had made this statement. Certainly there is no record of Mr Churchill having made it direct to General Brooke.

These telephone conversations continued throughout the evening. In some Mr Churchill took part. The eventual outcome was that, very reluctanly, the Prime Minister agreed that all further shipments of troops and stores should be stopped and that all troops not required to sustain immediate requirements should be evacuated. Finally, after General Brooke had at last convinced Mr Churchill that the remainder of the Canadian Army should be held back, by giving the most depressing picture of the situation, it was agreed that General Brooke should cease to be under French command. The Secretary of State, therefore, sent the necessary authority for this in the following signal:

> You are no longer under French command but will co-operate with

any French forces which may be fighting in your vicinity. In view of your report stating that organized resistance has come to an end, you must now prepare for the withdrawal of your force to the U.K.

Though this message was received on the night of the 14th, the messages of a similar nature sent to the French Government and General Weygand (the latter by the CIGS) did not reach their destinations until the following day. At this time General Weygand was attending a meeting at Bordeaux, the seat of the Government. He had the opportunity to read the message sent by Mr Eden to M. Reynaud, which read as follows:

> General Brooke has informed the CIGS that General Weygand told him that French organized resistance had ceased. In these circumstances I am sure that you will agree with me in thinking that the Allied cause will be better served by the suspension of landings of new British forces in France until the situation becomes clearer.
>
> Orders have been given in this sense, and also for the evacuation of a large number of personnel of the lines of communication between Rennes and Nantes. As you know, we have very large stocks of goods in the ports, which are also being evacuated. The British troops are continuing, and will continue, to fight with the 10th Army. If General Altmayer decided on a fighting withdrawal to a port, we should do our utmost to aid the evacuation of his troops if he so desired.

It was not until the 16th, when he went to his new HQ at Vichy, that General Weygand was able to read the text of the message sent to him on the subject. This was couched in the following terms:

> Message from General Dill to General Weygand. In view of the existing situation and the difficulty of communications, General Brooke can no longer count on receiving orders from the High Command. I have told him that he should no longer consider himself under the orders of the French High Command but should continue to co-operate with the French troops operating in his neighbourhood. I am sure that you will agree.

Owing to the pressure of work occasioned by the developing situation, General Weygand was unable to reply to General Dill until the

18th. He wrote:

> On 14 June at 2.30 pm General Brooke was received by General Weygand, who took him to the staff offices of General Georges. After a discussion between the three Generals, a note was drawn up and signed by each of them.
> This note defined the dispositions laid down by common agreement for the utilization of the British Divisions landed or about to land.
> General Weygand cannot understand how it could have been written on the same date by General Brooke that the French resistance has ceased. It was made clear, on the contrary, to General Brooke that resistance was continuing (and still is continuing today, 18 June), but that General Weygand did not want to risk placing the British units in difficulty by sending them too far forward. Nor does he understand how it could have been contemplated that the British forces should continue to fight with the Tenth Army if French resistance had ceased. [See above]
> Once the note was signed, General Brooke asked whether it would not be preferable to stop the British landings. General Weygand replied to him that it would not be a good way to sustain morale of the French Armies, who were fighting to their last breath.
> Next day, 15 June, General Weygand learned to his astonishment that the British command was resuming its liberty because it was no longer receiving orders from the French Command. General Weygand then warned the British High Command that he considered himself relieved in regard to the British troops.

With this letter all contact between the British and French Commands ceased. It must be left to the reader to judge the rights and wrongs of the situation. The question which must be asked is whether General Brooke mistook the statements made to him by General Weygand prior to their meeting with General Georges. As the conversations were carried on in French, this is a possibility. On the other hand, it must be remembered that General Brooke had been brought up in France and French was his second language.

When General Brooke arrived at Le Mans on the afternoon of the 13th, he only brought with him Major-General Eastwood. The whole of the remainder of his full Corps Staff had been left in St Malo. During his sojourn in France, only one other officer joined him at Le Mans, Brigadier N. Ritchie, his BGS. This officer remained for only one day before he was sent back to England.[1] It should be noted that General Brooke's staff at Le Mans was at no time greater than that of General Karslake — and that was known to be totally inadequate for the job envisaged. It would be interesting to know what influenced General Brooke, even before his meeting with General Weygand, to decide not to call forward the Staff that he had assiduously collected on his appointment to command, and which he knew to be vital if he was to carry out the operations with which he had been entrusted.

As soon as General Brooke was informed that he was no longer under French Command, he relates how he immediately gave instructions for the following moves:

> The elements of the Canadian Division which had landed to leave at once through Brest.
> The Corps troops from St Malo.
> 52nd Division, less 157th Brigade with the French, from Cherbourg. [By then this Division had concentrated near Le Mans.]
> All the rest of the troops and material from St Malo, Brest, St Nazaire, Nantes and La Pallice.

At the same time he sent a message to General Marshall-Cornwall giving details of what had occurred and requiring him to report to Le Mans at once.

On General Marshall-Cornwall's arrival in the early hours of the 15th General Brooke told him that he had managed to obtain the consent of the Authorities at home for the evacuation of most of the British Troops. He hoped that it would not be long before permission would be granted for the remainder to leave. In the meantime those troops actively engaged with the French 10th Army were to continue to co-operate. However, General Brooke anticipated that it would not be long before all British troops would cease to be subject to French orders.

General Brooke had decided that, in view of circumstances, General Marshall-Cornwall should assume command of all those troops still in action with the French. As soon as there appeared any likelihood of the French giving way, General Marshall-Cornwall was to disengage and withdraw the troops to the nearest available port; this seemed likely to be Cherbourg. Thus at 0300 on the morning of 15 June General Brooke had finally decided that the campaign in France was over.

The decision to form an independent Force (now to be referred to as 'Normanforce') was sound — at least on paper. Unfortunately, certain matters had been overlooked. In the first place General Marshall-Cornwall possessed a totally inadequate staff to conduct any form of military enterprise. Secondly, though troops, in the form of the balance of the 52nd Division, which on that day had been ordered back to Cherbourg, together with units of 'A' Brigade, were available should occasion arise, General Marshall-Cornwall had no authority over them. Finally General Marshall-Cornwall had had no experience of handling troops in the field; he had spent most of his career in the role of a Liaison Officer to various foreign HQs, a role for which he was eminently fitted. It is curious that General Brooke, knowing the weakness of General Marshall-Cornwall's staff and the complexity of the problems with which that officer was likely to be faced, never directed some of his massive staff who were still 'kicking their heels' at St Malo to supplement that of General Marshall-Cornwall. Instead these officers were sent back to England having accomplished nothing.

It is now time to look over the 'other side of the hill'. After the very successful termination of the campaign north of the Seine the German High Command, on 13 June, directed its main effort towards Paris. Of Von Kluge's 4th Army, one Armoured Corps, the XVI of the Hoth Armoured Group, together with the whole of the Kleist Armoured Group, was directed to this end. This left one Armoured Corps only in the area of the French 10th Army. On the other hand, the greater part of the infantry was retained for operations. Of the Armour, only the 5th Panzer Division had partially crossed the Seine on 14 June. This was owing to the very thorough destruction of the bridges and removal of the ferries. In addition, owing to the tremendous effort of the Armoured Divisions since 5 June, they required a maximum of repairs and maintenance. In fact the 7th Panzer Division (Rommel), which was located in Le Havre, was in such poor condition that its commander considered that it was unlikely that he could place more than half his tanks in the field. In addition to lack of spares there was little in the way of ammunition and other supplies. To sum up, the enemy were, on this day, in no fit state to begin another major offensive in the Rouen sector. Had Allied aircraft been available, it is doubtful if the right wing of the German forces could have made any progress. Unfortunately for the Allies, no aircraft were available, the greater part of the air effort being directed further East. As a result, the Germans were able to bring forward vital supplies without interruption.

During the 14th and again on the 15th, the enemy applied pressure through their infantry only. Then, to his astonishment, Rommel received orders to move with the utmost dispatch. His object was Cherbourg, there to intercept and capture the British forces who were directing their axis on that port *for evacuation*. As this order was received early on the 15th, it would be interesting to learn from whom the German command received the information that General Brooke had won his battle with the Authorities over the evacuation of the British troops! One must assume that reports received from the Luftwaffe indicated that a build-up of shipping at Cherbourg indicated that evacuation was intended.

Rommel, with his accustomed energy, moved off quickly. However, he was disconcerted to find that his command had been reduced to a shadow of its former self. He wondered what would happen if he came up against serious resistance. Indeed he wondered if he would achieve his object at all. Owing to the thorough destruction of the bridges, it was necessary for him to proceed east as far as Vernon before turning westwards in the direction of Cherbourg. Would his tanks stay the course? Another serious discovery was made. The tractors pulling his field and medium artillery were incapable of further effort until they had received maintenance. He was told that it would be quite impossible for his guns to move off for a further twenty-four hours!

To most men the prospect would have been daunting. In Rommel's case, however, it presented a challenge. Giving instructions that his artillery should follow as soon as possible, Rommel ordered the advance. By the 16th he had reached L'Aigle without encountering any undue difficulties. He drove on, praying that his luck would hold.

Hoth, in the meantime, had ordered the 5th Panzer Division and the 2nd Motorized Division to exert the utmost pressure on the extreme left of the Allied Line, the object being to cut off the French forces from Brittany. It would seem that the Breton Redoubt project had also been reported to the German High Command. However, before dealing with the operations that developed as a result of the German activity, it is necessary to 'clear the stage' of the 'supporting players'.

Not long after General Marshall-Cornwall had left Le Mans to assume his new command, General Brooke considered that his present HQ was likely to prove in too advanced a position. He decided, therefore, to move to Vitré. From there he would be in a position to evacuate either from Brest or St Nazaire, should the occasion arise.

Colonel Roberts was awakened at dawn on the 15th. A message from GHQ had just been delivered and was marked 'urgent'. Colonel Roberts tore open the envelope and studied the contents. He could scarcely believe his eyes! The orders were, however, quite clear. His command was to proceed at once to Brest for re-embarkation for England! It was signed by Major-General de Fonblanque himself.

There could be no question of querying the orders. Colonel Roberts called his officers to a conference at which he issued the necessary instructions for the move. It was quite evident that all those present were staggered, indeed furious, at the news. For the third time the unit was to be disappointed by being prevented from 'having a go at the Hun'.

Meanwhile GHQ had issued orders for the return of the other parts of the 1st Canadian Division which had landed in France. The portion which had only just disembarked that morning at Brest was re-embarked immediately and sailed for England. Of the three trains carrying the main body of the 1st Brigade, two were intercepted before they reached Sablé. The locomotives were changed to the other end of the trains and they returned to Brest. They arrived that evening and embarked. However, the ships did not sail till the evening of the 16th. The train carrying Brigade HQ actually arrived at Sablé before the order to return was received. Unfortunately some trouble was given by both the driver and the fireman. Brigadier Smith was quite determined that there should be no hold up. He detailed an armed guard for the cab of the locomotive. The guard in the cab was also a qualified locomotive engineer. With one other armed guard on the tender the locomotive changed ends and was soon puffing on its way westwards. It seemed that all the trouble was over. Unfortunately someone quite inadvertantly switched the train onto the wrong lines at Rennes which took it in a northerly direction. Eventually it arrived at St Malo. Fortunately room was found on a ship loading British service troops. All returned to England safely.

In a surprisingly short time both Colonel Roberts and the 1st Field Regiment RCHA, together with all the other parts of the road party that had arrived on the 13th at Sablé, were assembled and ready to move off. Just as they were about to do so, they were joined by a cavalcade of staff cars and lorries. These bore General Brooke and his staff from Le Mans who were hastening away to their new HQ at Vitré. As Colonel Roberts reported: 'They appeared to be in abject fear of being overtaken by the Germans at any minute. Although there was evidently no enemy within 200 miles, the withdrawal was conducted as a rout.'[2]

On arrival at Brest Colonel Roberts found a state bordering on panic among the Embarkation staff. No ships were available. In accordance with the orders which had been received from General de Fonblanque, all transport had to be left outside the Port area; only guns, limbers and tractors, together with important technical vehicles, were allowed near the quays. When the ships did become available on the 17th, a direct order came through from the General that *all* vehicles including the guns, were to be destroyed; only troops could be accepted. This was too much for the Canadians and in particular for Colonel Roberts. Having trained his men to a high standard on the brand new guns, then not being able to use them, and now receiving an order to destroy these guns without a struggle, was something that no Gunner could be expected to accept. For two hours he 'fought' the General over the telephone. At last, grudgingly, the General granted a concession (but two precious hours had been wasted). Roberts could load as many of his guns as possible up to 1600; it was then 1415, but it was enough for Roberts. Everyone worked with a will. By the deadline not only had the Regiment's twenty-four guns been loaded, but also twelve Bofors guns, (from the Port's defences,) seven Predictors, three Bren-gun carriers and a number of Technical vehicles. Unfortunately the Regimental limbers and tractors had to be abandoned as no latitude of time was allowed. This was particularly unfortunate as there was ample room for their accommodation on the ships — and the Germans did not enter the Port until 19 June.[3]

It is interesting to note that General de Fonblanque's order of 17 June for the destruction of the Canadian guns was much the same as that which he had issued on 21 May for a similar, unnecessary act.

In passing, it may be noted that all those parts of the 1st Canadian Division that had left England with such high hopes between 11 and 15 June returned safely. It was to be a very long time before they were to see the action for which they had come to Europe.

On arrival at Vitré General de Fonblanque issued a quite remarkable order to the Commander of the Southern District of the L of C, Brigadier F. Bissett. He was to disband his HQ at once and evacuate all his staff. Whether General Brooke was aware of this order is not known. One feels that it is unlikely, as he would have appreciated what chaos was likely to arise as a result of its reception. As will be shown in due course it was to have the most serious effects on the future movements of personnel and stores south of the Brittany Peninsula.

At 1230 Mr Churchill telephoned to General Brooke at his new HQ. He was anxious that the 52nd Division should not be embarked as it would have a bad effect on the French. General Brooke replied that, as all arrangements had now been made for its embarkation, it would be difficult to alter them at this stage. Mr Churchill was, however, adamant that the Division should not be embarked.

At 2115 General Brooke spoke to General Dill over the telephone. He informed him of the situation as it appeared to him at that time. Though curiously inaccurate, it was sufficiently alarming to obtain the CIGS's permission for one Field Regiment and some minor details of the 52nd Division to be embarked. Later that night at the request of General Marshall-Cornwall, who had, it will be remembered, no authority over the 52nd Division and was not at all happy over the provisions for the defence of Cherbourg, General

Brooke agreed that one battalion and a troop of anti-tank guns should be deployed for that purpose.

On 16th June at 0700 the CIGS telephoned to say that all arrangements could now be made to embark the Division, but that no actual movement was to take place. However, an hour and a half later permission was given for the embarkation to begin. It was emphasized that the troops acting with the French were to continue to do so. At 1330 General Brooke was again on the telephone to General Dill. He told him that the French had started their move towards Brittany; as a result he wanted permission to disengage the British forces as such a movement would bring them away from their port of embarkation. Permission, however, was not forthcoming. General Dill suggested that General Brooke should telephone him from the new HQ, which he intended to set up at Redon some thirty miles north of St Nazaire. At 2115 General Brooke again spoke to General Dill. He was told that Mr Churchill had decided that the troops with the French should *not* disengage, but should remain with them until the French Army *disintegrated*, when General Marshall-Cornwall could withdraw his force to Cherbourg or *the nearest available port*. This order from Mr Churchill is of considerable interest as it definitely tends to show that there had been second thoughts on the question of the knowledge of the Breton Redoubt scheme.

At 2300 that evening the ubiquitous Colonel Briggs arrived at Redon from General Marshall-Cornwall. He stated that, 'in his opinion, the French 10th Army would disintegrate if it was seriously attacked'. At this point it should be noted that, in spite of what General Brooke stated in his despatch concerning the lack of information regarding the enemy, mainly owing to bad weather conditions, this is contradicted by those whose responsibility it was to mark up the War Map. In fact, it has been categorically stated that, other than the visit he made to the room containing the map on the afternoon of 13 June, General Brooke never entered it either at Le Mans or at the other two HQs.[4]

It will be appreciated that the scene was being set for the final withdrawal of the fighting force. Early in the morning of the 17th a message was received at GHQ from General Marshall-Cornwall to the effect that the 10th French Army was 'in full retreat on Laval and Rennes'. In other words, it was carrying out General Weygand's orders to withdraw to the Breton Redoubt. The General continued that he was withdrawing his forces for embarkation at Cherbourg. This manoeuvre can only be accounted for by the fact that he must have received orders from General Brooke that if the French attempted to move towards Brittany, he was to take such action. It should be noted that there was no suggestion that the French Army was 'disintegrating', it was just 'in full retreat'.

At 1330 General Dill telephoned Brooke to say that the BBC had monitored a speech by Marshal Pétain in which it was alleged that he had asked the Germans for an Armistice. General Brooke, in his despatch, says 'it was subsequently confirmed by Capitaine Meric of the French Mission', (but see Appendix F on the subject of the Armistice.) In view of this alarming intelligence, General Dill agreed that every effort should be made to evacuate all the troops and then, if possible, any material. General Brooke goes on to say that he saw General de Fonblanque and Captain Allen RN (the Senior Naval Officer). Having explained the situation to them, he ordered them to make every effort to get away all personnel, and also as many guns and vehicles as possible. What action General de Fonblanque was able to take after his orders of the 15th is difficult to say. One thing is certain, that when the Naval party had arrived at St Nazaire and Nantes on the 16th, they were unable to obtain any information as to the number of troops to be embarked or schedule of stores and equipment that were to be lifted.[5] It is difficult to imagine that conditions had improved by the 17th.

In the meantime, the un-brigaded troops, together with the remains of 'A' Brigade, were leaving France. In order that there shall be a complete record of the evacuation and the 'efficiency' of its organization, the following account is given.

The 14th Royal Fusiliers had been stationed in Le Havre since 20 May, forming the British part of the garrison. On the morning of 13 June they were ordered to embark on SS *St Briac*. The Battalion, less 'W' Company and its transport, landed at Cherbourg that evening. They then proceeded to Rennes where, to their astonishment, they saw their transport awaiting them. The quartermaster, by tremendous efforts, had moved it overland. On the 15th, the Battalion was ordered to destroy its transport and to proceed to St Malo for embarkation. To their surprise, they found that their missing 'W' Company had arrived at the port the previous day. On the 16th, the united Battalion re-embarked on the *St Briac* for England. 'Y' Company, which had been working north of the Somme prior to the Panzer breakthrough, had already been evacuated through Dunkirk.

'A' Brigade had left Le Havre piecemeal, the 1/5th Sherwood Foresters leaving on the 12th and landing at Cherbourg. There it remained in a transit camp until it moved by rail to Brest, embarking for England on the 16th. The 4th Buffs, less 'C' and 'D' Companies, had arrived in Cherbourg on the 11th. They re-embarked on the 13th for Southampton. 'C' and 'D' Companies, not having received orders to withdraw, had attached themselves to the 154th Brigade. They were instructed to make their own arrangements for evacuation. Major Reid, the senior officer, was lucky to find a small French collier which, though permitting him and his men to embark, refused to take them to England. Instead they were landed at Cherbourg on the evening of the 13th. For some reason they were entrained and dispatched to Rennes. Eventually they joined up with Colonel Roberts' party and left France through Brest on the 17th.

The 4th Border Regiment embarked at Le Havre at midnight 13-14th, in the middle of an air-raid. The following morning (14th), they landed at Cherbourg and moved to a transit camp. That night, the Battalion was moved by an M.T. Company that had just arrived from England to a château some ten miles inland. On the 16th one half of the battalion was made into a Company under Captain J.L. Burgess. It was then entrained for an unknown destination. Early on the 17th the train arrived at Rennes where it remained in a marshalling yard; the locomotive had been removed. In spite of enquiries, Captain Burgess was unable to obtain any orders. Late that evening, a locomotive was attached to the rear of the train. Still no orders had been received. Early in the morning of the 18th the train moved off and that afternoon arrived at Brest. There the Company embarked on the SS *Yorktown*. This ship had just arrived from England fully loaded with artillery and ammunition for the 52nd Division!

The remainder of the Battalion, under Lt-Colonel Tomlinson, remained at the Château. On the 17th, however, orders were received to embark at Cherbourg that morning. They arrived in

Poole the same night.

The 6th Royal Sussex were still at Blain stacking ammunition and petrol. On the 15th they were ordered to move to the Forêt de Savernay for further stacking duties. However, on the morning of the 16th they were ordered to march to St Nazaire, 'after watching and hearing the distant dumps on which they had been working for the past three weeks being destroyed during the night'.[6] At St Nazaire the Battalion took up defensive positions around the quays, they being the only 'combatant' unit in the area. No one had any idea what was happening or whether the Germans might appear at any moment. Eventually an ESo ordered three companies to embark on the SS *Floristan* and a further company on the SS *Glenaffric*. The CO had noticed a large number of loaded lorries on the quay. On investigation it was discovered that many of them were filled with Bren-guns in mint condition. He instructed his men to break open the boxes and to carry away as many of the guns as possible. Boxes of ammunition were also found and the men filled their pockets and any other container they could find. The *Floristan* was lucky. It was the next ship to clear after the unfortunate liner *Lancastria*, which was bombed and sank with the loss of over 3,000 lives.[7] Fortunately the loss of lives during the final evacuation was comparatively small. Besides the sinking of the *Lancastria* on the 17th only one other disaster occurred involving substantial loss of life. This was the complete destruction of a troop train at Rennes on the same day, caused by enemy aerial action.[8] The three companies on the *Floristan* opened a devastating fire from nearly 300 Bren-guns on the attacking aircraft. It is claimed that one aircraft was brought down and the remainder driven off. The final company was unable to embark until the 19th, owing to interference by the French authorities. The Commander was unwilling to use force and it was only by much cajoling that the company was able to cross the swingbridge that divided them from their ship, the SS *City of Mobile*. As the ship was pulling away from the quay, the troops saw a number of German motor-cyclists arrive on the other side of the bridge. In fact, had the French delayed them for another half hour, there is no doubt that the company would have been captured.[9]

With the departure of the 6th Royal Sussex, though several small parties drifted into various enemy-free ports for some time afterwards, the main body of both the new BEF and the L of C personnel had gone. Even to this day the actual numbers are uncertain. Though lesser figures have been mentioned, it is calculated that about 200,000 men were involved. The amount of material removed after the 13th was minimal. Indeed, there is little trace of anything having been loaded other than the pieces mentioned. Though both time and space were available, owing to the breakdown of the normal port and internal administration, no advantage was taken of the opportunities given by the enemy. As a consenquence vast quantities of valuable material were abandoned, much of it being utilized by the enemy.

Probably one of the most remarkable examples of the loss of material is provided by the 2nd Armoured Brigade. This Brigade, having been relieved by the 3rd Armoured Brigade, had returned to the Le Mans area for refitting. There it joined the balance of the 3rd Armoured Brigade, which was still undergoing repairs.

Early on the 16th, the Brigade received orders (dated 15th) to entrain all its tanks, together with those of the 3rd Armoured Brigade, at Le Mans station. Not having received this order until 0100, it was quite impossible to carry out the instructions to start at 0200. However, the main body and transport left at 0315. At 0500 all the tanks were driven by skeleton crews to the station and loaded on a train equipped with special flat trucks. The crews, who then embussed in lorries, were instructed to follow the main body to Brest for evacuation.[10] It should be noted that *no military personnel accompanied the train*. The main body proceeded to Brest without difficulty, where they were joined by the following tank crews. They embarked at 1500 on SS *Lady of Man*, sailing for England at 1620 that same day. The train carrying the tanks was never seen again. After the conclusion of hostilities, the tanks were found on the ranges at Putloss, north of Lubeck, where they had been used for target practice by the Germans.[11]

It should be noted that the tanks were under the command of the 9th Lancers as both the other Regiments of the Brigade had handed over all their tanks to them.[12] In fact, the 10th Royal Hussars left Brest for England on the 17th. It is unlikely that it will ever be known what exactly happened to the train carrying the tanks. Whether through the medium of some Fifth Column activity or breakdown of the French railway system, it is impossible to say. What, however, is certain is that, at the time of the journey, there were no enemy troops in the vicinity or indeed anywhere along the route between Le Mans and Brest. It is remarkable that the tanks were allowed to proceed without any escort, something that is completely contrary to Military Regulations.

VIII

The Final Phase

'Nevertheless it must be conceded that Marmont, to use Wellington's phrase, made but a feeble effort; and it is perfectly true that he disliked the advance into Beira, expected no good from it, and was not displeased when that expectation was realised.'
History of the British Army, Fortescue, Book XIV, 1917

RQMS Brown, of Harrowing's 2nd Provisional Battalion, B Brigade, Beauman Division, wrote in his Diary after the Division had been handed over to the French:

'Wednesday, 12 June, 1940.
Rekitting men during the morning. Much cooler today. Yesterday was intolerable. Lots of men with wind up about going back to the front. Left Le Mans for the front at 1600 by trucks. Passed a memorial commemorating the Franco-Prussian war. Entered forest near L'Aigle (?) at 2130, remained there until midnight. Had to guide the driver. Convoy in total darkness. Plenty of aircraft about. Passed through village which had been bombed to bits. Arrived in wood near Rouen at 0500. Felt hungry and tired. Had very little sleep for a week now, no food since yesterday breakfast. Dozed off in truck but awakened at 0800 by enemy planes flying at a height of about 100 feet and machine-gunning wood.
Thursday, 13 June, 1940.
Yesterday's journey was another heart-wracking one. Refugees and disorganized French troops in a constant stream going towards Le Mans. They all put their thumbs up to us, even the tiny kids. Girls by the hundred in the towns and villages waved and threw kisses to us. That is because we were going to the Front. If we had been going in the opposite direction, they would not have looked at us. We have now mounted a Bren for AA defence and I have taken it over, but planes too high to fire at, or either our own or French. Very pleasant

lying on blankets on the thick turf under the trees beside the LMG. The only indication that there is a war on is the soldiers and the distant rumble of gun fire. Heard this morning that there are only 128 survivors of the Battalion [2/4th KOYLI]. Why we are being sent back into the line Heaven only knows. We are all tired and nerve-wracked. I have not had twelve hours sleep since a week last night. In the past week I have only had my clothes and boots off once. We take up our new positions in the Line tonight. I am tired out but cannot sleep. Arrived in district of Authon where reconnaissance made and billets marked up. Found many dogs chained to kennels and released them. Finished at 1830 very tired and hungry. Had first wash since yesterday morning. Troops arrived and took party to force open doors. Awful job that I detest. Found cats locked up in houses and in house two cage birds. Finished billeting at 2130 and had slice of dry bread, chunk of bully and mug of tea. Then to bed for the first time for many weary weeks. Asleep before my head reached the pillow. Plenty of artillery fire from east.

Friday 14 June, 1940.
Woke up at 0600 and got up at 0700. Surveyed my new abode. It is a pretty little black and white cottage of ancient vintage. It is difficult to judge its age. In England it would be definitely Tudor. Over the doorway there is carved in a wooden beam 'R F 1786'. Around the doorway roses are in bloom, and at the side of the house honeysuckle is also in bloom. There is a lack of artillery fire this morning. Colonel Harrowing told me yesterday that my own Battalion is up this way and I told him that he had better watch me otherwise I might hop back to them. He said that he would watch me closely enough. I saw the first wild roses this year in a hedgerow. The job we are on here is obviously another suicide one and if we get out we shall be very lucky. The men have definitely the wind up. I am wondering if the lack of artillery fire is an indication that the artillery has bunked. At 1400, Colonel Harrowing addressed the men on the situation, and whilst doing so, two attacks by enemy aircraft were made. Lot of AA fire was opened. Apparently, the vanguard of the second BEF are here and many more are following. I think that the AA batteries must belong to the new BEF. They were not evident yesterday afternoon. They did a pretty bit of shooting about 1500, splitting up a formation of six enemy aircraft. 2130, just having supper when orders to pack up and stand-by to move off because the enemy has crossed the Risle. Stood-to till 0400. No sleep and very cold. Plenty

to think about though.

Saturday, 15 June, 1940.

Just about to go to bed at 0430 when orders to stand-to again given. Three platoons came in from their positions and we moved off by trucks to a wood near Pont L'Eveque about 13 kilos from Honfleur. Unloaded trucks and lay down in wood. Left wood at 0700 and proceeded westward to new reserve position in another wood. Total food today, two slices of bread, one rasher of bacon and one piece of bully. Slept out in open under a tree. Lovely moonlight night.

Sunday, 16 June, 1940.

Got up at 0600. Woke up at 0400 by barrage and lay listening to it. Took Holy Communion at 0800. Service outside farm house with small table for altar. About 15 men attended. Received a great deal of consolation from it. The guns were silent during the service and a bird sang beautifully. Worked all the morning on the lists of missing men and also prepared an Acquittance role on which men were paid at dinner time. We are not much bothered by aircraft here. Barrage rose in intensity during mid-morning. Dinner of stew with thoughts of Sunday dinner at home. Finished extracting missing men. As near as we can say at the moment, there are 500 missing. Quiet uneventful afternoon with one exception — the receipt of two letters from ... Very excited, nearly afraid to open them. Turned chilly in evening with a touch of dampness. 2000 hrs news received that the French had retired on our right flank and had occupied Lisieux due south of our position. Orders given to be ready to move at 0300 tomorrow. 2200 hrs orders to accompany ... and L O to new position. Apparently, two bridges are to be blown up and we must get across before they go up. Left 2330 and arrived at a farm at Calvados. Very cold night and dazed with lack of sleep. On arrival, all three of us lay in road to await convoy. Couldn't sleep owing to cold. Remainder of Battalion arrived at 0400. Great fear that the French will capitulate and that we shall be taken prisoner.

Monday, 17 June, 1940.

Did not go to bed. Had small quantity of Eau de Calvados in farm house which brought tears into my eyes. 0800 orders to move immediately. Passed through Caen, Creully, Bayeux to cross-roads at Coty where we stopped. 1430 Hun twin-engine bomber came along at a height of about 100 feet going in the direction of Cherbourg. He didn't bomb or machine-gun. As I had reached the first L in Creully when writing this up the same Hun or his pal came down the road again machine-gunning this time. We are on our way to Cherbourg to embark for home and it looks as if the Hun intends making our last journey in France an exciting one and, if possible, our last journey ever. Left Coty at 1400 and stopped in a field at Montebourg at 1500. Immediate orders for small Austin to move off. Discover that one of the 3-tonners has got ditched at entrance to field. Moved into lane on opposite side of road. Road packed with Army vehicles, guns, Bren carriers and DRs all going in the direction of Cherbourg. 20 kilos to go when Hun bombers flying low came along road machine-gunning. Got into ditch but planes too fast to attempt shot with rifle. Then several minutes later they returned along road. Stuck up owing to traffic jam. Half an hour later orders given to fall in and march. Hot, boiling hot afternoon. 1700 took up defensive positions outside Cherbourg. Streams of troops and motor transport going down hill into town. 1800 news that French had capitulated and that we had twelve hours to get out of the Country from 1400 today. 1915 orders received to fall in and march into Cherbourg ... Very exhuasted and feet which have not recovered from the last march giving out. Into Cherbourg where I saw one of the 2/4th officers. Went across and shook hands with him. Mutual pleasure in the meeting. After a moment or so with him, hurried after Battalion and marched at rear through the town. People watched us pass through. There was no cheering. Then to the docks. As we crossed some open ground to the boat, Hun aircraft came over machine-gunning. I was too tired, footsore and exhausted to look at them or even care whether I was hit or not. At last, on board a crowded ship. Off with equipment and collapsed on deck. Sweat right through clothing. Left Cherbourg at 2145. Harbour full of troopships loading men as fast as possible and getting away. Finally assisted below to bunk and had feet to attend to. News that U-boats were trying to sink troopships. Last glimpse of France in the dusk. Then to bunk where fell asleep. Woke up at 0130. Thought light of electrics was sunlight, couldn't understand where I was. Then pulled myself together and had good wash and shaved three days beard off. Docked at 0400.

Perhaps the most interesting detail in the above extract is the remarkable statement that 'we had twelve hours to get out of the Country'. It has been impossible to discover from whom this mischievous rumour emanated. It would appear that its object was to create panic among the troops and, above all, to prevent as much equipment as possible from being loaded. There is little doubt that a certain amount of panic did prevail and much equipment was lost unnecessarily. Was it because of this rumour?

The Beauman Division, spread out along the River Risle, together with the 3rd (Composite) Armoured Brigade and the 157th Brigade, both located in the Conches area, represented the total sum of the British contribution to the Allied cause.

On 14 June Beauman's Division was ordered by General Altmayer to take up a position to the south of the River Dives. The Division was designed to act as a 'stop' through which the French could retire in case of necessity. As a result of this order General Beauman moved his force, now much reduced by losses, first to the area of Pont L'Eveque and thence to an area near Caen. He noticed that the French, though declaring that they were going to hold the line of the River Dives, had made no effort to prepare any positions of defence; in fact, it was most evident that the estaminets to the west of the river were doing an enormous trade. War, it appeared, was farthest from the thoughts of the alleged defenders of the 'Dives Line'.

When near Caen General Beauman received instructions from General Marshall-Cornwall. Having informed General Beauman that he was now in command of the British forces operating with the French 10th Army, General Marshall-Cornwall ordered General Beauman to withdraw his force to Cherbourg and, at the same time, to collaborate with the French. As this latter part of the order was patently impossible, General Beauman withdrew towards Cherbourg. General Beauman writes of the 15th, 'As I had no means of communication with my new commander, except by Despatch Rider, and as the whereabouts of his Headquarters was uncertain I decided to stand fast during the next day until I could get the matter cleared up'. (That is to say cooperating with the French). He continues (16th), 'In the evening, I received instructions to continue my retirement towards Cherbourg. The instruction regarding co-operating with the French was, apparently, never meant to be taken seriously.'[1]

During the night of the 16-17th news came through that the

French had abandoned the 'Line' of the Dives; orders were given to move within the hour. Beauman recorded, 'There were now no Allied troops between the Division and the enemy, as far as I knew.' He was not aware that the 157th Brigade was following him up the Peninsula. No one had seen fit to acquaint him of the fact.

General Beauman arrived in Cherbourg in time for lunch. Immediately he was asked by Brigadier Thorpe, the sub-area commander, to take up a defensive position astride the base of the Peninsula. The General pointed out that his formation had been engaged in a fighting withdrawal for the past ten days, whereas the 52nd Division had never been in action. However he agreed to cover the Carentan approach. To this end he planned to have the eastern road covered by a strong anti-tank artillery screen supported by three battalions of infantry, the Field guns and the balance of the infantry to be held in reserve.

Just as lunch was finishing the local Field Security Officer, Captain Rolfe, arrived and informed those present that the French had 'packed it in'. On being asked from whom he had obtained this information, Captain Rolfe replied that 'it has just come over the wireless from the BBC'. In view of this development the General, considering that Armistice terms might include the closing of the port, thereby trapping his men, ordered the Division to move at once into Cherbourg.

Arriving on the quays, the General found that no one had received any orders as to embarkation. There were masses of troops wandering about and quantities of loaded lorries and other valuable material. He was asked, as senior officer present, to assume command of the troops in Cherbourg. He pointed out that he was unable to do so as General Marshall-Cornwall had already received that appointment. He suggested, however, that as no one apparently had any idea where that General might be, a telephone call should be made to the War Office in order to obtain some instructions. This was done and, to his great relief, the General was ordered by a Staff Officer to embark his Division without delay. This was carried out most expeditiously. As a result, all the guns that had been brought back were loaded. These included eight Field pieces, twenty anti-tank guns and four Bofors. At the time of the formation of the Beauman Division, the artillery had consisted of thirty-six pieces of all kinds.[2] The records show that Major Elliott, commanding the Divisional artillery, had performed marvels of improvisation, not only to ensure that his guns remained in action, but also to withdraw them safely when necessary.

On the 14 the day began early for the 157th Brigade.[3] At 0430 two sapper officers and two sections of Royal Engineers arrived at Brigade HQ. They had had orders to prepare the bridges on the Brigade's front for demolition. During the remainder of the morning, the three Battalions of the Brigade, together with their supporting anti-tank artillery, continued to strengthen their positions. It was as well that they did so for just before noon the 5th HLI reported that the enemy were massing on their front opposite Ferrière; it was obvious that an attack could be expected at any time. Indeed by 1215 the attack had started, supported by heavy mortar fire both on Ferrière and Portes. Further west, the French also were undergoing a similar experience. Brigadier Laurie called on the 72nd French Field Regiment, which had been instructed to support the Brigade, to open fire. Unfortunately the Regiment had already limbered up and was moving to a position north-west of Conches. When at length the guns came into action, it was found that, as they were far back, their rounds (even when fired at maximum elevation) dropped only just in front of the British positions. It was, therefore, quite impossible for the artillery to provide the essential counter-preparation fire. It should be noted in the above connection that the French Regimental Commander was severely censured by the French Corps Commander.

In the meantime the attack had increased in intensity. The French guns provided a somewhat desultory reply with little result. By 1300 the enemy had penetrated into the woods between Portes and Ferrière. The French guns had now lowered their sights and their rounds began to fall within the British positions. The engagement lasted about an hour, the enemy finding that they were unable to make any further progress through the woods owing to the British resistance. A long lull then ensued; Brigadier Laurie took advantage of this respite to order up the remainder of the 5th HLI and a Company of the 6th HLI, in support.

At 1800 the enemy renewed his attacks, this time with increased violence. The French artillery were, once again, asked for supporting fire. It only came after about three-quarters of an hour and proved very ineffective. It was soon after this that Brigadier Laurie was informed that the 236th Demi-Brigade on his left had been forced to withdraw owing to heavy casualties. This left his left flank 'in the air'. It became obvious that withdrawal was essential if his command was not to be cut off through the enemy turning his flank by penetrating between him and the French. Nevertheless Brigadier Laurie ordered up a further Company of the 6th HLI in the hope of closing the gap left by the French. At the same time he sent an urgent message to the 3rd Armoured Brigade at Barquet for help. He had been informed that he could count on Brigadier Crocker's command for support. The movement of the new company, however, seems to have had the effect of making the Germans believe that the British were much stronger than they had anticipated. They failed to exploit their advantage by pressing through the gap.

At 1900 the Brigade received orders from III French Corps to move to a general line some three miles east of Conches. Though the engagement continued with unbated fury, by skilful handling the 5th HLI were gradually withdrawn. At 2230 with the falling of darkness, the rest of the Battalions were able to disengage, and one hour later had taken up their new positions. No further attacks were made on the Brigade that night. At 0335 on the 15th, as a result of orders received during the night, the Brigade moved off to a new position some fifty miles westward.

It was not until 0700 that Brigadier Laurie learned, for the first time, of the existence of the new 'Normanforce'; that its object was to embark the Brigade as soon as it was relieved from its obligations to the French; most important of all, that the Brigade was no longer under French command. Also, at this time, Brigadier Laurie learned something of more immediate importance; namely that a Supply Column was to report to the new Normanforce Headquarters at Orbec. This column was vital as the Brigade was beginning to run seriously short of rations and, indeed, all other supplies including ammunition for both small arms and A/T guns. As the matter was urgent the Brigadier himself went straight to Orbec at 0800 so as to intercept the Column and direct it on to the Brigade which was now en route.

On arrival at Orbec the Brigadier learned that the Column had arrived some time previously. It had inquired for the HQ of No 17 Military Mission (now re-christened Normanforce). The Column Commander, having been informed that the Mission was no longer there, withdrew and was never seen again! By 1100 the Brigade had arrived at its new location. It took up the following positions:

> 5HLI in a wood south of Villiers-sous-Mortagne.
> 6HLI in the Fôret du Perche.
> 1 Glasgow Highlanders in the Fôret de Longui.
> Brigade HQ and the 213 Anti-tank Battery at Autheuil.

In the meantime General Drew, commanding the 52nd Division, feeling extremely uneasy about the situation in which one of his Brigades was placed, ordered on his own initiative the 71st Field Regiment to make contact with the 157th Brigade as soon as the Regiment was ready to move. This proved a great asset. Now the Brigade had a strong arm on which it could rely. On arrival the Regiment took up positions in the Bois du Valdieu.

After an abortive search of Orbec for the elusive Normanforce, Brigadier Laurie finally located its HQ at Mortagne. There he had confirmed to him the defensive positions at Autheuil which he had already assumed. Soon after the Brigadier had returned to Autheuil, General Marshall-Cornwall arrived together with a number of French officers. When this party left at 1830 a great variety of orders had been issued, most of them conflicting. Brigadier Laurie gave his own orders that the Brigade should concentrate on strengthening its positions. He felt that there was a reasonable chance of the situation clarifying in due course. In the meantime he would ensure the safety of his command.

At 2000 hrs the French Cavalry Corps on the Brigade's left reported that the enemy were pushing on in the area of Verneuil and Brezolles. In view of this development the Brigadier set off to see General Marshall-Cornwall at his HQ at Mortagne; it seemed more than probable that the Brigade would have to withdraw once again. On arrival at Mortagne Sir John Laurie found that Normanforce had, once again, moved. This time also it had left no liaison officer to give any indication as to where it could be found. This, notwithstanding the fact that in Normanforce's Operation Order No. 1 it had been clearly stated that such a course would be adopted. Some French officers thought that it might have gone to Alençon. With the present uncertainty, the shortage of supplies and the complete lack of orders, the Brigadier decided that he should make every effort to withdraw his command to Cherbourg. With this in mind, he despatched one of his officers, accompanied by the French Liaison officer, to try and locate some petrol. The two officers found some in Alençon. They loaded up their lorries with two thousand gallons, returning about midnight with their prize. The Brigadier then decided to send a message to Normanforce stating that he considered that it was essential for him to leave for Cherbourg at latest by midday on the 16th. Lieutenant Hillis, the Brigade Intelligence officer, was ordered to try Alençon first, then, if there was no trace of Normanforce there, he was to proceed to Viré. By 1230 Hillis was nearing Alençon. On arrival in the town, he made enquiries in the Mairie and from anybody whom he met. No one had heard of Normanforce. (In fact Normanforce was in the town but had given no indication of its presence.) Hillis went on to Viré, but of course found no trace of it. He therefore rang up 52nd Divisional HQ, which had now returned to Cherbourg, who in turn telephoned to GHQ. He was told to remain at Viré. This he did for the rest of the day, keeping in touch with 52nd Division in the vague hope that they might succeed where he had failed. As their efforts proved hopeless, he was told to report back to Cherbourg.

It was not until 1200 that Colonel Briggs, now GSO I of Normanforce, arrived at Brigade Headquarters. He was informed that the Brigade was rapidly nearing the end of its resources. In reply he suggested that supplies might be obtained from 52nd Division. It was pointed out to him that, as the Division was now located at Cherbourg, it was in no position to help. He was unable to offer any further suggestions. Finally he agreed that if no supplies turned up or any orders were received by 1800 the Brigadier should use his own discretion to withdraw. How this was to be achieved was not stated. Brigadier Laurie had made it quite clear that without supplies his command would find it virtually impossible to make the journey. In fact by 1800 neither supplies nor orders were received. Brigadier Laurie was, therefore, on his own. In view of what had happened when 'under command', perhaps it was just as well!

It will be remembered that the French 127th Groupe de Reconnaissance had been placed under the command of the 157th Brigade. Now it was employed in its proper role and brought in valuable information regarding enemy movements. It sent in continuous reports which enabled the Brigade to take appropriate action. At 1030 it had sent in a report that the enemy had captured Marchainville. Heavy mortar fire could also be heard from the direction of Randonnai. Unquestionably the situation was developing dangerously. At 1330 it was becoming so serious that the Brigadier decided to put down a concentration of fire on the Moulicent and Marchainville areas. This in spite of the French saying that the latter town was still in their hands. As this statement was palpably untrue it was ignored. He was proved to be quite right. The 71st Regiment put down a most effective barrage which temporarily checked any further enemy advance in those areas.

It was necessary at this time for the Brigade to make new dispositions. This was done by assuming a line in the Feings — St Hilaire-le-Chatel area. At 1630 the 71st Regiment put down another concentration of fire in the original area, again with salutary effect on the Germans who were massing for an attack. It was at this time that the French said that they were sending forward British tanks for support, but the tanks never appeared.[4]

Owing to the increased pressure by the enemy and the appearance of tanks in the neighbourhood of L'Aigle (Advanced party of Rommel's 7th Panzer Division), the Brigadier decided that he must make every effort to withdraw even though neither supplies nor orders had arrived.

Prior to the move Brigadier Laurie had received information that the French on the left of the Brigade had been withdrawn without warning. However, at 2000 hrs on the 16th a Liaison Officer from the French 1st DLM arrived and reported that his Division was coming up at once to take up a position from Malétable to Boissy Maugis in the south. Brigadier Laurie told him, however, that his Brigade was withdrawing and it would be appreciated if the French would 'refuse' their left flank so as to link up with the Brigade at Feings. At 2100 the Brigadier gave the order for the Brigade to start its withdrawal. A quarter of an hour later a message was received from HQ French III Corps asking the Brigade to take up a new line. As this did not conform to the plan the Brigadier had made, it was pointed out to III Corps that the Brigade was no longer under its command. Apparently this news came as a great surprise to General de la Laurencie. An hour later the 1st DLM informed Brigadier Laurie that they were withdrawing, thereby leaving the British flank 'in the air'.

At 2245 a staff officer from Normanforce suddenly appeared with the following message

> You will extricate your Brigade Group forthwith and move to Cherbourg by the following route ...
> Petrol can be obtained from the French dump at Rue de la Gare at Domfront. HQ Normanforce moves to Avranches at 4.0am on 17th.

At long last the Brigadier had an idea as to where his Commander was located, though, as he admitted privately, he was by no means convinced that the information would prove accurate should an occasion arise when it had to be tested. So far all messages received from the Headquarters had proved unreliable to say the least!

At quarter to four on the morning of the 17th the convoy began to move. The orders, which had been sent out previously, ensured that the move went like clockwork. The final part of the column left the area by 0615. Other than by some air attacks and jamming on the roads caused by having to cross the front of the Cavalry Corps at right-angles, the column experienced no unexpected interference. It arrived at Domfront some two hours later where it stopped for petrol. Having reported to General Marshall-Cornwall who was, to his surprise, at Avranches, the Brigadier went back along the column to ensure its smooth flow. At 1600 on his return to Avranches, he found that the General and his Staff had left for Cherbourg.

The Brigade continued up the Cotentin Peninsula on its way to the port. Unfortunately no arrangements had been made to provide guides or instructions as to the disposal of the convoy. Indeed, it was not until it reached Virandelle that orders were received.

Colonel Balfour, GSO I 52nd Division, anticipating that the Brigade would soon be approaching, had gone forward in the hope of meeting it. The orders issued to Brigadier Laurie were quite explicit. Regrettably, owing to the almost complete breakdown of the port organization, they were impossible to carry out. The Brigade Staff did all they could to embark their stores and vehicles, but owing to 'panic' orders, few drivers were available to move additional vehicles to the quay. The Brigadier himself went to the quay to watch his men embark. He was horrified to discover that no efforts had been made by the embarkation staff to provide either tea or rations. Luckily he was able to detach some of his own people for this purpose. They soon had dixies boiling, fired by driftwood and any other fuel which came to hand. It was not long before the troops were provided with mugs of tea. Rations, on the other hand, proved an insoluble problem.[5]

By 0230 on the 18th all the personnel of the 157th Brigade had been safely embarked. It was not until 1330 that the ship carrying them actually sailed. For some nine hours it had remained tied up, the cranes and derricks idle. The ship's holds were largely empty. There is little doubt that had calm prevailed much in the way of stores and many valuable vehicles could have been saved.

The final formation with which we have to deal is the 3rd (Composite) Armoured Brigade. It will be recalled that General Karslake had sent it forward so as to provide the 157th Brigade with a force on which it could rely. Its Commander had, with the utmost reluctance, complied with the order. On arrival in the Conches area Brigadier Crocker had been ordered by the French Commander to position the Brigade so as to be able to support either *the right flank of the French 237th Division or the left flank of the 157th Brigade.* In the meantime the French 236th Demi-Brigade of two Battalions and a machine-gun Battalion had moved into position between the 237th Division and the British Infantry Brigade, thereby linking the two formations and forming a slender but continuous front. Prior to the arrival of the Demi-Brigade, it seemed that the Armoured Brigade might well have to fill the gap; luckily now it was able to concentrate on the work for which it was originally intended.

The morning of the 14th opened quietly. There was no activity other than that of a patrol which had been sent out by the 2nd Royal Tank Regiment to ascertain whether an aerodrome at Bernienville had been occupied by the Germans. At noon, however, there was a sound of firing, both of small arms and mortars, from the north-east and south-west of the Brigade position. A few minutes later a message arrived from 237th Divisional Headquarters stating that the Germans were infiltrating north of Tilleul and requesting Brigadier Crocker to arrange for a patrol to be sent out to investigate. The patrol, which had been sent out to recconnoitre the aerodrome, was accordingly diverted to carry out this new task. At this point it should be noted that Brigadier Crocker had provided no liaison officer for either formation with which he was supposed to co-operate.

By 1400 the firing from both the original directions had greatly increased. Brigadier Crocker received information that the enemy were pushing forward against *the right flank of the 237th Division*, and *the left flank of 157th Brigade* in the neighbourhood of Portes. In view of these developments Brigadier Crocker went up to General François's Headquarters at Le Plessis to find out for himself the true position on his front. General François said that the enemy were advancing along the main road towards Le Tremblay in considerable strength. He felt that it might be necessary to withdraw his right flank and requested Brigadier Crocker to help by covering the road during this operation. To this appeal Brigadier Crocker agreed. The significance of this move by the 237th Division seems to have escaped him; the 157th Brigade would have been left virtually 'in the air'. He decided that the 2nd RTR (Major Brown) should take up a position astride the main road south-west of Le Tremblay.

The Brigadier accompanied the squadron forward so as to ensure its correct positioning. Having accomplished this task, he was just about to leave when he was handed a message from the Headquarters of the 1st Armoured Division. This stated that two German Divisions were moving south-west on the axis Les Planches — Ormes. The French Tenth Army, of which the 157th Brigade formed the right flank, was to withdraw its left flank to the general line Neubourg — Montfort — Pont Audemer that night. The 3rd Armoured Brigade was to revert to the 3rd DCL (General Petiet). Brigadier Crocker was to report to this General at once at his Headquarters at Fontaine-l'Abbé.

Having returned to his Headquarters to inform his staff of the latest developments, Brigadier Crocker left for Fontaine-l'Abbé to meet General Petiet. The General told the Brigadier that the 3rd Armoured Brigade, together with the 3rd DCL, was to form part of the 10th Army reserve. It would move west to Courtomer some time that night. Detailed instructions would be sent to him in due course.

On his return to his Headquarters at 2000 Brigadier Crocker learned that the 2nd RTR had not been engaged but the 5th RTR had been attacked by aircraft at its position at Barquet. It had suffered no casualties, but a number of vehicles had been hit. He was also told that two requests for help had been received from 157th Brigade, as a result of the increasing enemy pressure on its position at Ferrière. But, as Brigadier Crocker writes in his Report, 'we had no alternative but to refuse regretfully'. As will have been seen, the 157th Brigade survived these attacks through the efficiency of Brigadier Laurie and the devoted men under his command.

Orders were now issued to prepare to withdraw. At 2130 the actual order to move was received from General Petiet. The Brigade moved off at once and crossed the River Risle at Beaumont-le-Roger between 2200 and 2230. The bridges across the river were blown up shortly afterwards. The Brigade reached Courtomer at 0600 on the 15th. There it rested for the remainder of the day. This halt proved invaluable, as it made considerable maintenance possible. During the day a message was received from 1st Armoured Division giving a warning order that the Brigade would be moving direct to Cherbourg for embarkation. This was confirmed later by a message from General Marshall-Cornwall explaining that he was now in command of all the British troops fighting with the French 10th Army, and that they were to be evacuated to England 'as soon as they are released from their obligations to co-operate with the French'.

On the morning of the 16th orders were received to withdraw to Montigny, which the Brigade reached at 1300. Here lorries which had been sent to Viré to obtain fuel returned with about 1,000 gallons of petrol and one and a half day's rations. Notwithstanding the fact that Brigadier Crocker had been informed by General Marshall-Cornwall that ample supplies would be available, this was all that could be collected. This rendered the position of the Brigade somewhat precarious. Any move which might lengthen the journey to Cherbourg could bring the Brigade to a complete stand-still through lack of supplies. When, therefore, Brigadier Crocker received an order from General Petiet for him to withdraw his command a further fifty miles in a south-westerly direction, in other words away from the direct route to Cherbourg, he sent a message to General Marshall-Cornwall (who was now at Alençon) representing the position. He received a reply at 1000:

'You will proceed forthwith to Cherbourg via Domfront — Viré — St Lo . . . My Headquarters moves to Avranches . . . 10th French Army is withdrawing tonight south-westwards' (in other words to the Breton Redoubt position). Shortly afterwards a liaison officer from General Petiet arrived and told Brigadier Crocker that he was no longer under that General's command.

At midnight on the 16th the Brigade moved off on its last journey. After a march of considerable difficulty, owing to having to cross the line of the French XII Corps retreating from its position along the River Dives, the Brigade reached Domfront. There, it halted for maintenance purposes and to obtain further supplies. At 1330 it arrived near Villedieu. There the information was received by wireless from the BBC that the French had asked for 'peace terms'. As a result the Brigade pushed on at increased speed. It was not until midnight of the 17th, however, that the whole Brigade reached its allotted parking area. 'During the morning, amid scenes of considerable confusion, embarkation started'. 'The bulk of the 52nd Division had already left. Our personnel marched in good order to SS *St Briac* and embarked. All tanks and vehicles were put on board and we sailed.' During the early afternoon all power was cut off from the cranes and the stevedores abandoned the docks. As it was considered that the enemy were close, the remainder of the Brigade's personnel were embarked at 1630 on the SS *Manxman* and sailed at once for England. Thus ends the story of the last formation of what was, hopefully, called the new BEF.

It will have been noticed that reference has been made on several occasions to the chaos that existed at Cherbourg and other ports at the time of the evacuation. It is time, therefore, to discover whether the haste which occasioned this state of affairs was really justified.

It will be remembered that Rommel's 7th Panzer Division entered L'Aigle on 16 June. By that time the French 10th Army was retreating south-westwards in the hope of achieving the problematical security of Brittany. Von Hartlieb's 5th Panzers, accompanied by the 2nd Motorised Division, was pressing forward on the westward part of the front. So fast was it moving that it was able to overtake the left flank of the French and interpose itself between the French and the Breton Peninsula. The Germans actually entered Rennes on the 18th. However, they were unable to capture Brest until the 19th — in other words two days after the majority of the British had sailed from that port. Rommel reached St Lo, at the base of the Cherbourg peninsula, in the early hours of the 18th. Here he discovered that the eastern coast road was mined and blocked. He had to move westwards and continue his advance through Coutances. This road was defended by the French. They had cut down trees across the road and did their best to man some primitive road blocks. It should be realized that these French troops consisted of men who had returned via Dunkirk. Not only had they suffered from their actions in the north but they were almost completely devoid of weapons other than rifles. Their artillery consisted of a few field guns only. It was not until 0900 that Rommel was able to reach La Haye-du-Puits, the road junction on the western approach to Cherbourg. The direct road through St Sauveur de Pierre Pont was defended by the 5th KOSB and a troop of A/T guns. So accurate was the fire from these latter that Rommel decided to take the western route. Once again the ill-equipped French struggled to prevent the German advance. However, the enemy managed to travel a further twenty miles in the next three hours, arriving at Les Pieux soon after 1200. By so doing, they had successfully out-flanked the small British force. It was not, however, until 1515 that these were withdrawn, embarking soon after. The French, meanwhile, had strengthened their positions. Though the Germans were able to make a certain amount of progress towards the east, they were brought to a complete stop in the west. It soon became evident to Rommel that, until his artillery caught up, it would be quite impossible for him to make any serious attack on the town. By way of bravado he lobbed a few 88mm shells into the town. So light a projectile could do little damage. The nearest approach he could make was three miles. With no field guns this was of little value. But worse was to come. At 1600 the great fortress guns opened up. Only then had the enemy come into range. They caused considerable casualties among the German lorried infantry. The Panzers were, of course, quite helpless in the face of such opposition. For five hours Rommel found himself pinned down, notwithstanding the fact that the fortress guns had ceased to fire after an hour. At length, at 2100 he essayed an attack on Querqueville but made little progress. It was not until after midnight when, at last, his artillery had caught up that he was able to prepare for a major assault. At dawn on the 19th, his guns opened a furious bombardment and at 1700 that evening the port of Cherbourg capitulated, twenty-four hours after the last British ship had sailed.

The strength of the Allied forces in the Cherbourg Peninsula had been known to the enemy before Rommel had started his dash for Cherbourg. Reports, however, that the British were evacuating indicated that there was every hope that they would not stand and fight. When Rommel reached St Sauveur, it seemed that the High Command's calculations might be wrong, that the British were going to counter-attack. He realized that if they did he would be in a very serious position. No artillery, no aerial support and a division greatly under strength indicated that his chance of survival was negligible. However, he acted in a way which was to make him famous in the years to come. He used his resources to the best advantage, causing as much confusion as possible without giving away his weakness. Luckily, the British command had already decided that there was to be no further fighting. A comparison of the relative strengths of the antagonists is interesting. The Germans had about 200 tanks in various stages of decrepitude, some light guns and a brigade of lorried infantry. The Allies had a composite brigade of tanks, five brigades of infantry and over 80 guns, plus, of course, the French contribution, including the backing of the Fortress artillery. There seems little doubt that the course of the war in North Africa would have been different if only action had been taken to eliminate the man who was to gain eternal fame as 'the Desert Fox,' to say nothing of the saving of vast quantities of valuable equipment and stores.

At Brest some two days were to elapse before light German forces were to enter the town. What could not have been achieved in those two days in the saving of equipment? Finally, at the great ports of Nantes and St Nazaire the vast amount of booty acquired by the Germans would never have been available had the organization not been prematurely abandoned.[6]

To complete the saga of the new BEF, it only remains to recount the story of the departure of its commander. General Brooke's account of his last hours in France, as given in his despatch, bears repeating.

> (17 June)
> 34. At 2130 hours I left St Nazaire in the armed trawler *Cambridgeshire*. The destroyer which had been sent for my use by the Commander-in-Chief, Western Approaches, was not available as she was being used to assist in carrying survivors from the *Lancastria* which had been sunk by enemy aircraft that afternoon. The *Cambridgeshire* remained in the harbour during the night. During that time, three enemy raids took place, but no damage was done though a few bombs were dropped ashore.

It will be seen from the above extract that there had been plenty of time to hear the correction to Marshal Pétain's broadcast and obtain the position of the enemy troops. Even if he had wanted to dissassociate himself with the evacuation, he had with him two officers of the rank of Major-General who had sufficient authority to undertake such action as was necessary to ensure that every effort was made to salvage the huge quantity of stores which were being abandoned on the quays. He had the precedent of Lord Gort who had left General Alexander in charge to make certain that all British personnel were safely cleared from the beaches of Dunkirk.

At 0900 on 20 June, General Brooke reported to the CIGS at the War Officer. In *The Turn of the Tide* he expresses surprise that he was rebuked for 'leaving so much valuable material behind.'

IX

Summary

> There were many cases in the late war (1914-18) where incompatability of temperament failed to get good results, and happily many brilliant examples of sympathy and understanding. It behoves our Officers to combat the national feeling of insularity, and to study the characteristics and points of view of our Continental neighbours, so that we may be able to give a good account of ourselves when called upon to act either with or against them in any future struggle. Failure to achieve results through personal prejudice is inexcusable.
> *Tannenberg*, Sir Edmund Ironside, 1925.

WHILE it has to be admitted that the principal causes of the final débâcle were the weakness of the French forces and the failure of their Commanders to employ the forces to hand satisfactorily, nevertheless the British cannot escape criticism. There is no doubt whatsoever that had all the British troops south of the Somme been under a single Commander the formations available could have been deployed and utilized correctly, thereby using their considerable strength to the best advantage. This, in turn, would have prevented their dissipation and constant misuse. No effort was made by the War Office to support the troops in France by providing an operational HQ staff under a Commander-in-Chief. Insufficient authority was given to the senior General. This prevented him from taking such measures as were essential to ensure the safety of the troops.

When the 51st Division arrived from the Saar, it was positioned by the French on the left of the Allied line. This was an obvious situation as it prolonged the front of the French IX Corps to the sea. Though the frontage occupied was excessive in the strictly military sense, namely 16 miles, nevertheless under the circumstances it was reasonable. The Armoured Division, such as it was, was considered to be available as a supporting formation. Also, it had been planned by the French that further formations that were being constituted further south would soon be available to take over part of the line. It will be remembered that the 51st Division was considerably overstrength; in fact, if employed correctly, it would have proved a formidable fighting formation. Unfortunately it was ordered into action before it, and the other troops with which it was to collaborate, was ready. Furthermore the artillery preparation was totally inadequate and no form of reconnaissance, either from the air or on the ground, had been undertaken. General Fortune, who commanded the Division and had another French division placed under his command, had no one to who he could appeal against this premature employment of his command. This was not the first occasion when the absence of an overall British Commander was felt. Even the French High Command realized the necessity for such an appointment. In spite of representations, General Dill continued to be obdurate on the subject of not having a senior British operational commander in France at that time. He did compromise to the extent of appointing Lieutenant-General Marshall-Cornwall as head of a new Military Mission, No 17, at the Headquarters of the newly-formed French X Army, commanded by General Robert Altmayer. However, this in no way compensated for a missing Commander, the head of a Mission having no command or reponsibility for the troops in his area. It may well be wondered why, when a command appointment was so obviously essential, if only for the good of the troops, General Dill persistently refused to make it. The reason, feeble though it was, is not far to seek. Mr Churchill had decided, even before the evacuation through Dunkirk had been completed, that a new BEF should be formed and sent over to France as quickly as possible. General Dill considered that his great personal friend, the erstwhile commander of II Corps, the newly-knighted Sir Alan Brooke, should command the first new corps to be despatched to France. If he had appointed General Karslake as Corps Commander on 27 May, all troops sent to France after that date would automatically have come under his command. This would leave no position for General Brooke for some time. Besides, General Karslake was considerably senior to General Brooke. There is no doubt whatever that the failure of General Dill to implement General Ironside's instructions was directly responsible for the destruction of the 51st Division, the decimation of the

Armoured Division and the loss of many valuable stores at the end.

With the development of the German offensive on 6 June, and the 51st Division in conjunction with the French IX Corps being held on the River Bresle, it became increasingly obvious to the Commander of the L of C and, subsequently, to the War Office, that it was vital that both these formations should withdraw on Rouen if both wings of the French 10th Army were not to be split apart. Karslake tried to persuade General Georges to get Weygand to give the necessary orders for the retirement of IX Corps, under whose orders the 51st Division was serving. General Dill, when he finally realized the danger in which the 51st Division stood, spoke to General Weygand without success. Both Generals Evans and Beauman tried to get General Marshall-Cornwall to induce General Altmayer to take some action in the matter. Marshall-Cornwall told them that there was nothing he could do. This statement is of considerable importance. After the campaign General Marshall-Cornwall stated that when he had been appointed by General Dill to head No 17 Military Mission part of his job was to watch over the interests of the British troops under command of French 10th Army and to report on any unsuitable orders given to British troops under his command. In other words, he had been given the vital authority that had been denied by General Dill to General Karslake. Had there been a Corps Commander of whose Corps the 51st Division had formed part, he would never have allowed it to be endangered in that way. If necessary, he could have used his right of appeal to the British Government. As there was no such Commander and the right of appeal was vested in another, the Division was lost. Even as early as 4 June, General Karslake, not knowing that General Marshall-Cornwall had been provided with the right of appeal, had begged General Dill to expedite the departure of General Brooke to France; he considered his presence vital if disaster was to be avoided. In reply, General Dill said that it was quite impossible for General Brook to leave at that time as he was fully engaged in organizing the forthcoming force. By this decision the terrible tragedies that followed were made inevitable.

In the case of the Armoured Division, from the first this unfortunate formation found itself in a most unsatisfactory position. Arriving in France piecemeal, it was both under-equipped and undertrained. Its Commander had had very little experience in the deployment and use of such a formation. Also a vital part of the Division had been diverted at the last moment. In the beginning of its career in France it was directed by GHQ in a particularly futile enterprise, then by the War Office in an equally fatuous role. Thereafter by any French Commander who chose to exercise his authority. As, like General Fortune, General Evans had no one to whom he could appeal, he found his command woefully misused and, in due course, so cut up that it ceased to have any real cohesion. Never did the Division serve as a whole, being broken up into not less than three parts. Not having the support of a Commander, and General Marshall-Cornwall not exercising his right of appeal, General Evans was unable to obtain command of his Division at any time. More often than not he found himself completely out of touch with the widely separated parts of his command; this led, ultimately, to the Conches Affair.[1]

From the moment that the new formations began to arrive in France, the situation as regards the British command became most peculiar. On 7 June General Karslake had had it confirmed that the new divisions were to come under his command. However, they were not to be used piecemeal. This meant that, until a formation had assembled complete in every detail, it was not to be employed in actual hostilities. It was a very wise decision as formations had hitherto been thrown into battle before they were ready — with tragic consequences. The situation on 10 June seemed quite reasonable. The 52nd Division was arriving at Cherbourg, its 157th Brigade having advanced to the new base for assembly at Le Mans. The Canadian Division was on the point of embarkation in England, its advanced Brigade being expected within two or three days. In France, the Beauman Division was under Karslake's direct command, together with the additional units of the 12th and 46th Divisions that were still in the area. It can be seen, therefore, that when the new formations arrived and the remainder of the British troops in France were assembled in position along the prescribed front at the base of the Breton peninsula, together with the French troops that had been allotted for the defence of the 'Redoubt', plus the various formations of the French 10th Army, there was just a chance that this strong-point could be held until reinforcements arrived from England. It will be recalled that the 51st Division had been included in the British Defence Force. On 10 June, however, it had become quite obvious that it was extremely unlikely that this latter formation would be available. Nevertheless on paper it seemed as if the situation was not altogether hopeless.

When the 157th Brigade arrived in his area it came as a shock to General Karslake to find that it had had so little training. However, with the knowledge that the rest of the 52nd Division would not arrive in the assembly area for a few days, together with the fact that when it did arrive it was to be used for the defence of Brittany, he set about arranging for the Brigade to have some practical experience in the employment of its weapons.

On 11 June the situation had radically changed. The General was ordered by the War Office to place the Beauman Division under command of the French Tenth Army. He also received orders direct from General Dill that the 157th Brigade should be placed under French command. Naturally, this series of orders came as a great shock as they completely upset the plans that had been formulated with such care for the employment of the British troops in France. However, he had no alternative but to carry out the orders that were subsequently received from the French High Command to send the 157th Brigade forward to Conches to operate under the French III Corps.

In the above connection there is one formation that, hitherto, has not been mentioned. This is the Armoured Division, or rather its remains. This Division was technically operating under the command of General Georges, or was it General Altmayer? No one was quite sure. Certainly, its commander was with the French 10th Army, together with the remnants of the 2nd Armoured Brigade. The rear HQ, together with the 3rd Armoured Brigade, was located near Le Mans. This latter Brigade was undergoing a most necessary refit. It is important to remember that these rear parts of the Armoured Division were completely out of contact with their commander. However, rear HQ received a direct order from No 17 Military Mission at 1145 on 12 June to arrange for every possible tank to be moved to Conches.[2] This instruction confirms that issued by General Karslake to help 157th Brigade.

It will be appreciated that, once again, British formations were being committed piecemeal and without a Commander. However, in this instance, the reason is clear. General Brooke was scheduled to arrive in France on 12 June, in time, it was hoped, to assume command of the troops engaged. As far as it is possible to discover, General Brooke had not been informed of the change of plan prior to his leaving England. As is now known he did not arrive at his command HQ at Le Mans until the afternoon of 13 June. He left almost immediately for Briare to see General Weygand. Indeed, he did not begin to exercise any form of control until the evening of the 14th. During the whole of this period he had issued no orders, nor had he given any indication of his policy. His Headquarters was completely stagnant; indeed it was wondered who was actually in command. As far as a staff was concerned, though a complete Corps staff had been assembled by General Brooke while he was in England, this staff had arrived in St Malo on a separate ship to that in which General Brooke had travelled. And there the staff stayed. With the exception of General Eastwood, who had travelled with General Brooke, and Brigadier Ritchie, who reached Le Mans on the 14th, no other member ever arrived at Corps HQ nor was ever employed in any capacity in France. It seems curious that when General Brooke appointed General Marshall-Cornwall to assume command of Normanforce on 15 June he did not allot some of this idle staff to help him. He must have been aware that General Marshall-Cornwall did not possess the facilities to conduct operations.

At the interview between General Brooke and General Weygand (together with General Georges), General Brooke, who prided himself on his command of the French language, either deliberately, or mistakenly, misinterpreted the statements made by General Weygand on the state of the French Army. Time after time General Weygand has insisted that this was so. Whatever the truth may be, General Brooke telephoned to General Dill during the late morning of 14 June and told him that General Weygand had indicated that the French forces had ceased to have a unified command and were, therefore, finished. The CIGS accepted these comments at their face value and passed the information to Mr Churchill, primarily to support General Brooke's plea to evacuate all the British troops as soon as possible. General Brooke's remarks eventually met with the desired result and he was informed that he was no longer under

French command and that the evacuation of the troops could begin. From his actions thereafter it is quite clear that he directed all his energies to evacuating the troops and returning to England as soon as possible. The staggering order to Brigadier Bissett, District Commander Southern District, is a case in point. From this it is obvious that he had no enthusiasm for prolonging the period of his command. He must have known that the result of such an order would be disastrous, both from the point of view of the troops and the loss of stores located in the Lower Loire area. No explanation has ever been forthcoming as to the reasons behind this fateful order. General Brooke does not even refer to it in his Diary (as edited by Sir Arthur Bryant).

It would seem that a quite unnecessary and excessive sense of urgency existed at Le Mans on the return of General Brooke from Briare. This is borne out by the hasty departure of the whole of the Headquarters staff, together with General Brooke, from Le Mans on the morning of 15 June.[3] In extenuation, General Brooke has said that accurate information regarding the movements of the enemy was not received at his HQ. In view of the extreme speed displayed by the Germans and the exposed position of Le Mans, General Brooke considered that it was essential to move further west so as to be behind British forces which could give, at least, some protection in case of an unexpected German thrust.

As regards the non-reception of information, this is contradicted by the RAF reports. These are confirmed by the GSO III who was responsible for collating all the information received and marking the results up on the War Map at the HQ L of C. Indeed, the War Diary shows that information was being received hourly and was meticulously entered.[4] While it has to be admitted that, with the advent of General Brooke, the special officer motor-cyclist patrols were discontinued, nevertheless the RAF reports largely compensated for them.

With the departure of GHQ from Le Mans communications became extremely tenuous with the other formations under command. Whereas for some eight months the L of C HQ had been built up with extreme care, lines being laid where necessary to every district and area, now any messages that had to be sent were confined to the increasingly unreliable civilian telephone system. However, the RAF were able to continue to supply up-to-date information regarding the enemy's movements right up to the time General Brooke boarded the *Cambridgeshire* on the evening of the 17th. In view of this it seems a pity that it was not found possible to inform the various embarkation staffs at the ports in Brittany and on the Loire, to say nothing of Marseilles. Had that been done, the evacuation of both personnel and stores could have been carried out in due order, with the consequent salvation of huge quantities of the latter. The evacuation of HQ Southern District on the afternoon of the 15th broke the connecting links to the Southern Ports, rendering GHQ's task of controlling the various units under its command almost impossible, there being no reliable form of communication from either Vitré or Redon. As will be appreciated, the only information that the Port Commandants were able to obtain was both vague and inaccurate, emanating as it did largely from refugees. Naturally, it was both exaggerated and alarming. Unfortunately the Commandants had no means by which the reports could be checked.

As far as the withdrawal of the combat troops is concerned, it will have been seen that, but for the very high qualities of the formation commanders, these movements could have ended in disaster. Fortunately in the Cherbourg peninsula there was a minimum of trouble and little interference from the enemy. It is this final move that requires further examination. As is known, General Brooke's main object was to evacuate the troops; the question of fighting the enemy did not, it would seem, arise. It is, however, interesting to see what might have happened if all the forces in the peninsula had been commanded by a 'fighting' soldier. Within a radius of twenty miles and including the port of Cherbourg was a British force of some 22,000 fighting men well equipped with artillery and supplies. In addition, there were at least five battalions of French infantry for use in the field plus the garrison troops in the forts. These latter had a considerable number of heavy guns mounted in them. They proved most effective when Rommel approached the town. There is no doubt that, in Cherbourg at least, the French forces were tenacious. Even after the British had left, the French garrison did not surrender for a further twenty-four hours.

Rommel, who commanded the 7th Panzer Division in its attack

on Cherbourg, admits that when he was held up at a point some twenty miles from the port he grew extremely anxious. He knew that the Allies were nearly three times as numerous as his own troops and very much better equipped since his lightning march of 150 miles from Le Havre.

When he had turned west and approached Cherbourg along the coast road, owing to the strength of the resistance and the mining of the direct route, the whole mass of the British forces could have been hurled against his flank and rear. There is no doubt that the 7th Panzer would have ceased to exist and Rommel would not have become the 'Desert Fox'. The result of this manoeuvre would have left the remainder of Schmidt's corps on its own in Brittany. This consisted of the 5th Panzer and a motorized division of infantry. Against them could have been arraigned General de la Laurencie's III Corps together with the various other formations of the 10th Army, also a fresh, well-equipped British Division, (if somewhat undertrained) the 1st Canadians. These forces do not take into account those that had already been moved to Brittany to help garrison the 'Redoubt'. A firm stand and an encircling movement could have liquidated the western assault. Both the above operations had been made possible owing to the diversion of the main German forces in the west by Von Rundstedt into a southeasterly thrust. Likewise, most of the Luftwaffe was being employed in dealing with the French in the east. There is no doubt that the results of such disasters on Von Rundstedts' command would have had considerable influence on German tactics, indeed strategy, throughout the remainder of France. However, it is more than probable that the final outcome would have been the same. Even allowing this, at least the enemy would have suffered severely and their immediate future plans upset.

While all the guns and vehicles of the BEF north of the Somme, together with ammunition and equipment, had been lost, there was still a considerable quantity in the south, all of which was vital to England if the war was to be carried on with any hope of success. In the *Official History* appears a table showing the amounts of the various items returned to England. In this context it is important to remember that *all* the items mentioned were evacuated from the *south*. The figures bear studying. First, there are 322 guns of all types. (Ellis) It is interesting to see how this total can be reconciled.

51st Division	17 (ex Le Havre)
52nd Division	120 (ex Cherbourg)
1st Canadian Division	24 (ex Brest)
Beauman Division	33 (ex Cherbourg)
	194

This leaves a balance of 128 to be accounted for. Owing to Ellis having included in the totals of other equipment material that was never landed in France, it seems possible that this also applied to guns. From the available records it is impossible to account for the balance of 128 guns as belonging to the two AA Brigades. If, however, the Canadian Division was reckoned as complete then the total of 312 guns for those returned by the AA Brigades seems much more realistic. The only other artillery units in France were those belonging to the L of C Anti-Aircraft Brigade and a second Anti-Aircraft Brigade that had been allotted to the A.A.S.F. for the defence of airfields, the grand total of these guns being a maximum of 170. Of these, two batteries had been lost north of the Somme. At least two more had been destroyed in action south of the Somme. Various other units had lost one or more guns prior to evacuation from one cause or another. When the evacuation began, units reported to the various ports for embarkation. Luckily, before panic began, a number of guns had been embarked. Thereafter the situation deteriorated rapidly. The story of the saving of the guns at Brest by the Canadians has already been told. There is one other story that serves to illustrate the situation further. The 53rd AA Regiment had ended up at Marseilles. It appears that this was a 'mixed' regiment consisting of two Batteries of Heavy and one of Light guns. Owing to the lack of cranes and, it would seem, no 'Jumbo' derrick on the ship allotted to the Regiment, only the light Battery could be loaded. The 13 surviving 3" guns were lined up on the quay. The Commanding Officer of the 53rd managed to persuade the French authorities to bring over a floating crane early the following morning to load the guns. That night, however, after the troops had turned in, certain senior Royal Naval officers appeared and said that the ship could not wait owing to the threatened Armistice; the guns would have to be abandoned. As a result the troops had to rise and render the guns useless. The ship sailed shortly afterwards. Failure to load guns for similar reasons occurred at other ports. The loss of guns and stores together with other equipment has been excused on the grounds that there was the possibility of the proposed Armistice including terms requiring all British troops in France to be interned. When, on the 17th, General Brooke heard from General Dill that Marshal Pétain had made his broadcast, he declared that the French had behaved disgracefully in not having warned him of the proposed action. It should be pointed out that he had no one but himself to blame. At his request, both Military Missions had been withdrawn. There was, therefore, no communication between his HQ and GQG. Further, he had declared that, as there was no chance of the French having control over military affairs through lack of communication, he should no longer be under their command. As his force was acting independently of the French and was completely out of touch with them, one asks the question, how could he reasonably expect to be notified in advance? In any case, as is known, the impression of an immediate ceasefire was removed that evening. As General Brooke, by his own decision, was completely out of touch with his command, he was in no position to reassure the various port commanders.

The loss of vehicles was considerable, only 4,739 returning to England. The great majority of these had not been unloaded as they belonged to both the 52nd and Canadian Divisions. A few had been saved by the 154th Brigade and the remainder represented those that had been loaded before the panic orders were received at the ports.

The amount of ammunition recovered seems, at first glance, to be surprisingly large — a total of 32,303 tons. It is necessary to see how this total is made up. General Karslake had been issued with a priority list of ammunition. This included small arms, 25 Pdr and, above all, the enormous dump of chemical warfare equipment at Fécamp. All this latter was cleared by the beginning of June. The remainder of the ammunition can be largely accounted for by a full shipload that had not been unloaded at Cherbourg on 15 June and a further shipload at St Nazaire on the same date. Other supplies and stores saved amounted to some 33,000 tons. Those, other than the ones actually still on board ships at the time the evacuation was ordered, had been returned to England by the end of May. Finally, the 1,071 tons of petrol can be accounted for by the partially loaded ship that left St Nazaire on 16 June.

As early as 4 June General Karslake had represented to the CIGS the absolute necessity for holding up further shipments of supplies for France. In spite of this, however, ships containing stores, petrol and ammunition continued to arrive. Indeed, as several officers remarked, it was provoking to see ships being loaded at the quays when others containing similar material were being discharged! The 6th Royal Sussex were employed in stacking newly arrived petrol from 26 May until *15 June!* One can appreciate the enormous amount that must have arrived during this period. The battalion had the mortification of seeing all their hard work going up in smoke when they left the forest of Savernay on their way to St Nazaire on 16 June. This continuous supply of fuel, including aviation spirit, was far in excess of any forseeable requirements, certainly by 5 June. The RAF had virtually disappeared from France. Their re-fuelling requirements grew less and less as time passed. The armour, likewise, had been reduced to a minimum and there was little likelihood of it being reinforced. In fact, the only use for the fuel was for the transport of the units and formations operating in the battle area together with the supply Services. Even had the proposed arrival of the 3rd Division materialized, which was problematical to say the least of it, the supply existing in France at the end of May was quite adequate to meet all needs until it was possible to calculate for the future. Unfortunately, no notice was taken of the advice from those on the spot, with the consequent unnecessary loss.

The reasons for the small number of armoured vehicles returned to England will, one presumes, remain a mystery. As has been related, the train bearing the remaining tanks of the 2nd Armoured Brigade and the balance of those of the 3rd Armoured Brigade that had not proceeded to Conches, left Le Mans for St Malo — and was never seen again. It has been said that, at some point, the French authorities had diverted the train onto a siding, removing the locomotive for some other purpose. Before the train could be moved again, the Germans arrived and captured it. In view of the fact that the Armoured Brigade's road parties were forced to remain outside

Brest for a further twenty-four hours, it is surprising that no effort was made to try and locate the missing train, especially as its escort had arrived without it. No explanation as to why the train was unaccompanied has ever been forthcoming. Had there been the original skeleton crews aboard, they would have been in a position to prevent the train being abandoned or, if this proved impossible, then it seems probable that they could have removed the vehicles from the train, travelling by road as the 3rd Brigade had done to Cherbourg. It is equally surprising that no recovery detachment was sent to find the train. It must have appeared obvious that something serious had occurred when the train did not arrive, even allowing for the inevitable delays. The Brigade had ample vehicles and supplies. The enemy were nowhere near the Brittany peninsula at the time. Further, a message to GHQ might have provoked the use of an aircraft to try and spot the train thereby guiding a recovery party to its location. In this connection, it must be admitted that at the time GHQ was a somewhat 'fluid' organization. In fact, nothing whatever was done. Whilst the actual loss of vehicles was comparatively small, it is surprising that Regimental pride did not insist that some effort was made to recover the tanks.

Bearing in mind the warnings that General Ironside had given both to Lord Gort and to General Dill prior to their departure for France in 1939, Lord Gort's Despatch shows that, too late, he had appreciated the advice he had received but had ignored. Lord Gort had written:

'In more rearward areas, schemes must be prepared for the manning at short notice of centres of communication and other important defiles. Therefore, all units, even those designed for purely administrative purposes, must prepare to take part in the battle and they must receive the necessary preliminary training'.

During the period up to the actual outbreak of hostilities, nothing whatever was organized in the event of the most unlikely occurrence of the enemy appearing on the door-step of the L of C. No plans of any kind had been drawn up for such an emergency. Fortunately, the presence of Brigadier Beauman, a retired but 'fighting' soldier, helped to remedy the deficiency to a small extent. The advent of General Karslake, had he been properly supported, could have added immeasurably to the success of the defence of the L of

C. While all those who tried to carry out operations did their best, the disadvantages under which they were operating were insurmountable. The fact that there was no unified British command prevented effective use of the available troops and the lack of experienced commanders proved a great handicap. When, at long last, a commander appeared the situation had passed the point of redemption, and in any case, he had no faith in the enterprise, the French or his troops. His sole object was to evacuate the troops as quickly as possible; engaging in 'fisticuffs' with the enemy did not cross his mind. This is proved conclusively by the fact that he did not call forward his operational staff on arrival.

But the final comment must be given to Gregory Blaxland. In his book *Destination Dunkirk* he says:

'There were men enough for the defence of Britian, once arms could be provided for them. *However, they had not been sent to France with the object of returning.*'*

---

* Author's italics.

References

Introduction
1. Report by a committee under the chairmanship of Lieutenant-General Sir Geoffrey Howard, 1940; hereafter referred to as 'Howard Report'.
2. General Sir James Marshall-Cornwall's Report.
3. 'G' file, L of C (PRO).

Chapter 1
1. Howard Report.
2. Ibid.
3. *Ironside Diaries*, edited by Colonel R. Macleod and Dennis Kelly.
4. Ibid.
5. Letter, Colonel M. Ryan, 26.11.70.
6. Howard Report.
7. Interview, Author and Macleod, 22.1.71.

Chapter 2
1. Diary of RQMS Brown, Imperial War Museum.
2. Interview, Macleod, 22.1.71.
3. Howard Report.
4. Ibid.
5. *Chief of Staff*, Vol I, Edited by Brian Bond.
6. War Diary, Beauman Division.
7. Report of Major-General P. de Fonblanque, 1940.

Chapter 3
1. Interivew, Sergeant Glover 7.12.70.
2. *Roussillon Gazette*, 1946.
3. Letter, Colonel G. Alms RE, 2.5.71.
4. 'G' file, L of C HQ (PRO).

Chapter 4
1. Letter, Brigadier A. Abel Smith, 14.4.70. In fact Major-General de Fonblanque had been appointed Major-General (A and Q) — Howard Report.
2. Letter and Diary, Mrs Elliott, 18.10.70.
3. Based on notes written between 23.5. and 13.6.40 by Colonel E.L. Fanshawe; see also General Karslake's Report (Appendix C)
4. Letters, Colonel E.L. Fanshawe, 10.10.72, and Brigadier J.R.T. Aldous, 5.7.72.
5. Letter, Mrs Brittorous, 7.6.71.
6. Beauman Division Signals War Diary and correspondence with Sir William Scott.
7. Letter Major General R. Briggs, 19.11.71. AFV No 6, Appx 'A' Report, 25.5.40-10.6.40.
8. Beauman Division War Diary.
9. Major General R. Evans' Report.
10. 51st Division War Diary.

Chapter 5
1. General Marshall-Cornwall's Report, published with General Sir Alan Brooke's Despatch, 1946.

2. *Keep the Memory Green* by Lt-Colonel E. Butler and Major T. Selly-Bradford.
3. Beauman Divisional Signals War Diary.
4. Howard Report.
5. 'G' file, L of C HQ (PRO).
6. Howard Report.

Chapter 6
1. Attached to Pownall's Report (PRO).
2. All details regarding the activities of the Support Group and its Commander are drawn from W/D 101st LAA and A/TK Regt and correspondence with Colonel A.L. Cameron, General H.R.S. Swinburn, Brigadier W. Radford, Major H.H. Walker, J.L. d'e Darby, Colonel W.M. Broomhall and General Sir Charles Dunphie, and from General R. Evans' Report, the *Official History* and *The History of the East Surrey Regiment.*
3. Letter, General Sir Charles Dunphie, 23.11.71.
4. Letter, Lt-Colonel H. Vere-Laurie, 28.1.72 — 28.4.72.
5. General Evans's Report.
6. Letter, General Sir Charles Dunphie, 23.11.71.
7. Lt-General H.R. Pownall's Report.
8. Sgt Brown's Diary.
9. General Sir John Crocker's Report.
10. General Sir Henry Karslake's Report.
11. War Diary, 157th Bde.
12. *The Business of War*, Brigadier Sir John Kennedy.
13. Letter, Major-General Sir John Laurie, 9.7.72. Letter, Field-Marshal Sir James Cassels, 2.8.72.
14. War Diary, 157th Bde.
15. General Sir Henry Karslake's Report: General Sir John Crocker's Report.
16. But see War Diary of Rear HQ 1st Armoured Div (PRO).
17. General Evans's Report.
18. General Sir John Crocker's Report.
19. Letter, Viscount Younger of Leckie, 13.6.71; Howard Report.
20. *The Canadian Army 1939-45*, Stacey.
21. Ibid.

Chapter 7
1. Letter, General Sir Neil Ritchie, 30.9.72.
2. *The Canadian Army, 1939-45*.
3. Ibid.
4. Letter, Brigadier A. Abel Smith, 29.4.71.
5. *Official History, The War At Sea.*
6. *Roussillon Gazette*, 1946.
7. Howard Report.
8. Major-General de Fonblanque's Report, 25.6.40.
9. Interview, B.P.V. Elsden, 30.10.70.
10. Letters, Major R.M. Collins, 9.2.71 and 18.3.71.
11. Letter, Major R.A. Archer-Shee, 13.1.70.
12. Letter, Brigadier E. Prior-Palmer, 30.5.71.

Chapter 8
1. *Then a Soldier*, Brigadier A.B. Beauman, 1960.
2. Howard Report.
3. Details of the operations and movements of the 157th Brigade Group have been largely obtained from the Brigade's War Diary. Also from correspondence with Sir James Cassels and Sir John Laurie.
4. War Diary, 157th Bde.
5. Ibid.
6. Howard Report.

Chapter 9
1. Letter, Sir James Cassels.

2. Rear HQ Armoured Divisional War Diary.
3. *The Canadian Army, 1939-45*, The Howard Report.
4. Letters, Brigadier A. Abel Smith, 20.4.70.

APPENDICES

APPENDIX A

ORDER OF BATTLE ON THE L OF C

Those Formations and Units which were not employed south of the Somme after 20 May 1940 are in italics.

1st ARMOURED DIVISION (from 20 May, et seq)
Major-General R. Evans
2nd Armoured Brigade — Brigadier R.L. McCreery
  Queen's Bays
  9th Lancers
  10th Hussars.
3rd Armoured Brigade — Brigadier J.T. Crocker
  2nd Bn, RTR
  3rd Bn, RTR (in Calais from 23 May)
  5th Bn, RTR
1st Support Group — Brigadier F.E. Morgan
  1st RHA Regt (with GHQ reserve; also see 51st Div)
  101st Light AA and Anti-tank Regt
  1st Bn, K.R.R.C. (Calais from 23 May)
  2nd Bn, Rifle Brigade. (Calais from 23 May)
  4th Border Regt (from L of C troops) from 23 May to 3 June
  2/6th East Surrey Regt (from 12th Div) from 3 June
  Royal Engineers: 1st Field and 1st Field Park Squadrons
12th (EASTERN) DIVISION
  Major-General R.L. Petre (until 18 May)
35th Brigade — Lt-Colonel A.F.F. Young (acting until 13 May) — Brigadier V.L. de Cordova (from 13 May)
  2/5th, 2/6th and 2/7th Bns, Queen's Regt
  36th Brigade — Brigadier G.R.P. Roupell VC
  5th Bn, The Buffs
  6th and 7th Bns, Queen's Own (Royal West Kent) Regt
37th Brigade — Brigadier R.J.P. Wyatt
  2/6th Bns, East Surrey Regt
  6th Bn, Royal Sussex Regt
  7th Bn, Royal Sussex Regt (destroyed 20 May)
  262nd, 263rd and 264th Field Coys; 265th Field Park Coy, RE
46th (NORTH MIDLAND AND WEST RIDING) DIVISION
  Major-General H.O. Curtis
137th Brigade — Brigadier J.B. Gawthorpe
  2/5th Bn, West Yorkshire Regt
  2/6th and 2/7th Bns, Duke of Wellingtons' Regt
138th Brigade — Brigadier E.J. Grinling
  6th Bn, Lincolnshire Regt
  2/4th Bn, King's Own Yorkshire Light Infantry

6th Bn, York and Lancaster Regt
139th Brigade — Brigadier H.A.F. Crewdson
2/5th Bn, Leicestershire Regt.
2/5th and 9th Bns, Sherwood Foresters
270th, 271st and 272nd Field Coys; 273rd Field Park Coy RE
51st (HIGHLAND) DIVISION
Major-General V.M. Fortune
152nd Brigade — Brigadier H.W.V. Stewart (until 6 June) — Lt-Colonel I.C. Barclay (from 6 June)
2nd and 4th Bns, Seaforth Highlanders
4th Bn, Queen's Own Cameron Highlanders
153rd Brigade — Brigadier G.T. Burney
1st and 5th Bn, Gordon Highlanders
4th Bn, Black Watch
154th Brigade — Brigadier A.C.L. Stanley-Clarke
1st Bn, Black Watch
7th and 8th Bns, Argyll and Sutherland Highlanders
Royal Artillery
17th, 23rd and 75th Field Regiments; 51st Anti-tank Regt
Royal Engineers
26th, 236th and 237th Field Coys; 238th Field Park Coy
TROOPS ATTACHED TO THE DIVISION FROM APRIL, 1949
Royal Armoured Corps
1st Lothian and Border Horse (GHQ troops)
Royal Artillery
1st RHA Regt, less one battery (GHQ troops and 1st Armoured Div)
385 Battery of the 97th Field Regiment (III Corps)
51st Medium Regiment (GHQ troops)
Royal Engineers
213 Field Park Coy (III Corps)
Infantry
7th Bn, Royal Northumberland Fusiliers (MG) (III Corps)
1st Bn, Princess Louise's Kensington Regiment (MG) (III Corps)
7th Bn, Royal Norfolk Regiment (Pioneers) (GHQ troops)
6th Bn, Royal Scots Fusiliers (Pioneers) (GHQ troops)
ATTACHED TO THE DIVISION FROM 7 JUNE, 1940
'A' Brigade (Beauman Division) — Brigadier M.A. Green
2/7th Duke of Wellington's Regt (L of C troops)

LINES OF COMMUNICATION
GOC — Major-General P de Fonblanque (23 May and from 13 June)
GSO I — Lt-Colonel F.A.S. Clarke (until 23 May)
GOC — Lt-General Sir Henry Karslake, late RA (from 23 May to 13 June)
BGS — Brigadier G. Bruce (until 25 May)
GSO I — Lt-Colonel J.R.T. Aldous
GSO II — Major E.L. Fanshawe (from 23 May until 13 June)
Royal Artillery
3rd Anti-aircraft Brigade — Brigadier W.R. Shilstone
2nd, 8th and 79th Anti-aircraft Regts

4th Light Anti-aircraft Regt
Royal Engineers
104th, 106th and 110th Army Troops Coys
212th and 218th Army Troops Coys
270th and 272 Field Coys; 273rd Field Park Coy (from 46 Div) Together with Road and Rail Construction Coys etc
Also numerous Ordnance Depots and RASC Coys and Medical Services including Hospitals and Hospital trains.
Infantry
4th Bn, The Buffs (to Beauman Div 27 May)
14th Bn, Royal Fusiliers
12th Bn, Royal Warwickshire Regt
4th Bn, Border Regt (to 1st Armoured Div from 23 May to 3 June)
1/5th Bn, Sherwood Foresters, (to Beauman Div from 27 May)
2/6th Bn, East Surrey Regt (from 12th Div to 1st Armoured Div 3 June)
2/4th Bn, KOYLI (from 46th Div 21 May; to Beauman Div 7 June)
2/6th and 2/7th Bns, Duke of Wellington's Regt (from 46th Div 21 May)
2/5th, 2/6th and 2/7th Bns Queen's Regt (from 12th Div 21 May)
6th Bn, Royal Sussex Regt (from 12th Div 20 May)

52nd (LOWLAND) DIVISION
Major-General J.S. Drew
155th Brigade — Brigadier T. Grainger-Stewart
7/9th Bn, Royal Scots
4th and 5th Bns, KOSB
156th Brigade — Brigadier J.S.N. Fitzgerald
4/5th Bn, Royal Scots Fusiliers
6th and 7th Bns, Cameronians
157th Brigade — Brigadier Sir John Laurie Bt
5th and 6th Bns, Highland Light Infantry
1st Bn, Glasgow Highlanders
Royal Artillery
70th, 71st and 78th Field Regts
54th Anti-tank Regt
Royal Engineers
202nd, 241st and 554th Field Coys; 243rd Field Park Coy

1st CANADIAN DIVISION (from UK 11 June)
Major-General A.G.L. McNaughton
1st Brigade — Brigadier A.A. Smith
48th Highlanders
Royal Canadian Regiment
Hastings and Prince Edward Regiment
Royal Canadian Artillery
1st Field Regiment RCHA
The remainder of the Division did not land in France

BEAUMAN DIVISION (formed 27 May)
As this formation was unique, its organization is given in detail. It is felt that it is worthy of study as it was an excellent example of effective improvisation.
Commander — A/Major-General A.B. Beauman

Staff
  GSO I — Major A.N.S. Corbett, RA
  GSO II — Captain J.G. Churcher, KSLI
  GSO III — Captain G.S. Lowden, Y and L
  GSO III(I) — Captain D.G. Dawes, RA
  Attached — Major D.G.I.A. Gordon, Gordon H
A and Q
  AA and QMG — Colonel H.F. Grant-Suttie, RA
  DAAG — Major R.A. Lake, Northants
  DAQMG — Major M.C.E. Sharpe, S. Lancs
  Attached — Captain D.M. Gall, Cameronians (Camp Commandant)
  Attached — Captain E.P. Dickson, RE

  CRA — Major G. Elliot, RA
  CRE — Lt-Colonel J.B.H. Doyle, RE
  CSO — Major W.A. Salt, R. Sigs
Troops
A Brigade (late Beauforce) — Brigadier M.A. Green (to 51st Div 7 June)
  Brigade Major — Captain Rennie, KOSB
  4th Bn, The Buffs — Lt-Colonel F.J.E. Marshall
  2/6th Bn, East Surrey Regt (till 3 June) — Lt-Colonel H.S. Burgess
  4th Bn, Border Regt — Lt-Colonel T.W.A. Tomlinson (from 3 June)
  1/5th Bn, Sherwood Foresters — Major B.D. Shaw
  D Machine Gun Coy (elements of Cheshire and Manchester Regts)
  Carrier Platoon
B Brigade — Brigadier Kent-Lemon (late Vickforce)
  Brigade Major — Major White, Beds and Herts
  'Merry's Rifles', Major H.R.H. Davies, Coldstream Guards (1st Provisional Bn)
  'Davies Rifles', Major W.W. Harrowing, DCLI (2nd Provisional Bn)
  'Newcombe's Rifles', Major L.E.C.M. Perowne, RE (3rd Provisional Bn)
  Carrier Platoon
C Brigade (late Digforce) Lt-Colonel J.B.H. Diggle, 9th Lancers
  Major Brittorous (from 1 June to 11 June)
  Brigade Major — Major N.W. Gwatkin, Coldstream Guards
  P, Q and R Battalions of the AMPC
Divisional Troops
  2/7th Bn, Duke of Wellington's Regt (to 51st Division 7 June) — Lt-Colonel G. Taylor
  2/4th Bn, KOYLI (to C Brigade 5 June) — Lt-Colonel J. Hodgkinson
  4th Provisional Bn (to B Brigade 6 June) — Major Syme, Royal Scots
  2/6th Bn, Duke of Wellington's Regt (to C Brigade 5 June) — Lt-Colonel E.H. Llewelyn
  23rd AA Battery, RA (to C Brigade 8 June) — Major Unsworth, RA
  Divisional Tank Coy (to 3rd Armoured Brigade 7 June) — Captain P.W.C. Colan, RTR
  E Anti-tank Regiment RA (P and Q Batteries)   (formed 23 May)
  X Field Battery RA
'Ark Force' — Brigadier A.C.L. Stanley-Clarke (formed 9 June)
  4th Bn, Black Watch (from 153rd Bde)

7th Bn, Argyll and Sutherland Highlanders (from 154th Bde)
8th Bn, Argyll and Sutherland Highlanders (from 154th Bde)
6th Bn, Royal Scots Fusiliers (Pioneers)
A Brigade (Beauman Division)
1st Bn, Princess Louise's Kensington Regiment (less 2 Coys)
17th Field Regiment RA
75th Field Regiment RA
51st Anti-tank Regiment RA (one Battery)
236th Field Coy RE
237th Field Coy RE
239 Field Coy RE
154th Field Ambulance
'**Normanforce**' — Lt-General J.H. Marshall-Cornwall (from 15 June)
3rd (Composite) Armoured Brigade — Brigadier J.G. Crocker
Beauman Division (less A Brigade) — A/Major-General A.B. Beauman
157th Brigade Group (52nd Division) Brigadier Sir John Laurie
71st Field Regiment R.A. (52nd Division)
5th Battalion the King's own Scottish Borderers. (52nd Division)
One troop of Anti-tank guns and a company of Sappers.
It will be noted that, beside the Regular Divisions, there were some 20 Battalions of Infantry on the L of C after 20 May, viz:
L of C troops 5 Battalions
Beauman Div (excluding above) 7 Battalions
12th Division 5 Battalions
46th Division 3 Battalions. Total 20 Battalions
Regular Infantry actually in France south of the Somme between 20 May and 20 June 1940
51st Division 13 Battalions
52nd Division 9 Battalions
1st Canadian Division 3 Battalions. Total 25 Battalions
This shows a grand total of 45 Battalions or nearly 32,000 infantry. Also there were 17 Regiments of Artillery present South of the Somme between 20 May and 19 June.

APPENDIX B

Administrative Position in B.A.F.F. at 1800 Hrs, 2 June, 1940

HQ B.A.F.F.
1. Now located at OLIVET, south of ORLEANS.
Advanced Headquarters (North) remains at COULOMMIERS and Advanced Headquarters (East) is still at NANCY.

A.A.S.F.
2. The A.A.S.F. is now composed of 3 fighter and 6 bomber squadrons with the necessary ancillary units. Orders have been issued for it to move to a new location in the VENDOME area on 3 June. The provisional new locations are shown at Appendix 'A'.
3. A small operations Headquarters, together with Nos 7 and 8 Servicing Sections have been left in the TROYES area to provide refuelling and rearming facilities for fighters and bombers at ECHEMINES and VILLECERF aerodromes, should these be required as advanced landing grounds for operations.

SOUTH COMPONENT
4. This has now been reduced to four composite wing servicing units as ESTREES ST DENIS has been abandoned as it was considered to have become vulnerable. Only ROUEN BOOS, DREUX, ETREPAGNY and BEAUMONT aerodromes are therefore now manned.
5. ...
6. The force is constituted mainly for the operation of up to 6 fighter squadrons from either the A.A.S.F. and/or the U.K. and is also responsible for the operation of aircraft of Rear Component.

SOUTHERN FORCE (HADDOCK)
7. No 71 Wing and Nos 16 & 17 Servicing Flights, together with petrol and bombs for 14 days sustained effort for Wellingtons have been prepared for dispatch at short notice.
They will probably move on 3 June and should be ready to operate by 9 June.

LOCATION OF A.S.S.F. UNITS IN LE MANS — BLOIS AREA

HQ A.A.S.F.	Chateau de la Cressoiniere
HQ No. 67 Wing (Fighter)	Laigne (8 miles south of Le Mans)
No. 1 Squadron	Chateaudun
73 Squadron	Le Mans
501 Squadron	Le Mans
62 W.S.U.	Le Mans
HQ No. 75 Wing (Bomber)	Ecoman (20 miles N.E. of Vendome)
No. 88 Squadron	Herouville (5 miles north of Ecoman)
103 Squadron	Herouville
HQ No. 76 Wing (Bomber)	Montoire (13 miles west of Vendome)
12 Squadron	Souge (10 miles west of Montoire)
226 Squadron	Houssay (6 miles east of Montoire)
150 Squadron	Houssay
142 Squadron	Houssay

APPENDIX C

Report On
Operations in France between 23 May and 13 June, 1940
By
Lt-General Sir Henry Karslake

Arriving at Cherbourg at 6.0am on Thursday May 23rd, I left by air for Le Mans, the HQ of the L of C at 7.30am. As soon as possible, I left by car for the Swayne Mission, arriving there at about 8.0pm.* On my way, I visited the HQ of the 1st Armoured Division which was already on the way northward. The 3rd Brigade of this Division† arrived by the same boat as I did at Cherbourg and was not expected to reach the neighbourhood of the Division until Saturday.

At the Swayne Mission, I was informed that the Armoured Division had received an order from Lord Gort, via London, and approved by General Georges, to make a dash across the Somme the next day between Picquigny and Pont-Rémy, for Arras, to open up maintenance communication with the BEF. I enquired if this was in conjunction with a big attack by the French between Amiens and Peronne, due to take place next day. This, Brigadier Swayne thought, was most unlikely. This was confirmed by the Chef de Cabinet of General Georges,** whom I met the next morning. He explained that nothing of the sort was anticipated, and that the Armoured Division exploit was entirely independant. Brigadier Swayne was very pessimistic about the French carrying on much longer.

On Friday [24th] I went to Rouen to visit Rouen sub-area HQ. I learned that one L of C Territorial battalion [4th Border Regt] had been lent to the Armoured Division to replace its two battalions that had been sent to Calais with the 3rd Tank Battalion of the 3rd Brigade.

The Armoured Division, apparently, started its mission but, except for the Infantry battalion which crossed the river [Somme] at Ailly, unsupported by tanks or anything else, no crossing was effected. The battalion, I was told later by one of its officers, was forced back again by counter-attacks.

The next day [25th] the Germans bombed the Armoured Division, who asked for air assistance which was arranged as the result of my representations to the Swayne Mission, with satisfactory results.

Whilst at Rouen, I was advised of the force which General de Fonblanque had wisely constituted north of Rouen, including reinforcements.‡

Up to the time of the arrival of the Armoured Division, no Allied troops, except for the above scratch force, existed as far as is known, between Rouen and the Somme. On the other hand, officers' patrols from Rouen had established the fact

---

* Brigadier Swayne represented the British Commander-in-Chief at the HQ of General Georges, commanding the French north-east theatres of operations. The HQ was located at La Ferte-sous-Jouarre, some 180 miles from Le Mans.
† The 3rd Armoured Brigade had only two battalions, one having been sent to Calais just before the Brigade had sailed.
**General Roton.
‡ This consisted of a motley collection of Battalions made up of re-inforcements under the Command of Colonel Vicary. This officer was responsible for all reinforcing arrangements for the BEF.

of a German bridge-head south of Abbeville and at St Valéry-sur-Somme. Nobody knew if any of the bridges across the Somme between Amiens and Abbeville were intact or not, except the one at Ailly which one battalion reported to be intact.*

The next day [25th] I sent Brigadier Bruce to London to report the situation. Unfortunately, he had an accident on landing, so the 'plane returned for me. I reached the War Office at 9.0pm.

In the meantime, the remnants of two French light cavalry Divisions and a few tanks of a D.C.A. arrived south of Abbeville. Those were ordered with the Armoured Division to drive in the German bridgehead at Abbeville. This attack failed; the Armoured Division reported losing 40 tanks.†

On my return from London on Sunday evening [26th], I learned that the 51st Division, of which I had never heard before, was being sent round from the Saar front.

This Division, on arrival, was ordered to take over from the French Light Cavalry Divisions on the front inclusive Pont-Rémy to the sea, a distance of about 16 miles. Up to now this area was commanded by the French IX Corps. The IX Corps became the French 10th Army after the arrival of the 51st Division, but with no other troops than those already mentioned.**

I asked the Swayne Mission to have an Air reconnaissance made of the Somme between Amiens and the sea to try and discover the condition of the bridges. Although this was possibly interference on my part, I felt that I must do something to help the 51st Division to obtain information. The results, I am afraid, were not satisfactory.

I then visited General Frére's Seventh Army, and General Altmayer of the IX Corps‡, and asked them what their plans were. The former had some ideas but the latter was very problematical. They expected two French Divisions to come up at any time, but could not say when.

A few days after the complete arrival of the 51st Division, the French 31st Division arrived. General Fortune of the 51st Division was ordered to drive in the Abbeville bridgehead in conjunction with the French 31st Division which was put under his command, and some tanks of the French Light Cavalry.

The time for reconnaissance and preparation was, in my opinion, quite inadequate, with the result that the attack failed. Even those [troops] that had been successful had to be withdrawn.

Considering that an attack had failed a few days before, it was to be expected that the enemy would have made any adjustments to his defence that were found to be necessary.

    * This bridge was not at Ailly-sur-Somme, as was supposed, but at Ailly-sur-Noye. It had been reported by an officer of the 6th Royal Sussex when passing through Le Mans after the Amiens debacle.

    † 1st Armoured Division came under command of the French Seventh Army (General Frére) on 25 May and the attack took place on the 27th, by which time the Germans were strongly established along the Somme. The 'few tanks of a D.C.A.' (*Division Cavalrie Armoré*) may have been part of General de Gaulle's division which was now arriving in the area.

    ** It was, in fact, Group A, an intermediate formation between IX Corps and Seventh Army. It was commanded by General Robert Altmayer. It was this formation that became the 10th Army.

    ‡ General Altmayer was the new 10th Army Commander. In addition to the French troops he had also the 51st Division and the 1st Armoured Division under his command.

The method of attack adopted by the 51st Division was, I suppose, in accordance with our (modern) Army teaching. It extended over something like 5 miles in a semi-circle. The Artillery assistance consisted of ten-minute concentrations on certain points. Is it surprising that the whole thing was a fiasco?

With the guns available, a certainty could have been made of success on a front of 2,000 yards!

The Germans at St Valéry were informed with the result that they came out against the left of the 51st Division and captured (it is reported) one of our batteries.

After this action, General Marshall-Cornwall told me, the French were elated but, when the final results were known, accused General Fortune of treachery, saying that he should be court-martialled: why, I never discovered. This was not my first experience of the temperament of some of the French Generals. Within a few days of my arrival in France, Brigadier Swayne rang me up and said that the French General at Rouen had reported to General Georges that 'the British troops in an around Rouen were a thoroughly undisciplined rabble, and would not take orders from their Commander'. At once I went to see the General in question but was informed that he was in Paris, so I saw his Chief of Staff. Having told him the reason for my visit, he expressed himself astounded at the alleged report of his General. He declared that he had never heard of any such accusation being made, or even discussed. They had always been on the best of terms with Brigadier Beauman and his Staff. I asked him to convey to General Dufour my wish that, should he have any complaints, he would at once refer to Brigadier Beauman and *not* to the C-in-C.

During this time, the scratch force round Rouen had been organized into three Brigades; two Brigadiers, Green and Lemon, being sent out from England, and the third, a Lt-Colonel with three battalions of the A.M.P.C. I felt that, if it was to be of any use at all, it must be organized in this way *and be got together by experienced men.* Even though they had very few days to get hold of their Brigades, the results were very good.

I offered my services to Generals Frére and Altmayer as Commander of the British Divisions, should they consider it would help them; but it was not accepted, though they wanted it*. Fortunately, General Marshall-Cornwall was sent out as Mission (17th) to 10th Army to look after the interests of our troops.

The task of the Beauman Division, as the Force round Rouen was now called, was from the outset to form a very thin line of protection for Rouen, which would destroy all bridges and lay anti-tank mines, of which some 30,000 had been supplied. Later, it became a thin rearguard position through which troops could withdraw if driven back.

General Beauman worked out a plan with General Fortune for this. It would have been of considerable value if the original plans for the withdrawal had been carried out.

For the next few days, after the 51st Division's attack [on 4 June] had failed, there was necessarily some confusion, and the Germans were able to penetrate the very thin line of the 51st Division in various places, capturing a considerable

---

* A hopeless situation existed which was recognized by the French Commanders. General Karslake's statement [see Supplement, p. 261] that GQG had been responsible for the failure to appoint him as Corps Commander, was unjustified. The fault lay with the CIGS who refused to implement his predecessor's recommendation of the appointment being made.

number of men, and actually crossing the River Bresle near the coast. [This was the beginning of the new German Offensive.]

The men of the 51st Division had suffered considerable casualties and were getting very tired, so I agreed to one of Beauman's Brigades [A Brigade] going foward and being replaced by a tired Brigade in the Beauman line. I have grounds for believing this was a considerable relief and could never have been accomplished if these Brigades of Beauman's Division had not been organized.

During the whole of this period, it was most difficult to discover the French policy of protecting this part of France. All that they could say was 'The Line of the Somme will be held at all costs'. This meant nothing of course because the French never did hold the Line of the Somme! Two Tank officers, who had escaped from Arras, crossed the Somme one morning at Etoile and met some German patrols south of the river! Then the 'Line of the Bresle' was to be held at all costs and so on. As regards the Seine, the bridges were prepared for demolition by the Commander of the garrison of Rouen, who had five battalions for holding the bridges. No preparations for a reserve south of the Seine was, apparently, contemplated.

The Beauman Division, with 9 Battalions and 20 anti-tank guns, was stretched over some 50 miles and was, of course, never intended to hold anybody anywhere by itself.

When, eventually, the Germans did attack [5 June], two Armoured Divisions broke across the Somme near Amiens, and made the first day Forges-les-Eaux.* There the 10th Army brought up our Armoured Division; but it does not seem to have had any effect. Some of Beauman's troops carried out a successful little counter-attack at Serqueux, but there was nothing to stop the Armoured Divisions from eventually reaching Rouen, thereby getting behind Beauman's troops all along the Andelle, and those immediately in rear of the French IX Corps.

In spite of these operations, the IX Corps and the 51st Division do not appear to have withdrawn or attempted to counterattack. All the other French troops on the other side of the gap (eastern side) moved off in the direction of Paris. The IX Corps and the 51st Division were ordered to withdraw on Le Havre and to take up positions to defend this port; this was the very thing that everyone knew would be fatal.†

Having blown up the bridges, the troops of Beauman's Division, after our Armoured Division had passed through, withdrew to the bridges over the Seine, and the inner defences of Rouen, putting up a certain amount of resistance where possible but quite rightly getting across the Seine in order to allow the bridges to be blown up before the Germans could cross them.

Vile accusations have been made by a certain French General [General Dufour] against Beauman's troops which, from all I have heard, are absolutely unjustifiable. The Right Brigade [C Brigade] held on to two bridges, and one party

---

* This is not correct. The Panzer Corps did not reach Forges-les-Eaux until 8 June.

† There were no bridges across the Seine below Rouen so that the recapture of the town from the Germans was essential for the extrication of the forces in the Le Havre peninsula. The complexity of command was a fatal barrier to any such attempt. The 51st Division was under IX Corps; 1st Armoured Division was under French 10th Army and the Beauman Division was under General Karslake, under General Georges. Both General Weygand, when visiting HQ Tenth Army, and General Karslake had stressed the importance of keeping open the Rouen line of withdrawal and, in the case of the Beauman Division and 1st Armoured Division, this was successfully achieved. See also Churchill's *Second World War*, Volume II, page 134.

was left on the Right bank because the bridge was blown up before it could cross. On arrival on the Left bank, this Brigade (or what was left of it, many men having been taken prisoner, as testified to by an NCO's report, of the F.S.P. who was also captured but escaped) put themselves under the command of General Maillard, of some cavalry formation, for two or three days in the vicinity of Les Andelys, until told by him to rejoin the Division which was being collected in an area agreed by General Dufour commanding the Left section.

The other Brigade [B Brigade] of this Division, [the third, A Brigade, being with the 51st Division] withdrew through and to the west of Rouen, crossing by the ferries.

The day after the troops had been withdrawn across the Seine [9 June], I went up to Evreux to meet General Beauman, and explained to him that he would continue to watch the crossings until relieved by French troops, when he would collect his command towards the west, with a view to preventing the Germans from moving towards Cherbourg; the new Division [52nd] just arriving would probably move north and deliver a blow against the Left flank of the enemy. During the night [11th], in reply to General Beauman, I told him to put himself under the senior French General.*

I then went to see Generals Cornwall and Evans at the HQ of a French Division which was just arriving. I understood that the French Tenth Army Commander was temporarily 'out of the picture'. The situation was most interesting; for some unexplained reason, the bridge at Les Andelys had not been blown up, nor the one at Vernon some miles upstream.† Apparently, quite small parties of Germans had crossed these bridges.

Some French Commander had issued orders for a defensive line to be taken up inclusive Vernon to the ferries just below Rouen, the Left Sector being under General Dufour and consisting of all troops that had crossed the river at Rouen. [This was made clear later by the mention of British as well as French troops.] A very wise order and the only solution at the moment.

It was agreed that the Armoured Division should co-operate with the new French Division. We then discussed the possible future policy. It came to this: two divisions were arriving from England which when complete, though small, would be a valuable striking force. Whilst they were collecting, the mechanically unfit tanks should be collected with them so as to increase their striking power. Previously, the mechanically unfit tanks had been moved back too short a distance before they had had sufficient time for maintenance. It was agreed, as a matter of policy, that they should go well back to the Le Mans area where the new Divisions were collecting. This policy could only be acted upon if the French Commander, under whom the British troops were acting, approved. It was always possible that, by rapid moves south, German Armoured Divisions might get into the assembly area without any tanks in it: so it was an added advantage having them well back. It

---

* It was during 11 June that General Karslake heard from General Dill that all the available forces were to be handed over to the French as and when available.
† Major-General J.B. Churcher, formerly GSO II (ops) Beauman Division, cites several examples of the operations by Fifth Columnists; in particular, the case of a French Major. This officer used to appear at Divisional HQ just prior to the blowing up of a bridge. He would then request that there be a postponement so as to allow French troops that were approaching shortly to cross. In fact, no French troops did appear; instead German Armour would try and rush the crossing before the bridge was blown up.

had proved itself time and time again that short moves were unsuitable. The next evening [10 June], presumably with the approval of the French Commander, some of the Armoured Division arrived back at Alençon for refit, having left one Brigade and Divisional HQ up in the battle area [2nd Armoured Brigade].

The Germans made no effort on this day, and indeed for two days, to take advantage of their crossings, except at Vernon. Even then, it was not serious.

The Germans must have been very weak, as individuals from our side for two days crossed by the ferries, reaching the 51st Division [52nd Division?] and actually entered the outskirts of Rouen.

As late as the afternoon of 12 June, our patrols had been all along the bank of the river from west to east as far as, inclusive, Pont de l'Arche, and thence by, inclusive, Louviers and Evreux without seeing a sign of the Germans.

I came to the conclusion that the German move in this area was not serious, but meant to draw off reserves from Paris, which was the danger spot*. Also, judging by the large number of French troops in the villages further back (including Algerian troops), there appeared sufficient force at the moment to prevent a serious and rapid advance.

The optimism of Brigadier Swayne, who spent the night of 10-11 June at my HQ, and the continued arrival of the 52nd Division added to the situation on our particular front, made us very hopeful that the new BEF might after all be in time. I could not believe that the 52nd Division and the Canadians would continue to arrive in France if the situation was hopeless.

Of course, alarming reports kept coming in. During the night of 11-12 June, a report came in that the Germans were in Dreux. During that morning an Admiral, Fitzgerald by name, who had been 'hawking' floating mines round the country, said that he was in Dreux at 6.0am that morning and had seen no sign of anybody!

The following morning I arranged with the Senior Brigade Commander [actually it was Brigadier Crocker *not* Brigadier McCreery] of the armoured Division, and the Commander of the 157th Brigade, 52nd Division, which had just arrived and whose men had never seen a tank, to give them practical experience of them.

That evening, a wire came from the CIGS to say that General Laurencie had complained to General Weygand that General Evans was not co-operating, and that every ounce of help was to be given to the French. First thing next morning I went up to investigate, having warned the Armoured Division rear HQ to have as many tanks as possible worked on in case they were required. I met Generals Evans and Cornwall, and the former explained that he had met General Laurencie, who was perfectly satisfied with what he had done, and was most affable and pleasant.†
I noticed during my motor drive a large number of French troops in villages close up to the front area and not actually employed.

---

* The General was right. It was only when the Germans discovered that it was the intention to evacuate the British troops from Cherbourg that they made serious efforts to prevent this; also to cut off the Breton Peninsula.
† General de la Laurencie had recently been appointed commander of the reconstitued III Corps. Not being aware that the 3rd Armoured Brigade had been withdrawn for refit, he complained to Weygand that he was not being fully supported. He had not referred to HQ 10th Army first. Weygand had contacted the CIGS who had, in turn, signalled Karslake (with a copy to Marshall-Cornwall) that such a complaint had been made and that he should investigate. All was, ultimately, resolved. Subsequently, de la Laurencie apologised to General Evans.

On my return to HQ at 11.0pm, a message came in from GQG ordering the 157th Brigade at once to Conches, saying that this was supported by the CIGS who was actually present.

It was a wet night, and very dark, and the troops had received no warning. However, thanks to the excellence of the Commander of the 52nd Division, his CRA [Brigadier John Kennedy], as well as my Staff, the Brigade started at 6.0am and arrived at Conches at 6.0pm.

Realizing that a considerable change had taken place at GQG since the instructions to me about not allowing the 52nd Division to be used piece-meal, I rang up the rear HQ of the Armoured Division and asked if they had any tanks fit to go up with this Brigade, as they had never fired their anti-tank rifles or guns, or even seen a tank. They said they had, so I ordered the 3rd Brigade to move to the same destination as the 157th Brigade, and put themselves under the Brigade Commander until they could report to their own Divisional HQ, with which they were out of touch.

That evening the 3rd Brigade relieved the 2nd Brigade in the Line. These two Brigades remained with the 157th Brigade and the Beauman Division until, I understand, they were all evacuated at Cherbourg. I should like to pay tribute to the very high mechanical efficiency of our tanks as the result of the very long road movements*.

The next day [13 June] General Brooke and his Staff arrived from England and took over from me; I returned to England†.

During all this time, anti-aircraft and anti-parachute defence was organized. To show what difficulties do occur, Le Havre was being evacuated of everything and the future BEF was going to rely on ports further south. I asked permission for the non-static guns to be withdrawn to Nantes. General Weygand refused to allow it, but finally acquiesced — just in time! It took days to discover what AA guns the French had in various places. To show this ignorance; one night some AA guns round Le Mans blazed away for some time at some of our own machines. When I protested to the Regional Commander, he said they were ours! We had none within 50 miles! He and his Staff were apparently quite ignorant of the disposition of their own defences. The Regional Commander appeared to be quite out of touch with the remainder of the Army. When I returned from the Seine after the Germans had effected a crossing at Vernon, the Regional Commander had heard nothing of the operations but, at my suggestion, at once started to erect formidable blocks on all the roads leading into the town of Le Mans.

The area of the L of C was about twice the area of the British Isles,** and we only had *three* battalions available for anti-parachute work! These were completely mobile and placed near aerodromes ready to go out in any direction. We thought it

---

* The 3rd Armoured Brigade's connection with the 157th Brigade was very tenuous. The 2nd Armoured Brigade on being relieved, went back to the Le Mans area, taking no further part in operations. Though General Karslake's comments on the 'high mechanical efficiency of our tanks' has been questioned, there is no doubt that, considering the wear and tear imposed upon them, the tanks behaved well, owing to the unceasing efforts of their crews to maintain them.

† General Karslake and Major Fanshawe slipped away, virtually unnoticed, from Le Mans, after having put General Eastwood 'in the picture' when General Brooke had left to visit General Weygand.

**In this the General was exaggerating. The actual area covered by the L of C was some 600 miles from Amiens to Marseilles and 350 miles from Troyes to Cherbourg. It was, nevertheless, a vast area to defend with the resources that were available.

would be possible that the Germans might accompany their attack on Rouen by landing troops by air on the Left Bank of the Seine. One Battalion was actually placed for this purpose! That was all we could scrape up! The Germans made no use of airborne troops anywhere in our area. Again, as in the case of AA defences, I could not discover what the French arrangements were. Up to the end, I do not believe that they had any, as the Regional Commander was constantly calling upon us to deal with bogus parachutists.

Air cooperation was, of course, difficult but I have no hesitation in saying that whenever we asked for it, it was forthcoming, and most willingly. In the later stages Air-Commodore Cole-Hamilton, who was in charge of the maintenance aerodromes at Rouen (Boos) [see also Appendix B], was always most helpful.

The evacuation of stores and personnel was begun, or rather, continued more rapidly after my arrival. Gas had already been evacuated from Fécamp*.

I was given lists in the order of priority for the evacuation of stores, and at the same time, I was told to keep it secret from the French. As a matter of fact, when mentioning that such an evacuation of things like rifles, at that time necessary for Home purposes, when I was at GQG, it was accepted as a most reasonable and rational thing to do.

When one thinks of the amount of stuff collected in France and the position of the BEF at that time, it was only reasonable to want to reduce stock.

Obviously it was impossible to evacuate in a few weeks what had taken nine months to produce.

Later, the policy changed when it was decided to reconstitute a new BEF south of the Somme. Instructions from Home were to the effect that we were to hold stocks for a Force of four Ordinary, and one Armoured, Divisions.

It is not right for me to comment on the colossal amount of stuff that had been collected in France for the BEF, but it does strike me as being the case of over-insurance in the case of some articles. On the other hand, certain equipment was completely, or nearly, deficient!

When I was organizing the Beauman Division, there was not a single field gun available on the L of C and the machine guns did not fit the condenser tubes, nor the tripods, which were very scarce.

As regards the latter (weapons), it was impossible to obtain from the reinforcement camps more than a very few officers or men who, though alleged to be machine gunners, knew anything about the guns at all!

It takes a little time before a change of policy percolates through all the branches of the Staff. For instance, some days after the evacuation of reinforcements and other stores had begun, some 4,000 reinforcements arrived, and a large amount of Ordnance stores!

All this evacuation was most ably carried out under the direction of Major-General de Fonblanque.

I would like, in conclusion, to mention the following officers of the L of C who appeared to me outstanding:

Brigadiers Barry, Beauman, Bissett and Vicary.

Colonels Alms RE, who organized extra means for crossing the Seine, Diggle of the AMPC and Brittorous.

* It is difficult to understand this statement. Instructions had not been issued for the evacuation of the troops and stores before General Karslake received them on 21 May. Certainly, the clearance of the great chemical warfare depot at Fécamp did not start until 25 May.

Also Major Elliott RA for organizing a gunner 'regiment'.
Captain Colan RTR for organizing a tank unit.

I do not mention any of the others because General de Fonblanque, who knows them much better than I, will no doubt make a report on them.*

SUPPLEMENT TO THE ABOVE REPORT

1. LIAISON WITH THE FRENCH

It was apparent to me that the arrangements whereby the British Formations were acting independently under the orders of French Commanders produced considerable difficulties.

The British Formations were maintained from the British L of C but commanded by French Commanders. The orders of the latter were not sent to our L of C, so it was not always possible to foresee likely requirements. Many of their systems, both tactical and otherwise, are totally different from ours and lead to all sorts of misunderstandings.

My suggestion that I should act as Corps Commander for the 51st and Armoured Divisions was definitely turned down at GQG in spite of being considered desirable by Generals Dufour, Frére and Altmayer.† This, however, was greatly mitigated by the appointment of Lt-General Marshall-Cornwall as the head of a Mission with the French 10th Army, under which our Regular Divisions were operating.

The system, in my opinion, is definitely wrong. There must be a *Commander* of all formations acting with a foreign army, not just a Liaison Officer who has no responsibility of command.

Actually, poor General Fortune had the Armoured Division put under his command when he was busily fighting a battle with his own Division, and suddenly had it whisked away again by the French Army Commander. I cannot believe that General Altmayer would have dared to say what he did about the 51st Division if there had been a British Corps Commander.

Looking back on the series of outbursts made against British troops, I cannot help thinking that it was definite policy instigated by General Weygand, especially as, from what I had seen, we were the only people who had tried to do anything in this particular area, even in the way of fighting when the enemy did appear!

In spite of repeated requests, I could never discover the French intentions as regards the protection of France south of the Somme, nor for the thousands of French troops which poured into my area from Dunkirk. The CIGS did all he could but those on the spot would never commit themselves.

2. INFORMATION

As always in war, this was difficult to obtain. If it had not been for the organization

---

* Unfortunately, General de Fonblanque's Report contains few details of importance. Few references are made to the activities of individuals.
† As has been stated previously, GQG were not responsible for this decision. This was purely a personal matter between Ironside and Dill and the very strong feelings that existed between Karslake and Dill. It was one of the features of the whole campaign in France and Flanders that personalities were allowed to intrude so as to affect the smooth working of the Military Machine. Also, they occasioned serious and unnecessary loss of life and materiel.

of Brigadier Beauman, and later by my HQ, of officers from the Reinforcement Depot, mounted on motor-cycles, no accurate information would have been forthcoming.*

Most fantastic reports used to come in bearing no relation to the truth. It was most difficult to discover accurate information as to the dispositions of French Formations or the intentions of the various Commanders.

On more than one occasion I was given such information but at once discovered that it was not accurate, but merely in the nature of '*un projet*' which, it was hoped, would materialize sometime!

I impressed on Liaison Officers who brought in this information that it is not sufficient to produce the Staff Map, but to take actual steps to check it by actual contact with the French Formations, if they possibly could.

3. TRAINING

The lack of previous training for our formations showed itself in many ways. I have no doubt that everybody did their best and it is quite wrong in my opinion to be too harsh on mistakes which were, inevitably, made from time to time by those who had not been given the opportunity beforehand of meeting difficult situations.

When the 157th Brigade of the 52nd Division arrived in France, the Brigade Commander told me that:

(*a*) Most of their equipment had been issued only a day or two before they had left England. Bicycles, for instance, were still wrapped up in paper.

(*b*) Not a single man had fired an anti-tank rifle or anti-tank gun.

(*c*) None of them had seen a tank.

4. DISCIPLINE

The first British troops I met during my first day [in France] gave me a shock! It was a detachment of a Regular[?] Battalion which said it had been in Orchies at one time. Their behaviour was terrible! From all sides, I heard that this was typical of the 'New Army' discipline as the result of the 'democratizing' of the Army. Whether this was so or not, I am not in a position to say as I have not sufficient experience of it. I mention it in case it may have been noticed by others with more experience.†

What I can say is that what I saw of the 51st and 52nd Divisions gave me the

---

* Brigadier Beauman has stated that there were eight of these individuals originally, some four more being added later from HQ Le Mans. They were drawn from the reinforcement Depots of the Royal Armoured Corps and the Royal Artillery. He says: 'Their tasks took them well in front of the Allied Line and into country infested by the enemy. They brought back invaluable information as to the rate and direction of the enemy advance. Some never came back from their dangerous missions and all had hair-raising adventures.'

It is noteworthy that General Brooke never employed any of these officers on such essential duties. This is surprising as he has stated that information regarding the enemy was both scarce and unreliable.

† General Karslake had had no direct dealings with troops after he had relinquished his appointment as GOC Baluchistan District at the end of 1935, until he was appointed Representative Colonel-Commandant, Royal Artillery, in 1937, just prior to the advent of Leslie Hore-Belisha as Secretary of State for War. As Colonel-Commandant he had visited every possible Artillery unit in the United Kingdom and had been duly impressed by their bearing and turnout. It was just after this that the process of 'democratizing the Army', to which he refers, began.

impression that they were excellent.

One has to remember that most of the others had been through a severe trial, e.g. the 12th and 43rd [46th] Divisions which I am told had been used purely as 'labour' and not even equipped as Divisions were considered quite unfit to be used in the Front Line again — until they had been completely reorganized, equipped and given some training.

5. RATIONS

From what I saw in France, I am convinced that the scale of rations is excessive. I would urge that this question is seriously considered. The saving of even an ounce here and there, when multiplied by 1½ million, would not be noticed by the troops, but would save the Country an enormous amount of anxiety regarding food supply.*

    H. KARSLAKE
    Lt-General

East Wellow,
Romsey, Hants   12 July, 1940.

It should be noted that this Report was composed within one month of the General's return to England. He did not have the assistance of a Staff, files or diaries. He had to rely on his memory and the few scribbled notes that he had made from time to time. An edited version of the Report was published in the *Army Quarterly* of 1972. The Editor wrote:

> General Karslake's Report, which is here produced for the first time, is dated 11 [12] July, 1940, and was therefore written long before the more considered narratives of General Evans and Brigadier Beauman. What it loses in confirmed detail it gains in immediacy and it is remarkable how, written in haste from such notes as General Karslake was able to make at the time, supported by memory of very recent events, it is corroborated in every important detail by the later accounts.'

---

* From the outbreak of war, General Karslake had been living as a 'civilian' and receiving civilian rations. When he assumed his appointment in France he was staggered by the very generous rations that were being issued to Army personnel. This was most noticable at HQ where all ranks lived a sybaritic existence, as far as food was concerned. He considered it outrageous that such vast amounts were being used (and wasted) in France when the people at home were undergoing considerable privations.

APPENDIX D

The Breton Redoubt

One of the most vexed questions of the Second World War is that of the Breton Redoubt. Many details have been given of this enterprise by well-known public figures; in most cases the accounts are attempts to justify their failing to implement the scheme. In order that the reader may make his own judgement, all the known details are given below together with statements of the various individuals involved.

As early as 29 May, 1940, M. Reynaud, the French Prime Minister, in answer to a letter from General Weygand reporting on the existing military situation, wrote:

> In view of the decisive importance for the Allies of resistance along the line [Abbeville to Switzerland] the French Government entreats the British Government to accede to the request made in your note [Additional divisions, guns and planes].
>
> The fact that, in considered hypothesis, the whole territory of the Nation could no longer be defended does not necessarily mean that we could end hostilities in conditions compatible with the honour and vital interest of France. [This is referring to Weygand's recommendation that an armistice should be considered.]
>
> So, since in the considered hypothesis, the enemy would be likely to make rapid thrusts throughout the length and breadth of the country, I would ask you to be so kind as to look into the possibility of fortifying a national redoubt round a naval habour enabling us to use the freedom of the seas and, in particular, to communicate with our Allies. This national redoubt would have to be planned and supplied like a real fortress. *It would comprise the Brittany peninsula.*

The subject was brought up informally at the meeting of the Anglo-French Supreme War Council on 31 May, when it was approved by Mr Churchill. This is confirmed by Mr Churchill's memo to General Sir John Dill, and the Chiefs of Staff on 2 June. [See p. 122]

It would seem that the Chiefs of Staff took this matter seriously. Lieutenant-General Alan Brooke was selected to command the advanced portion of the reconstituted BEF on the day Mr Churchill's memo was received. Likewise, a draft Operation Instruction was undertaken, this being ready on 5 June.

Owing to the developments in the situation which occurred on 6 June, the Instruction was modified. It was decided to utilize Plan 'W', the original plan for the landing of the BEF in 1939, the 52nd Division being directed to Cherbourg, with assembly point at Evreux. This was to try and give support to the 51st Division.

Also on 6 June, General Weygand received a letter from M. Reynaud on the subject of the Breton Redoubt. It should be noted that the General had done little to implement Reynaud's suggestion of 29 May. On receipt of his letter, General Weygand issued definite instructions that work on the Redoubt should begin at once. He reported this action to Reynaud, adding that he had placed a 'good Corps Commander in charge'. This Commander was General Réné Altmayer, the brother of General Robert Altmayer, who was commanding the 10th French Army.

With the crossing of the Seine by the Germans on 9 June and the virtual cutting off of the 51st Division to the north of the river, the War Office decided that the advanced position of Evreux ceased to have any practical advantage. It was decided, therefore, to revert to the original plan. Plan 'W' was cancelled and the Rennes area substituted. The leading Brigade of the 52nd Division was directed to Beaumont, near Le Mans. The remainder of the Division, on arrival at Cherbourg, followed on for concentration.

The 1st Canadian Division's leading Brigade, the First, which began to arrive on 11 June at Brest, was directed to Sablé-sur-Sarthe. The reason why the original plan had been modified was because it was considered that two fresh divisions would enable the retreating French army, together with such British elements as were still engaged, to pass through them so as to take up the prepared positions covering the Brest peninsula.

On 11 June also, after the meeting of the Allied Supreme War Council at Briare, at which both Mr Churchill and General Dill were present, General de Gaulle, who had become Minister for War, was ordered by M. Reynaud to visit Rennes for the purpose of discovering the development of the Redoubt from General Altmayer. Mr Churchill had declared that he was willing to support the scheme if the report showed that it was a practicability. On 12 June General de Gaulle returned from Brittany and gave M. Reynaud the following details:

> Naturally I favoured Quimper [in the Brest peninsula]. Not that I had any illusions as to the chances of holding out in Brittany, but if the Government retired to Quimper, it would be bound to put to sea sooner or later ... Once on board ship, the ministers would, in all probability, make for Africa or stopping off in England. At all events, Quimper was a move towards forceful decisions.

General Altmayer stated to him that preparations had been put in hand. In spite of the serious lack of materials, strong points were under construction and labour was becoming gradually available for the project. The Polish Division alone had sent up over 3,000 men; a fair amount of civilian labour had also been recruited. The main trouble was the lack of suitable machinery, eg; concrete mixers and mechanical shovels. (One wonders where all the enormous mass of equipment gathered by the British in 1939 had gone to.)

As a result of M. Reynaud's urgent representation, Mr Churchill visited France (this was the last time) on the 13th. M. Reynaud then informed him of the report he had had from de Gaulle on the Redoubt. It would seem that they were in accord over the project.

In the meantime General Brooke had visited the 1st Canadian Division at Aldershot. He gave General MacNaughton, the Divisional Commander, the draft of the plan as given above. This was to be issued on the arrival of the Division in France.

General Brooke met both General Weygand and General Georges on the 14th at Briare. Though it was agreed by all three men that the scheme was likely to prove abortive owing to lack of resources, nevertheless, as it had been agreed by the two Governments, it was their duty to undertake it. The two French Generals considered that it was desirable to show their accord and, to ensure that there should be no misunderstanding on the part of the new BEF Commander, to sign a joint agreement on the subject. The French, rightly or wrongly, considered that in the past there had been other misunderstandings which had led to disaster.

Major Ellis, in the *Official History*, puts in italics the fact that the Breton Redoubt project was not included in General Brooke's orders. In fact, the same orders as had been issued to General Gort in 1939 had been given to him. These earlier orders had not included any specific strategic action.

After the meeting with the French Generals Brooke telephoned to the CIGS with the information. General Dill replied that no agreement had been made with the French; he would contact the Prime Minister on the subject. Soon after, he telephoned back to say that *Mr Churchill knew nothing about the Brittany project*. As Mr Churchill himself did not make this statement to General Brooke, it cannot in fairness be ascribed to him. It would seem, however, that in subsequent conversations (according to General Brooke) no reference was made to the Redoubt. Nevertheless, it is clear that Mr Churchill was exceedingly reluctant for the new Corps to be withdrawn. He said that certainly all British troops fighting with the French could be withdrawn after the French had collapsed and then from the nearest port to them at that time.

General Brooke's actions are recounted in full in Chapter VII and need not be repeated here. With the absence of the 52nd Division on its left flank, the various formations of the French 10th Army were cut off from the Brittany peninsula. General Schmidt directed two divisions of his Corps to cut in behind the French so as to get into the peninsula and thereby preventing the French from getting between them and Brest. The French, therefore, had no option but to withdraw to the River Loire. The remainder of the French troops located in the peninsula were able, after the departure of the Canadians, to link up with the retreating French forces.

The key to the Breton Redoubt affair rests largely on the meetings on 11 and 12 June at Briare. When the matter was raised on the 11th, General Dill had suggested that General Marshall-Cornwall should be sent to Brittany to survey the situation. General Weygand had objected as he considered that General Marshall-Cornwall lacked experience of such matters. While General Dill denies that any agreement was reached, General Ismay categorically states:

'12 June.
    The Council had a second short session that morning. The only conclusions that need be mentioned were *the agreement to try and organize a redoubt in Brittany* and the undertaking by the Prime Minister to dispatch divisions from England, as soon as they could be equipped and organized.'

And later on, on the way to the airport,

'I pleaded with him that the Brittany project, however attractive in theory, had not got the ghost of a chance of success. The best we could hope for was yet another evacuation. The greater the numbers that set foot in France, the greater would be our losses in men and material. We must, of course, keep our promise to send reinforcements to France soon, but need we be in too much of a hurry? Could we not unobtrusively delay their departure?' [*Churchill would have none of it.*] 'Certainly not. It would look very bad in history if we were to do any such thing.'

As a result of the 'agreement' and General de Gaulle's visit to Brittany, the French 10th Army was given orders to bar the way to the Breton Redoubt on 13 June. The order for this movement was written by General de Gaulle on the instruction of M. Reynaud, *after the meeting with Mr Churchill on that day*. The order is in the form of a directive and reads as follows:

> 'In the event of the final breaking up of our lines of defence, you [Weygand] indicated in your note of 10 June that our armies separated by this breakthrough would go on fighting until their supplies and strength were exhausted ...
>
> In this respect, it seems to me that two courses are open to us, both vitally important from the point of view of continuing the war.
>
> The first course would lead to our armies covering the very heart of the country for as long as possible, linking up with those of our forces that are defending the Alpine frontier.
>
> The second course would *lead to our establishing and defending a national Redoubt in Brittany.* I am glad that I have obtained your agreement on that point.'

[This latter statement has led to much confusion. There seems little doubt that Weygand had agreed, if reluctantly, to the decisions of the Supreme Council on the 11th and then only to the extent of obeying such orders as were given to him; *not* that he agreed with the policy as such.]

> 'Such a redoubt, lying close to England, which would send us troops and supplies [Churchill had promised this] and her Air Force might assist us in its defence, would enable us to maintain, to the Allies advantage, a bridgehead on the Continent for as long as possible.'

Finally, at a meeting of the French Cabinet, which took place after the departure of Mr Churchill on the 13th, M. Reynaud informed them that 'the French Government had decided not to conclude an armistice but to continue hostilities'. From this it can be concluded that M. Reynaud must have given Mr Churchill an indication as to how these hostilities were to be continued. Doubtless General de Gaulle's report would have been mentioned in this connection.

From the foregoing, it would seem that *all* the chief 'Actors' were fully aware of the scheme and equally, that *all* had agreed, if reluctantly and with little faith in its success, that the scheme should be implemented.

APPENDIX E

The Armistice Misunderstanding of 17 June, 1940

On 17 June at 1230, Marshal Pétain broadcast the following statement to the French people:

> 'Frenchmen, Answering the call of the President of the Republic, I am from today assuming control of the Government of France. Certain of the affection of our wonderful Army, fighting with a heroism worthy of its long military traditions against an enemy superior in numbers and equipment; certain, by its magnificent stand, it has fulfilled its duties to our Allies; certain of the support of the ex-servicemen whom it has been my honour to command, I bestow myself on France to palliate her misfortune.
>
> In these painful hours, my thoughts are with the unfortunate refugees suffering dire hardship on the roads. I send them my sympathy and concern. *It is with a heavy heart that today I tell you that we must stop the fighting.*
>
> Last night [16th] I communicated with the enemy, asking him whether he was prepared to join us in seeking ways — honourably, as between soldiers after the fray — of putting an end to hostilities.
>
> Let all Frenchmen rally round my Government in this time of tribulation, subduing their fears and hearkening only to their faith in our Country's destiny.'

The reaction in France to this speech was one of almost universal approbation. The words contained in the second paragraph indicated to most people that the fighting was over. It led to fatal vaccillation among the troops. They did not know whether they should continue to fire on the enemy or not. In fact, a number of regiments actually stopped fighting. When General Weygand was notified by General Georges of these occurrences he took immediate steps to counter the impression that had gained credence among the troops that the fighting was over. He ordered all Army Commanders to fight on. The French Government instructed the evening papers to alter the sentence to read "We must *try* and stop the fighting'. Also, in order to ensure that there should be no further misapprehension as to what had been meant in Pétain's broadcast, the French Foreign Minister broadcast at 2130 this statement:

> 'The French Government has decided to ask Germany for her conditions. It goes without saying that she will accept none that conflicts with her honour or dignity. France could not consent to clauses involving the end of all spiritual freedom for her people ...
>
> Our exhausted troops have been unable to compensate for the tanks, guns and planes which we lacked. Even without the threat of Italian invasion, we were only 40 million against 80 million ...
>
> *That is why the Government, led by Marshal Pétain, has had to ask the enemy what his peace conditions would be. But, for all that, it has not abandoned the struggle or laid down arms.* [Author's italics] As Marshal Pétain said this morning, the Country is prepared to seek ways, in honour, of putting an end to hostilities. It is not prepared, and never will be prepared, to accept dishonouring conditions, to forsake the spiritual freedom of our people, to betray the spirit of France.
>
> If the French can only preserve these spiritual values that they prize more than life, they will agree to any individual sacrifices. But, if they were asked to choose between

existence and honour, their choice is made, and by their total sacrifice they will preserve the spirit of France and all that it implies in the World.'

Unfortunately a period of nine hours had elapsed before the correction was issued. With the fast-moving changes in the situation, such a delay would have proved disastrous.

As was their custom, the BBC had monitored the Marshal's speech. On translation, deeming it to be of the utmost importance, they at once transmitted it to Whitehall. The CIGS took immediate steps to acquaint General Brooke with the situation. He instructed him that, as an Armistice had been sought by the French Government, all efforts must be made to evacuate the troops as soon as possible and then, if there was time, to evacuate such stores and other equipment as might be to hand; further, that General Brooke should embark for England that evening.

There is little doubt that General Brooke was very relieved to receive this message from Sir John Dill. He had been chafing all day at the delay of orders that would permit him to leave France. He states in his Despatch that the message he received from the CIGS was subsequently confirmed by the French Liaison Officer, Capitaine Meric. This seems curious as, if Capitaine Meric was from the Headquarters of either General Georges or General Weygand, he would have known the truth.* It is possible, however, that he was from the Headquarters of the French 10th Army. If so, then this formation might not have been informed of the true facts by General Weygand at that time.

It is interesting to note that, at the very moment when General Brooke was embarking at St Nazaire for England, the French Foreign Minister was announcing that a constriction had been placed on the Marshal's speech.† History does not relate whether General Dill tried to contact General Brooke to reassure him, or, indeed, whether General Brooke heard the broadcast on board the *Cambridgeshire*. Even at that late hour, the Royal Navy could have been asked to contact him and, as a result, he could have issued orders for the removal of the valuable stores which were lining the quays at Nantes and St Nazaire. Even if no resistance was contemplated, there still remained a further twenty-four hours at least before the Germans, with very light forces, approached the towns.

At Cherbourg the position was equally curious. The Port Admiral, Admiral Abrial, was fully aware of the French Government's decision to fight on. This is clearly shown by his orders and the remarks he made to General Rommel when the port eventually capitulated. When the original text of the first broadcast became known to the British at Cherbourg they were quite convinced that, should an Armistice take place, they would find themselves interned. For this reason a quite unnecessary speeding up of evacuation was ordered. What is particularly strange is the fact that, notwithstanding the corrections made to the original broadcast during the evening of 17 June, no news of this, *apparently*, was received by General Marshall-Cornwall. One must presume that this is so as otherwise there would not have been the extreme urgency as was shown by the acts of abandonment of stores and vehicles on the 18th.

Unfortunately the War Diary relating to No 17 Military Mission, subsequently

* In *The Turn of the Tide* (Bryant) it is stated that Meric received the news of the Armistice proposal from the French radio. He would, therefore, have known the details *before* Brooke

† One might wonder whether Meric heard this broadcast also. If so, whether he informed Brooke of the new facts.

Normanforce, is missing from the files deposited at the Public Records Office. It has not been possible, therefore, to discover the details of times and orders (and from whom they emanated) received at the HQ of the Mission.

Bibliography

BARCLAY, Brigadier C.N., (ed) *History of the Duke of Wellington's Regiment*, Clowes, 1953
BEAUFRE, General Andre, *1940, The Fall of France*, Cassell, 1967
BEAUMAN, Brigadier-General A.B., *Then A Soldier*, Macmillan, 1960
BENOIST-MECHIN, J., *60 Days That Shook the West*, Cape, 1963
BOND, Brian, (ed) *Chief of Staff, Diary of Lt-General Sir H. Pownall*, Leo Cooper, 1973/4
BROOKE, Lt-General Sir Alan, *Despatches*, London Gazette, 1946
BROWN, RQMS, *Diary*, Imperial War Museum
BRIGHT, Joan, *The Ninth Queen's Royal Lancers, 1936-1945*, Gale & Polden, 1951
BRYANT, Sir Arthur, *The Turn of the Tide*, Collins, 1957
CHURCHILL, Winston, S., *The Second World War*, Cassell, 1948-54
COLVILLE, J.R., *Man of Valour*, Collins, 1972
CROCKER, Brigadier J., *Report on Operations of 3rd Armoured Brigade in France, 1940*, RAC Museum
DANIELL D.S., *History of the East Surrey Regiment Vol IV*, Ernest Benn, 1957
DE FONBLANQUE, Maj-General P., *Report on L of C in France 1940*, Lord Southesk
DE GUINGAND, Maj-General Sir Francis, *Operation Victory*, Hodder & Stoughton, 1947
ELLIS, Major L.F., *The War in France and Flanders 1939-40*, HMSO
EVANS, Maj-General R., *Report on Operations of the 1st Armoured Division in France*, 1940, PRO
FOSTER, Major R.C.G., *History of the Queen's Royal Regiment*, Vols 8 & 9, Gale & Polden, 1953/61
GORT, General, *Despatches*, London Gazette
HAY, Ian, *The Battle of Flanders*, HMSO, 1941
HINGSTON, Lt-Colonel W., *Never Give Up*, History of the KOYLI
HORNE, Alistair, *To Lose a Battle*, Macmillan, 1969
ISMAY, Lord, *Memoirs*, Heinemann, 1960
KARSLAKE, Lt-General Sir Henry, *Leaders of the Army*, Hutchinson,1939; *Report*, Army Quarterly, 1972
KENNEDY, Maj-General Sir John, *The Business of War*, Hutchinson, 1957
KNIGHT, C.R.B., *Historical Records of the Buffs*, Medici Society, 1951
LEWIN, R., *Churchill as Warlord*, Batsford, 1973
LIDDELL HART, B.H., *The Tanks*, Cassell, 1959; *Memoirs*, Cassell, 1965; *The Rommel Papers*, Collins, 1953
LINKLATER, Eric, *The Highland Division*, HMSO, 1942
MACLEOD, Colonel R., *The Ironside Diaries*, Constable, 1962
MARSHALL-CORNWALL, General Sir James, *Despatch*, London Gazette
MINNEY, R.J., *The Private Papers of Hore-Belisha*, Collins, 1960
MORGAN, Lt-General Sir Frederick, *Peace and War*, Hodder & Stoughton, 1961

PARKINSON, C.N., *Always a Fusilier*, Sampson Lowe, 1949
REOCH, Ernest, *The St Valery Story*, Highland Printers, 1965
ROSKILL, Captain S.W., *The War at Sea, Vol I*, HMSO, 1954
SHEARS, Maj-General P.J., *The Story of the Border Regiment, 1939-45*, Nisbet, 1948
SPEARS, Maj-General Sir Edward, *Assignment to Catastrophe*, Heinemann, 1954
STRACEY, Colonel C.P., *The Canadian Army 1939-45*
WEYGAND, General M., *Recalled to Service*, Heinemann, 1952

In addition, all relevant Files and War Diaries have been consulted. Unfortunately, certain important papers have been abstracted from the files; also, certain files are missing altogether. Luckily, some of these omissions have been obtained from outside sources.

INDEX

Abancourt, 47, 60, 64, 68, 76, 77; dumps, 45; destruction of viaduct, 76
Abbeville, 27, 60, 64, 73, 84, 87, 89, 110, 114; fighting around it, 68-71, 77; attempted Allied advances on, 106, 150; continued French attempts to reduce bridgeheads, 114-16
Aigneville, 108
Ailly-sur-Noye, 65, 95
Ailly-sur-Somme, 95, 100, 101
Air Defence of Great Britain, 24, 130
Air Ministry, 144, 145
Aisne, River, 58, 95, 111, 123
Alanbrooke, Viscount, *see* Brooke
Alençon, 218, 224
Alexander of Tunis, Field-Marshal Earl, 29, 227
Alizay, 58, 168
Allen, Captain, R.N. 204
Alms, Colonel, 75; arrangements for crossing Seine, 116
Alpine 75 gun, 138 and n.
Altmayer, General Robert, 102, 106, 117, 128, 131, 132, 134, 143, 146, 147, 154, 156, 171, 178, 195, 213, 229, 232
Amiens, 27, 29, 73, 83, 84, 88, 95, 110, 114, 118, 119, 131, 143, 150; sub-area, 44; French H.Q., 60; fighting round it, 64-8, 76
Andelle, River, 74, 75, 126, 129, 154, 156; crossed by Germans, 162
Anti-tank (A/T): guns, 22, 26, 128; units, 84, 86, 104, 114
Appleyard, 2/Lt., 168
Ardennes, the, 49, 52, 54
Arkforce, 181
Armistice misunderstanding (June 17, 1940), 190, 204, 227, 238, 268-70
Armoured Divisions, different British and French conceptions, 113
Armoured vehicles, lost in France, 239
Arques-la-Bataille, 74, 181
Arras, 39, 56, 58, 61, 68, 69, 81, 88, 95, 100; sub-area, 44, 58, 59; Gort's attack from, 63, 84, 90, 95, 96; British withdrawal from, 111

Arrest (village), 109
Artillery, absence of reserves, 22-4, 26, 53, 91, 94, 99, 124-5
Aumale, 47, 120, 130, 146, 147, 150, 155, 157
Autheuil, 217
Authon, 210
Avranches, 220, 224

Bacquepuis, 175
Balfour, Colonel, 220
Bands, playing of, 43-4, 63
Barc, 179
Barker, General, 31
Barquet, 179, 216, 223
Barratt, Air Marshal, 101, 139-40, 144, 145
Barry, Brigadier, 44
Battle of Flanders, The (War Office booklet), 22-3, 30-1
Bayeux, 211
Beauchamps, 146
Beauforce, 62, 119, 130 *See also* Beauman Division
Beauman, Brigadier A.B., 58-62, 80, 81, 89-90, 94, 117, 126, 127, 148, 150, 151, 153, 154, 161, 168, 183, 213, 214, 230, 240; defensive measures, 58, 73-6; and movement forward of 'Labour' Divisions, 59-61; formation of Beauforce, 61-2; forms protective line on River Béthune, 74-6, 130, 144, 148, 151; covers approaches to Seine, 75, 90; talks with Karslake at Rouen, 98-9; to command his force on divisional lines, 103, 104; and 51st Division, 118-19; strengthening area north of Rouen, 149-50; reinforcements for him, 150; disposition of additional battalions, 163; moves to near Caen, 213; ordered to withdraw towards Cherbourg, 213; ordered to embark, 214
Beaumont-le-Roger, 223
Béhen, 116
Belgium, invaded by Germans, 51, 53, 56
Benoist-Méchin, 142
Bernay, 166, 168, 169, 171

273

Bernienville, 221
Berniéres, 170
Besson, General, 117, 131
Béthune, River, 148; protective line on, 74, 75, 118, 126, 129, 153, 179
Bienfay, 116
Billotte, General
Bissett, Brigadier F., 202, 234
Black Watch, 1st, 115-16

Blain, 47, 68, 188, 206
Blangy, 88, 129
Blaxland, Gregory, 241
Bois du Valdieu, 217
Bois Heroult, 162
Boismont, 109
Bolton, Lt-Colonel E.F., 47, 71
Bordeaux, 104, 195
Border Regiment, 4th, 43, 99, 105, 119, 127, 146; action of Somme bridges, 100-1; on Bresle, 119-20, 154, 179; embarked for England, 205
Bouillancourt, 115
Boulogne, 41, 82; sub-area, 44; reinforcements from England, 85
Bray, 107, 139
Bresle, River, 71, 106, 119, 129, 130, 137, 138, 152, 154, 179, 230; Germans held up, 154, 157; 51st Division withdrawn behind, 154, 157
Brest, 154, 186-8, 197, 200, 205, 207, 208, 226, 237; evacuation of Canadians, 200-2; capture by Germans, 225
Breteuil, 174
Breton Redoubt, question of, 122-3, 143, 154, 186, 187, 191-3, 200, 203, 204, 224, 231, 236, 264-7
Brezolles, 217
Briare, 173, 174, 189, 194, 233
Briggs, Lt-Colonel Raymond, 89, 95, 113, 203, 218
British Army units: (*see also* under names of individual regiments)
I Corps, 31, 41
II Corps, 40, 41, 185, 186, 193, 197
III Corps, 22, 45, 52
1st Armoured Division, 24, 26, 30, 31, 55, 85-9, 94-6, 110, 113, 115, 116, 120, 147, 153, 155, 156, 162-3, 172, 177, 186, 193, 223, 228, 230, 232; descent from 'Experimental Force' and 'Mobile Division', 85; establishment, 86; training, 87; arrival in France, 87-8; instructions for employment, 88-9, 94, 100; under control of GHQ, 97, 106 action of Somme bridges, 99-101; under French orders, 102, 105, 132; refurbishes tanks, 151, rejoined by Composite Regiment and Support Group, 159-60; conference on its state, 171: summary of its condition, 230-1
1st Canadian Division, 23, 133, 152, 167, 173, 176, 184-8, 193, 197, 231, 236-8; training, 185; operational instructions, 185-6; arrival of part in France, 187; evacuated from Brest, 202; saves its guns, 201-2, 237
3rd Division, 24, 125, 152, 239
5th Division, 84
12th 'Labour' Division, 27, 31, 46, 47, 50, 54-6, 63, 72-4, 124, 127, 231; movement forward, 59-61; fighting round Amiens and Abbeville, 66, 70
23rd 'Labour' Division, 46, 47, 50, 56, 127
46th 'Labour' Division, 27, 31, 46, 47, 50, 72, 124, 127, 153, 231; movement forward towards Abbeville, 59, 76; railway blocked, 76; diverted via Dieppe, 76-7
50th (Northumberland) Division, 44, 84
51st (Highland) Division, 26, 28, 73, 104, 120, 131, 132, 134, 155, 161, 163, 166, 181-4, 186, 323, 237; in Saar, 31, 50, 55, 57, 112, 115, 183, 228; returns from Saar, 104-5, 112, 116; changing orders, 112-13; brought into action, 115-16; War Diary, 118-19; dispositions, 129; and final attack on Somme bridgeheads, 137, 139; and German offensive, 143, 145-9, 151; fighting on Bresle, 154, 167, 179; evacuation of part, 183; surrender of remainder, 183; summary of its position, 228-30
52nd (Lowland) Division, 122, 124, 151, 152, 173, 184, 186, 187, 193, 197, 205, 218, 231, 232, 237, 238; arrival in France, 22, 167, 172; question of its employment, 152-4; ordered back to Cherbourg, 188
Beauman Division, 28, 58, 104, 110, 120, 129, 132, 148, 152, 153, 161-3, 166, 168-9, 172, 176, 181, 184, 193, 209, 213-15, 231, 131, 137; disbandment ordered by Dill, 125-6; order withdrawn, 126; composition, 126-8; on the Risle, 167, 171, 213; ordered to take up line on the Dives, 231; withdrawal towards Cherbourg, 212-14; embarkation, 212, 214
1st Army Tank Brigade, 83, 84, 104
1st Armoured Brigade, 24, 101, 102, 105, 113, 116, 119, 161, 171, 176, 178, 232,

274

239; lands in France, 26; and attack towards Abbeville, 106, 107; withdrawal, 110; refitting at Le Mans, 207; loss of train carrying tanks, 207; embarkation, 207
3rd AA Brigade, 81, 135
3rd Armoured Brigade, 24, 92, 93, 105, 120, 159, 164, 171, 172, 178, 179, 207, 213, 216, 221-4, 232; moves northwards, 102; and attack towards Abbeville, 106, 108; withdrawal, 110; reinforced with squadron of Bays, 161; withdrawal to Seine, 162, 163; forms part of French Army reserve, 223; withdrawal, 223; embarkation, 224; loss of train carrying tanks, 239-40
25th Brigade, 44, 127
35th Brigade, 27, 47, 64, 70; and fighting round Abbeville, 68-71; withdrawal across Somme, 71; ordered back to England, 184
36th Brigade, 47, 63, 69, 73
37th Brigade, 27, 47, 64, 69
137th Brigade, 47, 77
138th Brigade, 47, 59, 72
139th Brigade, 47, 59, 72
152nd Brigade, 116, 129, 141, 179; and German attack from Somme, 145, 146
153rd Brigade, 115, 129, 139, 141, 179; and German attack from Somme, 145
154th Brigade, 129, 139, 179, 181; and German attack from Somme, 145, evacuation from Le Havre, 182, 183; saving of vehicles, 238
157th Brigade, 154, 172, 174-9, 197, 213-23, 231, 232; under French command, 174, 184, 232, engagement with enemy, 215-16; no longer under French control, 216, 220; starts withdrawal, 219
'A' Brigade, Beauman Division, 28, 127, 146, 183, 184, 198; reinforces 51st Division, 148-50, 153, 154, 179; fighting on withdrawal to Le Havre, 181; evacuated from Le Havre, 182, 183; leaves France, 204, 205
'B' Brigade, Beauman Division, 127, 148, 162, 163, 209; crosses Seine, 166; on Risle, 166
'C' Brigade, Beauman Division, 127, 148, 150, 162-4; on Risle, 166
Auxiliary Military Pioneer Corps, 31, 44, 46, 127, 134; equipped as fighting force, 74
Royal Army Ordnance Corps, 39, 43, 45
Royal Army Service Corps, 39, 43, 45

Royal Artillery, 181; operating with RAF, 144
units:
    51st Medium Regiment, 182
    53rd AA Regiment, 227-8
    101st LAA and Anti-Tank Regiment; in Support Group, 86, 87, 101-2, 117, 129-31, 237; and the Seine crossings, 90; Regimental Diary, 129-31; surrender near St Valéry en Caux, 158-9
    X Field Battery, 104
    23rd AA Battery, 168
    44th AA Battery, 114-15
    213th Anti-Tank Battery, 172, 217
    157th Anti-Tank Company, 172
Royal Engineers, 39, 60, 78, 101, 128, 150, 161, 181; and covering of Seine approaches, 75; 264th Company, 64; in Support Group, 86, 87, 119, 130; operating with RAF, 144; with 157th Brigade, 215
Royal Tank Corps, 85
182nd Field Ambulance, 64
British Expeditionary Force (BEF); arrival in France, 22, 41; Plan 'D', 49, 51-2; position on May 15th, 1940, 55-60; consideration of evacuation, 82; cut off from south of Somme, 98
Brittorous, Major (Colonel), 103, 104
Brooke, Lieutenant-General A.F. (Sir Alan) (Viscount Alanbrooke), 28 and n., 41, 85, 133, 171, 185-9, 191-204, 227, 233-5, 238; GOG-in-C, Southern Command, 40; Commander of II Corps, 40; meeting with Dill, 123, 125; to command leading Corps of new BEF, 125, 133, 151-4, 229, 230; technically in command of British troops in France, 133; arrives in France, 184, 188-9, 231; his Terms of Reference, 191-2
and 1st Canadian Division, 185-7; sends Karslake back to England, 189; and Weygand, 189, 191-4, 233; and Breton Redoubt, 191-3; agreement with Weygand and Georges, 193-4; no longer under French command, 194-7, 233; and evacuation of British troops, 197-8, 233-5; Normanforce, 197-8; sends Staff home, 198; moves HQ to Vitre, 200, 201, 234; his order to Bissett, 202, 234, 235; and 52nd Division, 202-3; new HQ at Redon, 203; and Petain's reported request for armistice, 204, 238; last hours in France, 227, 235
Broomhill, Colonel, 120, 156, 157, 159-61;

275

captured, 160
Brown, Major (2nd RTR), 222
Bruce, Brigadier C.G., 91, 93, 94; sent to London with report for Ironside, 103; taken ill, 103
Brussels, 55, 96
Bryant, Sir Arthur, 234
Buchy, 67; ammunition dump, 43, 45, 58, 134
Buffs (East Kent Regiment): 4th, 43, 74; equipped as mobile unit, 61; embarked for England, 205
5th, 57, 58
Burey, 175
Burgess, Captain J.L., 205
Butler, Colonel R.B., 180

Caen, 44, 46, 211, 213
Calais, 44, 61, 82, 92, 119
Cambrai, 94-6
Cambron, 116
Cameron, Colonel, 115, 157-8
Cameron Highlanders, 4th, 116
Caubert, 132, 139
Caudebec, 166, 182, 183
Cave-Brown, General, 189
Chamberlain, Neville, 19, 22
Chateau de Muguet, 189; Supreme War Council meeting at, 173
Chepy, 108
Cherbourg, 41, 46, 88, 93, 113, 118, 135, 167, 174, 182, 183, 186, 188, 189, 197, 203-5, 211-14, 218, 220, 223-6, 231, 235-8, 240; sub-area, 44; intended evacuation from, 198, 199; Rommel's thrust towards, 199, 224-6; defence of, 202, 225-6; British evacuation, 224; capitulation, 226
Cherbourg Peninsula, 214, 225, 235; French troops from Dunkirk in, 167, 225; strength of Allied forces, 226, 235
Cheshire Regiment, 75
Churchill, (Sir) Winston, 22, 31, 32, 42, 44, 121, 194, 202, 203, 229, 233; visit to France, 82; telegram to Cabinet on situation, 82; and Karslake, 91, 124; at Supreme War Council in Paris, 122; considers France to be beaten, 122; and Breton Redoubt, 123, 187, 194; at Supreme War Council near Briare, 173; agrees to stopping of shipments and evacuation of troops, 194
Colan, Captain P.W.C., commands scratch Tank company, 104, 161, 170
Command system in Northern France, 116-18; priority of French orders, 117; precautions to safeguard British formations 118; complications, 132
Committee of Imperial Defence, 119
Composite Armoured Regiment 120, 129, 130, 132, 147, 151, 154, 171; sent back to Armoured Division, 156, 157, 159-61; skirmish with enemy on the way, 159-60; under Crocker's command, 163
Conches, 174, 175, 177, 178, 213, 215, 216, 221, 229, 231, 232, 239
Cotentin Peninsula, 220
Coty, 211, 212
Courtomer, 223
Coutances, 225
Crecy airfield, 45
Creully, 211, 212
Crocker, Brigadier J.T. (General Sir John), 102, 154, 161-3, 216, 221-4; withdraws across Seine, 162-3; and question of help for 157th Brigade, 177-8, 221, 223; and co-operation with French, 221-2
Curtis, Major-General H.O., 47, 54-5, 58

Darnetal, 160
De Fonblanque, Major-General Philip, commander of L. of C., 39, 44, 49, 61, 81, 90, 98, 117, 172, 188, 200-2, 204; replaced by Karslake, 93-4; orders Southern District to disband HQ, 202
De Gaulle, General de Brigade Charles, 127; attack on Abbeville, 114-16; at Supreme War Council, 173
Destination Dunkirk (Blaxland), 241
Deverell, Field-Marshal Sir Cyril, 40, 85
Dieppe, 41, 44, 74, 90, 118, 134, 148, 153, 180, 183; immunity as Red Cross port, 76; bombed by Germans, 77; arrival of three battalions from Abbeville, 79, 80; bombing of hospital ship, 80; raid (1942), 187
Diggle, Colonel J.B.H., 44, 74
Dill, General (Field-Marshal) Sir John, 40, 125-6, 132, 152, 187, 227, 230, 232, 233, 239, 240; G.O.C.-in-C., Aldershot Command, 40; commanding I Corps, 31, 43; VCIGS, 31; CIGS, 29; cancels Ironside's instructions, 29, 30, 229; and Brooke, 123, 125, 133, 151, 152, 229; rejects appointment of Karslake to command all British troops in France, 132, 229; sends Marshall-Cornwall to France, 132, 229, 230; decision for British Commander in France too late, 151, 152, 230; and 52nd Division, 151, 152, n. 202, 203; at Supreme War Council, 173, 174; offer of British troops to French, 173-4; and withdrawal on Le

Havre, 180; and Breton Redoubt, 192, 194; and withdrawal of Brooke's troops from French command, 202, 203; and Pétain's reported request for armistice, 204, 238
Dives, River, 213, 244 'Line' abandoned by French, 214
Domfront, 220, 224
Doyle, Colonel, 75
Dreuil, 100
Drucat, 69
Dragons Portées, 105, 109
Drew, General J.S., GOC 52nd Division, 174, 217
Duclair, 166
Dufour, General, 58
Duke of Wellington's Regiment:
2/6th, 47, 167, reaches Abbeville but forced to withdraw, 77; march back to Dieppe, 77-8; in Rouen area, 80; reinforces Beauman, 150, 153, 163; fighting on Seine, 169-71
2/7th, 47, 148, 184; reaches Abbeville but forced to withdraw, 77; march back to Dieppe, 77-8; as garrison in Dieppe, 80, 183; evacuated, 183
Dunkirk, 44, 82, 121, 123; defence of perimeter, 111, 121; evacuation through, 24, 25, 29, 142, 144, 205, 229; French troops from Dunkirk in Cherbourg peninsula, 167, 225
Dunphie, Major (General Sir Charles), 93n, 156
Dyle, River, 49, 51, 55, 61

East, Kent Regiment, *see* Buffs
East Surrey Regiment, 2/6th, 47, 57, 74, 127, 130, 146, 148, 158, 184; equipped as mobile unit, 60-1; fighting on Bresle, 155; surrender near St Valéry-en-Caux, 158-9
Eastwood, Major-General, 188, 196, 233
Eden, (Sir), Anthony (Earl of Avon), Secretary of State for War, 31-2, 91, 125, 135, 173; withdraws Brooke's forces from French command, 194-5; message to Reynaud, 195
Elbeuf, 161; Rommel's attack on it, 166-7; French blow bridges, 167
Elliott, Major G., 94, 124, 129, 215; his Field Battalion and Anti-Tank Regiment, 128, 162
Ellis, Major L.F., 191-2, 237
Eu, 74, 145, 146, 154; Basse Forêt, 155, 157
Eure, River, 171
Evans, Major-General Roger, Commander of 1st Armoured Corps, 85, 89, 90, 97, 102, 113, 115, 117, 120, 150, 151, 161, 177, 230, 231; and Karslake, 94-6, 99; and GQG Intelligence report, 95-6, 100; ordered by GHQ to attack, 94-7, 100; and battle of Somme bridges, 100; withdrawal, 101; and French reinforcements, 105; ordered by Altmayer to attack, 106; conference with Weygand, 156; conference on state of his Division, 171; and use of Armoured Brigades, 178
Evreux, 88, 153, 154, 175

Falls, Cyril, 142
Fanshawe, Major (Colonel) E.L., 91, 93, 99
Fauville, 88
Fécamp, 44, 180, 181; chemical warfare dump, 47, 57, 238; dump emptied, 134
Feings, 219
Ferrière, 215, 223
Feuquières, 110
Floristan, SS, attacked by aircraft, 206
Fontaine Bellenger, 169
Fontaine l'Abbe, 222
Forêt d'Eawy, 158
Forêt de Brittone, 166
Forêt de Helles, 119
Forêt de Lyons, 90, 156, 157
Forêt de Perseign, 171
Forêt de Savernay, 206, 239
Forêt du Hellet, 105
Forges-les-Eaux, 47, 73, 120, 130, 146, 148, 163
Fortune, Major-General V.M., Commander of 51st Division, 115, 117, 118, 132, 134, 153, 179-82, 229, 231; and final attack on Somme bridgeheads, 138, 140; and German offensive 146-9, 154-8; asks for relief of shortening of his line, 146; withdrawal behind Bresle agreed, 147; releases Composite Regiment and Support Group, 156-8; plans for withdrawal, 179-82
Franco-Belgian frontier line, 39, 41, 42, 51
François, General, 178-79, 222
Franleu, 109
French Air Force, 138
French Army units:
Army of the Alps, 111
1st Army, 83, 95
2nd Army, 54
3rd Army, 95
16th Army, 95, 131
7th Army, 75, 95, 102, 131
10th Army, 114, 120, 131, 132, 142, 143,

277

152, 154, 159, 167, 174, 176, 178, 184, 193, 195, 196, 203-4, 213, 222-4, 229-32, 236
Cavalry Corps, 84, 217, 220
  Corps, 107, 173, 174, 216, 220, 232, 236
  IX Corps, 120, 131, 132, 137, 140, 147, 148, 167, 181, 184, 228, 230
  X Corps, 131, 143, 147
  XII Corps, 224
  Armoured Divisions, 106, 110
  2nd Armoured Division, 131, 137-9, 143
  2nd DCL (Division Cavaliere Legere), 105, 106, 120, 131, 138, 143, 147, 155, 157
  3rd DCL, 142, 163, 222, 223
  1st DLM, 219, 220
  3rd DLM, 176, 178
  5th Colonial Division, 131, 138, 143, 146, 147
  5th DCL, 105, 106, 120, 131, 138, 143, 147, 155, 159
  17th Division, 143, 161, 162
  26th DCL, 105
  31st (Alpine) Division, 132, 138, 139, 143, 146, 147, 153, 155, 158, 161
  40th Division, 132, 138, 142, 143, 146, 147, 155
  237th Division, 179, 221, 222
  236th Demi-Brigade, 179, 216, 221
  32nd Depot Battalion, 58
  71st Artillery Regiment, 217, 219
  72nd Artillery Regiment, 175, 215
  127th Groupe de Reconnaissance, 176, 219
  Reserve Group III, 132
Frere, General, 75, 117, 131
Fresnoy, 105, 159
Fressenville, 71
Frieres, 145

Gamaches, 47, 74, 147
Gamelin, General, 49, 52-4; new plan, 82-3; replaced by Weygand, 83
George VI, King, 20-31
Georges, General, French C.in-C., North Eastern Armies, 28, 30, 50, 94, 97, 117, 126, 128, 132, 137, 151, 152, 191, 193, 194, 196, 230, 232, 233
German Army: 1937 manoeuvres, 25; offensive of May 10, 1945, 26, 51, 53, 56; crossing of Meuse, 54; half on Oise, 54; fighting round Amiens, 64-7, 76; crossing of Somme, 71, 76; gains Channel coast 84; defence of Somme bridgeheads, 140; 'Plan Red', 143; attack from St. Valery-sur-Somme, 145; crossing of Ardelle, 162; attack on Rouen held up, 163-6; enter Rouen, 166; main effort towards Paris, 198; thrust towards Cherbourg, 199, attack to cut off French from Brittany, 200
German Army units:
  4th Army, 143, 198
  XVI Armoured Corps, 198
  XXXIX Corps, 146
  2nd Motorised Division, 146, 200, 225, 236
  5th Panzer Division, 143, 146, 164, 167, 198, 200, 225, 236
  7th Panzer Division, 67, 143, 146, 198, 219, 224, 235, 236
Gethen, Lt-Colonel R., 47, 64-7; wounded in bombing, 64; taken prisoner, 67
Girling, Lt-Colonel F.F.B., 47
Glasgow Highlanders, 1st, 217
Gloucestershire Regiment, 75
Gormanston, Viscount, killed, 168
Gort, Field-Marshal Viscount, 26, 27, 41, 46, 53, 54, 87, 115, 125, 133, 184, 185, 191, 227, 240; and Hore-Belisha, 20; on lack of equipment and ammunition, 22-3; CIGS, 28, 29, 40, 41; Commander-in-Chief, 20, 28, 29, 40, 42, 43, 47-50, 57; and Brooke, 41; and Plan 'D', 52; and moving forward of 'Labour' Divisions, 54-6; and position of BEF, 55-6; instructed to withdraw to south, 83; discussions with Ironside, 83-4; agrees to attack, 84; ordered to evacuate his troops, 111
Gournay, 161
Gouy, 139
Graham, Lord Malise, 68
Grand Bois de Cambron, 115
Green, Brigadier M.A., 103, 149
Griffin, Brigadier, 44

Haig, Field-Marshal Earl, 21
Halluin, 41, 95
Hangest, 146
Harroway, Colonel W.W., 209, 210
Hartlieb General von, 143, 150, 164, 166, 167, 225
Hastings and Prince Edward Regiment, 188
Haughton, Captain, 168
Haute Foret d'Eu, 105, 113
Heselton, Lt-Colonel J.S., 45, 61, 74, 182
Highland Light Infantry:
  5th, 217; in action near Conches, 215, 216
  6th, 174, 217, in action near Conches, 215, 216

Highlanders (Canadian), 48th, 188
Hillis, Lieutenant, 218
Hind, Captain R.W., 100
Hitler, Adolf, 122
Hobart, Major-General (Sir) Percy, 85
Hodgkinson, Lt-Colonel J., 168
Holland, invaded by Germans, 51, 53, 56
Honfleur, 211
Hopkinson, Major J.F., 100-1, 179
Hore-Belisha, Leslie (Lord Hore-Belisha), Secretary of State for War, 23, 25, 29, 38, 40, 53, 98, 125; and Gort, 20, 50; replaced, 31
Hoth, General, 146, 198, 200
Howard-Vyse, Major-General Sir Richard, 117, 189, 194
Huppy, 107

Igoville, 168
Ihler, General, 117, 131, 180
Incheville, 179
Inverclyde, Lord, 94
Ironside, General Sir Edmund (Field-Marshal Lord Ironside), 20, 21, 29, 31, 45, 46, 49-50, 54, 56, 85, 97, 98, 103, 121, 123, 127, 228, 240; Inspector-General of the Forces, 40; expects to become C.in-C. Field Force, 40; CIGS, 20, 29, 40, 42-3; and the Norwegian Campaign, 32; and appointment of Commander for L of C, 29-30; and direction of likely German attack, 49, 52; and German reaction to Plan D, 52; visit to Gort, 83; plans for attack, 83-4; and de Fonblanque, 90; and appointment of Karslake, 91, 229; relinquishes his post, 29, 30; C.-in-C., Home Forces, 30, 103, 121-3; and question of German invasion, 121; and new BEF, 123
Isneauville, 150, 163

Jones, 2/Ltd., (KOYLI), 168

Karslake, Lieutenant-General Sir Henry, Commander of L of C., 30-1, 91-4, 97-9, 103, 106, 110, 114, 117, 124-6, 135-6, 145, 151, 154, 157, 161, 163, 184, 187, 197, 228-30, 239, 240; and German invasion of Belgium, 52-4; at Le Mans, 93; seeks to form Artillery Regiment, 94; and position of 1st Armoured Division, 94-6, 171; and Beauman Division, 98, 125-6, 176-9, 231; and battle of the Somme bridges, 101; asks RAF for fighters, 101-2; flies to London with report for Ironside, 103; Ironside puts him in charge of separate Command, 103; and 51st Highland Division, 104-5, 113, 148-9; and safety of all British troops, 118; appointment to command all British troops in France rejected by Dill, 132 and position north of Seine, 134; and final attack on Somme bridgeheads, 139; further appeal to RAF, 139-40; urges despatch of new Corps Commander, 152, 153, 230; and Pownall's visit, 153-4; and arrangements for crossing Seine, 166; and 157th Brigade, 172, 176, 177, 178, 184, 221, 232; and withdrawal on Le Havre, 180; and Brooke's arrival, 188-9; Brooke sends him back to England, 189; priority list of ammunition, 238; his Report, 103, 132, 253-63
Kennedy, Brigadier, 174, 176
Kent-Lemon, Brigadier, 103, 164, 166
Kind's Own Scottish Borderers (KOSB), 225
King's Own Yorkshire Light Infantry (KOYLI), 2/4th, 47, 59, 63, 72, 167, 210, 212; at Abbeville, 77, withdrawal and march back to Dieppe, 77-9; in Rouen area, 80; sent to reinforce Beauman, 150, 153, 163; fighting on Seine, 168-9
King's Royal Rifle Corps (KRRC), 2nd, 86
Kleist, General von, 198
Kluge, General von, 143, 198

Labour Party, 22
La Ferte-sous-Jouarre (Georges' HQ), 94, 97, 98

La Haye-du-Puits, 225
La Hutte, 172, 177
L'Aigle, 199, 209, 219
Lancastria, 206, 227
La Pallice, 197; as new port for BEF, 189; troops evacuated from it, 190
La Rochelle, 189
Laurencie, General de la, 143, 167, 173, 174, 220, 236
Laurie, Brigadier Sir John, Commander of 157th Bridge, 172, 173, 177, 178, 215-21; seeks help from 3rd Armoured Brigade, 216, 223; learns of Normanforce, 216; search for it, 216-17; and withdrawal to Cherbourg, 218-20; and embarkation, 221
Laval, 10th French Army retreats on, 203
Leaders of the Army (1940), 20
Le Chete, 178
Le Havre, 43-5, 57, 58, 61, 81, 88, 134-6, 153, 162, 167, 182, 189, 198, 205, 236, 237;

RASC dump, 45, 134; threat to, 112-13, 134-5, 179-80; plan to fall back on, 118-19, 149, 180; use of port discontinued, 134; proposal to withdraw AA guns, 135-6; garrison, 166, 180, 182, 204; AA guns withdrawn, 166; withdrawal on, 180-2; garrison's transport saved, 182; evacuation of troops, 182
Le Manoir Bridge, 168
Le Mans, 46, 103, 113, 154, 171, 172-4, 176, 185, 187-9, 193, 194, 196, 197, 203, 231-3, 239; L. of C. Headquarters, 39, 43, 56-8, 61, 68, 93, 98, 99, 149, 153, 166; sub-area, 44; withdrawal of HQ, 200, 201, 234
Le Montant, 108
Lens, 64, 68, 69
Le Plessis, 222
Le Translay, 74
Le Tremblay, 222
Le Tréport, 74
Les Andelys, 163, 167, 169, 170, 176
Les Hogues, 157, 159
Les Pieux, 225
Les Planches, 225
Liddell Hart, (Sir) Basil, 53
Lillebonne, 180, 181
Limeux, 116
Lincolnshire Regiment, 6th, 47
Lines of Communication (L of C), 24-31, 41-2, 45, 47-9, 56-7, area covered, 39; establishment of HQ, 39; sub-areas, 39, 45; supplies in area, 41-2; decentralization of control, 44; extension of lines, 56; HQ moves to Mantes and back to Le Mans, 61; operational HQ near Rouen, 98; order of battle, 247-51
Lisieux, 166, 211
Llewellyn, Lt Colonel E.H., 47
Loire, River, 235; stores in Lower Loire area, 234
Lothian and Border Horse, 1st, 120; and German offensive, 146, 154
Louviers, 120, 169-71
Luftwaffe, the, 41, 51, 61, 199, 236
Luxembourg, invaded by Germans, 51
Lyons-la-Forêt, 150
Lys, River, 41

Macdonnel, Major, 159, 160
Macleod, Colonel, 90
McMullen, Brigadier, 189
McNaughton, Major-General A.G.L., Commander of 1st Canadian Division, 184-7; Divisional War Diary, 186; his command sent forward to Le Mans, 187

Maginot Line, 42, 49, 52, 55, 111, 112
Maid of Kent, hospital ship, bombed off Dieppe, 80
Maillard, General, 171
Maisiniers, 108
Maletable, 219
Manstein, General von, 167
Mantes, 61
Marchainville, 219
Mareuil, 107, 138
Marseilles, 190, 235; 53rd AA Regiment at, 237-8
Marshall, Lt-Colonel F.A.J.E., 43
Marshall-Cornwall, Lieutenant-General J.H. (General Sir James) 132-3, 150, 154, 171, 213; heads No. 17 Military Mission to France, 132-3, 140, 146, 147, 149, 152, 156, 177, 178, 187, 229-31; no executive authority, 133; and Breton Redoubt, 192, 193; commands Normanforce, 197-8, 200, 203, 214, 217, 220, 223, 224, 233; and defence of Cherbourg, 202; and retreat of French Army 203-4; leaves for Cherbourg, 220
Martainville, 160

Martel, Major-General G. le Q. (General Sir Giffard), 44
Master-General of the Ordnance, post abolished, 21, 26, 38, 125
Maulde, 41, 95
Meric, Capitaine, 204
Meuse, River, 54, 96
Miannay, 108, 109
Miller, Lt. Colonel G.S., 46
Milne, Field-Marshal Sir George (Lord Milne), 85
Ministry of Supply, 23
Mont de Caubert, 138, 141
Montebourg, 212
Montfort, 222
Montgomery of Alamein, Field-Marshal Viscount, 29
Montmédy, 95, 112, 143
Montigny, 223
Morgan, Brigadier F.E., Commander of 1st Support Group, 88, 114, 115, 119, 147, 155, 157;61
Mortagne, 217
Moulicent, 219
Moyenneville, 107, 108, 116

Nantes, 43, 68, 110, 134, 135, 185, 188, 195, 197, 204, 226
Neubourg, 222
Neufchâtel, 90, 102, 150, 162

280

Ninove, 88
'Normanforce', 197-8, 216-18, 220, 233
Northern Army Group, 83-4
Norwegian Campaign (1940), 23-4, 32, 45
Nozay, 43

Official History of the War in France and Flanders (Ellis), 191, 236
Oise, River, 55, 95, 96; Canal, 95
Oisemont, 146
Orbec, 174, 178, 216-17
Ormes, 222

Pacy-sur-Eure, 88, 90, 93, 94, 102
Paris, 67, 68, 81, 82, 112, 113, 122, 123; plans to cover it, 112; German advance on, 198
Payne, Major, 87, 88
Péronne, 94-6
Pétain, Marshal, 173; reports of his request for armistice, 190, 204, 227, 238, 268-70
Petiet, General, and Group Petiet, 132, 142, 143, 163, 178, 222-4
Petre, Major-General R.L., 47, 69
Picquigny, 100, 101, 105, 131, 143
Plan 'D', 49, 51
Plan 'Red', 143
Plan 'W', 186
Poix, 151; airfield, 45
Pont de l'Arche, 90, 150, 160, 163, 167, 168
Pont l'Eveque, 211, 213
Portes, 215, 222
Port-le-Grand, 71
Pownall, General Sir Henry, 57, 95, 187; instructions to 1st Armoured Division, 88-90; sent to reassure French, 152-3; report on visit to Karslake, 153-4
Préaux, 160
Princess Louise's Kensington Regiment, 129, 157
Prioux, General, 84
Provisional Battalion, 2nd, 209
Provisional Battalion, 4th, 149; holds up German attack on Rouen, 163-7

Quartermaster-General's Department, 37, 48
Queen's Royal Regiment, 4th, 5th and 6th, 47, 68; fighting near Abbeville, 69; 71
Querqueville, 226
Quesnoy, 108
Quillebeuf, 166, 182

Railway construction, 27, 47
Ramburelles, 110
Randonnai, 219
Redon, 203, 235

Reid, Major, 205
Rennes, 46, 47, 51, 54, 153, 185, 195, 201, 204, 205; 10th French Army retreats on, 204; troop train destroyed by bombing, 206; entered by Germans, 225
Reynaud, Paul, French Premier, 82, 83, 123, 135, 173, 187, 194, 195
Reynolds, 2/Lt., 170
Richter, Oberleutenant Gerhard, 67
Rifle Brigade, 1st 86
Risle, River, 166, 167, 171, 188, 223
Ritchie, Brigadier N., 197, 233
Roberts, Lt-Colonel H. Sherriff, 86
Roberts, Lt-Colonel (Major-General) J.H., 187, 200, 201, 205
Rolfe, Captain, 214
Rommel, Major-General (Field-Marshal) Erwin, 67, 143, 181, 198, 219; foiled at Elbeuf, 166-7; races towards Channel, 167; thrust towards Cherbourg, 199, 224-6, 235-6; meets opposition, 225-6, 236
Roton, General, 97
Rouen, 45, 47, 58, 61, 75, 76, 90, 93, 94, 98, 102, 118, 126, 153, 154, 160, 162, 163, 165, 168, 181, 182, 199, 209; sub-area, 44, 76, 98, 166, 167; French District Command, 58; reinforcements sent to area, 80; threat to it, 126, 149, 156; strengthening of force to its north, 149-50; German attack held up, 163-6; bridges round Rouen, 164-6, 182; entered by Germans, 166
Rouvroy, 138
Rouxmesnil, 76
Royal Air Force, 95, 101-2, 137, 139-40, 144-5, 188-90, 252; role of, 24-6; Air Component with BEF, 25; Advanced Air Striking Force (AASF), 25, 144, 237, 252; French airfields, 46; directed from London, 97, 140, 144; BAFF (British Air Force, France), 144, 252; Air Component withdrawn, 144; South Component, 144, 252; supply of information, 234-5; virtual disappearance from France, 239; Southern Force, 252
Royal Canadian Horse Artillery (RCHA), 1st Field Regiment, 187, 201
Royal Canadian Regiment, 188
Royal Dragoon Guards, 2nd (Queen's Bays), 88, 90, 94, 113, 161; and action of Somme bridges, 100; in advance towards Abbeville, 107
Royal Fusiliers, 14th, 45; move to Le Havre, 58, 61; in Le Havre garrison, 182, 204; evacuated, 204-5

281

Royal Horse Artillery (RHA), 1st, 86, 87, 115
Royal Hussars, 10th, 113; in advance towards Abbeville, 107; cover withdrawal of Dukes from Seine, 171; leave for England, 207
Royal Lancers:
9th, 110, 113, 207
12th, 51
Royal Naval Air Service, 25
Royal Navy, and evacuation of troops, 183, 204
Royal Scots Fusiliers, 6th (Pioneer) Battalion, 129
Royal Sussex Regiment:
6th, 47, 64, 81, 95; and fighting round Amiens, 64-7; withdrawn to reserve, 67-8; as labour for supplies, 188; stacking of petrol, 206, 239; moved to St Nazaire, 206; embarkation, 206; their ship attacked by aircraft, 206
7th, 47; and fighting round Amiens, 64-7; heavy casualties, 67
Royal Tank Regiment, 99
2nd, 93, 179, 221-3; in advance towards Abbeville, 108-109
3rd, 92
5th, 93, 179, 223; in advance towards Abbeville, 108
Royal Warwickshire Regiment, 12th, 46; garrison battalion at L of C HQ, 81, 188
Royal West Kent Regiment, 73, 99
Rundstedt, Field-Marshal von, 55, 236

Saar, the 31, 55, 57, 105, 112, 115, 183, 228
Sable-sur-Sarthe, 187, 188, 200, 201
St Hilaire le Chatel, 219
St Just-en-Chaussée, 67
St Léger, 113
St Lo, 224, 225
St Malo, 196, 197, 201, 204, 233, 239
St Maurice-les-Charencey, 174
St Nazaire, 41, 43, 47, 68, 110, 134, 135, 185, 186, 188, 197, 200, 203, 204, 206, 226, 227, 238, 239
St Pierre-du-Vauvray, 169, 170
St Pol, 69
St Roche, 64, 65
St Saens, 180; ammunition dump, 43, 45, 58, 99, 134
St Sauveur-de-Pierre Pont, 225

St Valéry-en-Caus, 158-9, 183
St Valéry-sur-Somme, 78, 105, 107, 108, 137, 139; German attack from, 145

Saleux, 65
Saveuse, 100
Sausseuse-Mare, 130, 155, 157
Schmidt, General, 146, 236
Scott, Major (Lt-Colonel), Chief Signals Officer, 104, 128
Seaforth Highlanders, 2nd and 4th, 116; and final attack on Somme bridgeheads 141
Seclin, 59
Sedan, 49, 54, 96; German breakthrough near, 59
Sine, River, 73, 80, 81, 88, 90, 102, 118, 138, 139, 150, 151, 154, 156, 160, 161, 167, 172, 179, 181, 189; covering of approaches, 75, 120; German dash for, 146; Seine crossings, 162, 163, 165, 166, 168-71, 176, 182-3, 199
Senarpont, 119, 129, 147
Serqueux, 156, 159, 162
Shaw, Major E.D., 43
Sherwood Foresters, 1/5th, 43, 74; on River Bresle, 154, 119; embarkation for England, 205
Shilstone, Brigadier W.R., 81, 135, 166
Sigy, 163, 167
60 Days Which Shook the West (Benoist-Méchin), 142
Smith, Brigadier A.A., 188, 200
Somme River, 30-1, 47, 49, 68, 70, 73, 75, 77, 88-90, 95, 96, 105, 106, 108-12, 118-20, 123, 131, 143, 153, 205, 228, 236; fighting south of river, 25, 46, 66; crossed by Germans 71, 76, 84, 114; action of the Somme bridges, 99-101; situation north of river, 111; final effort to reduce German bridgeheads, 137-41; German attack from, 145, 146; equipment lost in battle, 237
Spears, General Sir Louis, 122
Staff talks between British and French (from March 1939), 37
Stanley, Oliver, 31-2
Stanley-Clarke, Brigadier, A.C.L., 181
Stewart, Brigadier, 116
Supply system in France, 26-7, 41-2
Supply Group, 22, 24, 86, 94, 99, 105, 120, 127, 129, 132, 146; 1st Group arrives in France, 87, 114-15; units taken from it, 115; dispositions, 119; and German offensive, 147, 154-5; sent back to Armoured Division, 156-9, 162
Swayne, Brigadier J. de R., and Swayne Mission to General Georges, 97, 117, 151, 152
Swinburne, Colonel, 157, 159
Syme, Lt-Colonel, Commander of 4th

Provisional Battalion, 149-50; holds up German attack on Rouen, 163-7

Tank Company, scratch force, 104
Taylor, Lt-Colonel G., 47
Thibouville, 178
Thomas, Colonel (French Artillery), 175
Thompson, Captain, A.W., 101
Thorpe, Brigadier, 44
Toeufles, 107, 108, 115, 145
Tomlinson, Lt-Colonel T.W.A., 43, 205
Toster, Sergeant, 70
Touchon, General, 131
Tours, 113
Trade Union attitudes, 22
Trouville, 180
Turn of the Tide, The 227

Usher, Colonel, 44

Varennes, 112
Vauchelles, 69
Vehicles, loss of, 238
Venables, 170
Vere-Laurie, Major, 159
Verneuil, 217
Vernon, 90, 167, 176, 199
Veules-les-Roses, 183
Vicary, Colonel Charles, 44, 61; and Vickerforce, 62, 75; raises reinforcements for 51st Division, 149
Vichy, 195
Vickforce, 62, 75
Vieux Manoir, 159
Villedieu, 224
Villelume, Colonel de, 173
Virandelles, 220
Vire, 218, 223, 224
Vitre, 200-3, 235

Walkington, Major, 66
Wannup, Lt-Colonel E.K.B., 47, 65-7
War Office, 20, 22, 23, 37, 40, 45, 81, 117, 135, 154, 187, 214, 230; 'War Book', 37; continues to send supplies to France, 110; Instruction of 6 June, 186-7; failure to provide operational HQ Staff under a C.-in-C., 228
Watteau, Colonel, 170
Wavell, General Sir Archibald (Field-Marshal Earl Wavell), 20, 21, 28-9
West Yorkshire Regiment, 2/5th, 47, 77
Weygand, General, 111, 117, 122, 132, 134, 152, 156, 178, 180, 181, 184, 230; succeeds Gamelin, 83; his plan, 83; considers Allied offensive dead, 111; and Breton Redoubt, 123, 204; and Le Havre AA guns, 135, 136, 166; and final effort to reduce German bridgeheads, 136-7; 'Weygand Line', 136-7; and Beauman Division, 152; at Supreme War Council meeting, 173; and Dill's offer, 173; and Brooke, 189, 191-4, 233; said to have reported end of organized resistance, 194-6, 233; and withdrawal of Brooke's troops from French command, 185-6
White, Colonel, 75
Wilford, Captain, 168
Wilmer, Brigadier, 44
Wilson, Colonel (RAMC), 44
Woincourt, 145
Wyatt, Brigadier, R.J.P., 70

York and Lancaster Regiment, 6th, 47
Young, Lt-Colonel A.F.F., 47

Zoteux, 145